IMAGES
of America

ITALIANS OF GREATER CINCINNATI

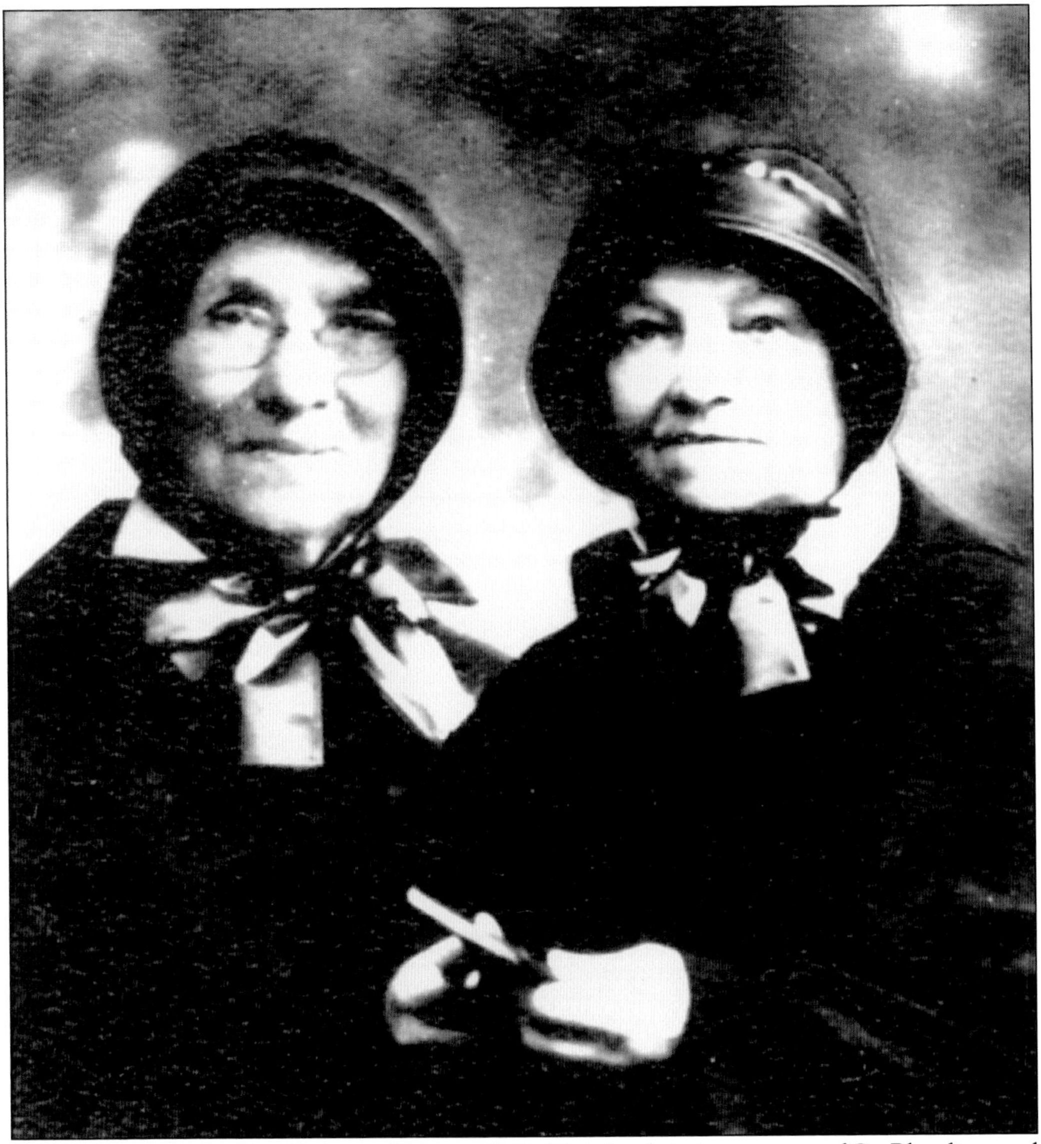

SR. BLANDINA AND SR. JUSTINA SEGALE, S.C. This book is in memory of Sr. Blandina and Sr. Justina Segale, who devoted over 30 years of their lives assisting poor immigrants, especially the Italians, by instructing them in their Catholic faith and guiding them through the Americanization process. (Courtesy of the Archives of the Sisters of Charity of Cincinnati and Santa Maria Community Services.)

On the cover: **CENTENNIAL EXPOSITION.** The 1888 Centennial Exposition of the Ohio Valley and Central States showcased the products of Cincinnati business owners as well as inventors, artists, and varied industries. A fleet of real Venetian gondolas carried dignitaries and partygoers to the centennial exposition via the Miami and Erie Canal. (Courtesy of the Cincinnati Museum Center, Cincinnati Historical Society Library.)

IMAGES
of America

ITALIANS OF GREATER CINCINNATI

Philip G. Ciafardini and Pamela Ciafardini Casebolt

ARCADIA
PUBLISHING

ISBN 978-0-7385-5214-9

Published by Arcadia Publishing
Charleston, South Carolina

Printed in the United States of America

Library of Congress Catalog Card Number: 2007943176

For all general information contact Arcadia Publishing at:
Telephone 843-853-2070
Fax 843-853-0044
E-mail sales@arcadiapublishing.com
For customer service and orders:
Toll-Free 1-888-313-2665

Visit us on the Internet at www.arcadiapublishing.com

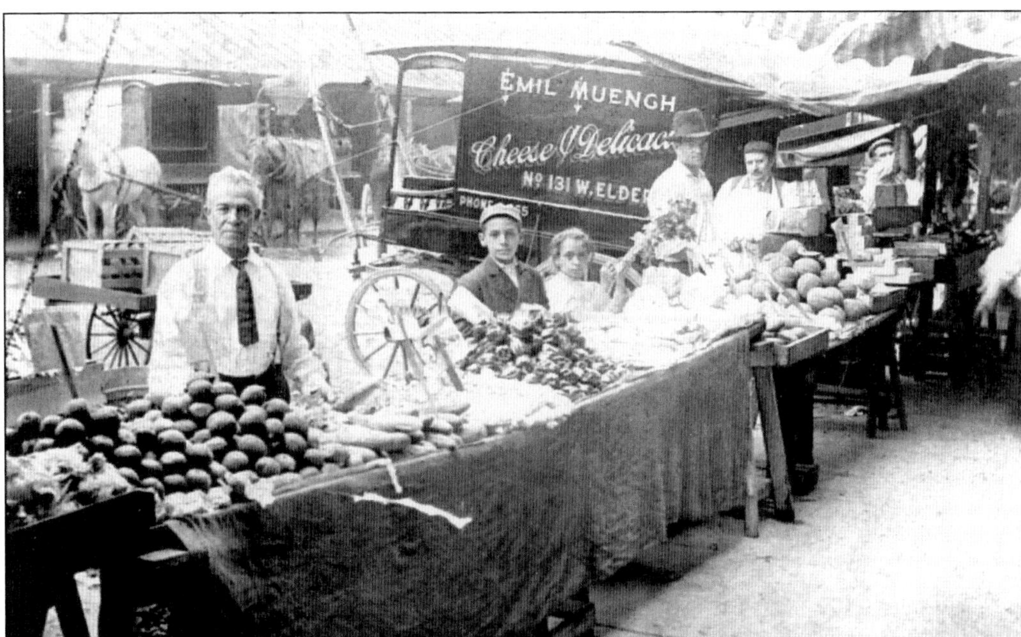

COURT STREET MARKET, C. 1906. Court Street Market, located between Vine and Walnut Streets, was built in 1864 as a replacement for the Canal Market, which was torn down in 1864. The Sansone family members are, from left to right, Carl Sansone, age 63, with his grandson Carl Sansone, age 9, and his granddaughter Carmella Sansone Geraci, age 7. The grandchildren were 2 of 11 children born to Fabiano Sansone and Filippa Palmisano Sansone. (Courtesy of Joe Geraci.)

CONTENTS

ACKNOWLEDGMENTS

It would not have been possible to write *Italians of Greater Cincinnati* without the help of those who either immigrated here or are of Italian descent living in the area. They are recognized in the courtesy lines or in the bibliography. We are most grateful to the Honorable Judge Ronald A. Panioto, president of the Order Sons of Italy in America, Cincinnatus Lodge No. 1191, and Phil Sabatelli, president of the United Italian Society, who permitted us to attend their meetings and provided family contacts for us to call upon. Our gratitude is also extended to Joe Pitocco, a founding member of the Mezzo-Mezzo Social Club who provided us with the rich history of the Italian societies in the Cincinnati area.

The early history of the Italian immigrants was made possible by the writings of the late Fr. Louis Bolzan, C.S., as written in his book *Memories of an Italian Parish*, as well as *The Santa Maria Institute* by Anna C. Minogue. We are also extremely grateful to Fr. Mario Rauzi, C.S., pastor of Sacred Heart Church, located in Camp Washington. He provided numerous church directories for our review, and he provided oral history of the church and clergy that served the Italian community at Sacred Heart Italian Church, which was formerly located in downtown Cincinnati. And to the wonderful Sisters of Charity of Cincinnati, namely, Sr. Victoria Marie Forde, S.C., Sr. Judith Metz, S.C., and Sr. Patricia McQuinn, S.C., who made the Santa Maria Journals of Sister Justina Segale, S.C., and dissertation of the journals by Mary Beth Fraser Connolly available to us to review. They also provided a host of photographs held by them and Santa Maria Community Services (SMCS). A heartfelt thank-you also goes to Nune Krayterman, development director of SMCS, and to Nancy Becker, coauthor of *Sister Blandina Segale: History of a Departure and a Return*, which documented the life of Sr. Blandina Segale and the dedication of the town square in Cicagna, Italy, in her honor.

We also wish to sincerely thank the *Kentucky Post*, *Kentucky Enquirer*, *Kentucky Times Star*, *Cincinnati Enquirer*, *Cincinnati Post*, Mario and Gina Onorini of WAIF 88.3 FM, and Alan Biondi, editor of *La Voce Italiana* newspaper, media outlets that allowed us to share our plans for the book and to request photographs from the Italian community.

INTRODUCTION

The Italian emigration from Italy and the eventual settling of Italian immigrants in Cincinnati began before 1800. According to the writings of Fr. Louis Bolzan, C.S., as stated in his book *Memories of an Italian Parish*, Italian merchants from Genoa, Italy, the birthplace of Christopher Columbus, came to America entering at the port of New Orleans. They then made their way up the Mississippi River and settled in the Ohio River basin in downtown Cincinnati, an ideal place to establish their businesses. By 1835, there were a large number of Italian immigrants living in the area, by 1892 the number had grown to 4,000, and by 1894 the number stood at 6,000.

Since most of the Italian immigrants were Roman Catholic, they began saving to build a Catholic church that would care for the Italian-speaking population. By March 1867, 75 persons had contributed $6,455 to a building fund. It would take 20 more years, however, to gain the momentum to move forward with their plan. On Columbus Day 1890, the parish was born. Construction began in the spring of 1892 at Fifth and Broadway Streets under the guidance of Fr. Peter Lotti of the Missionary Fathers of St. Charles Borromeo, known as the Scalabrini Fathers, whose mission was to maintain the Catholic faith among the Italian population. The cornerstone was laid on October 2, 1892, and by August 27, 1893, Sacred Heart Italian Church was dedicated with great respect, pageantry, and love to the sacred heart of Jesus.

Caring for the Italian immigrant population ironically also became the life's work of two biological Italian immigrant sisters, who joined the religious order of the Sisters of Charity of Cincinnati in 1866. Sr. Blandina and Sr. Justina Segale would enrich the lives of the Italians by instructing them in their Catholic faith and providing very basic help to fill the needs of these young, poor immigrant families.

The following chapters give readers an understanding of the early lives of the Italian immigrants and an appreciation of what they held dear to them as they learned to dedicate themselves to their church, their community, and their new country.

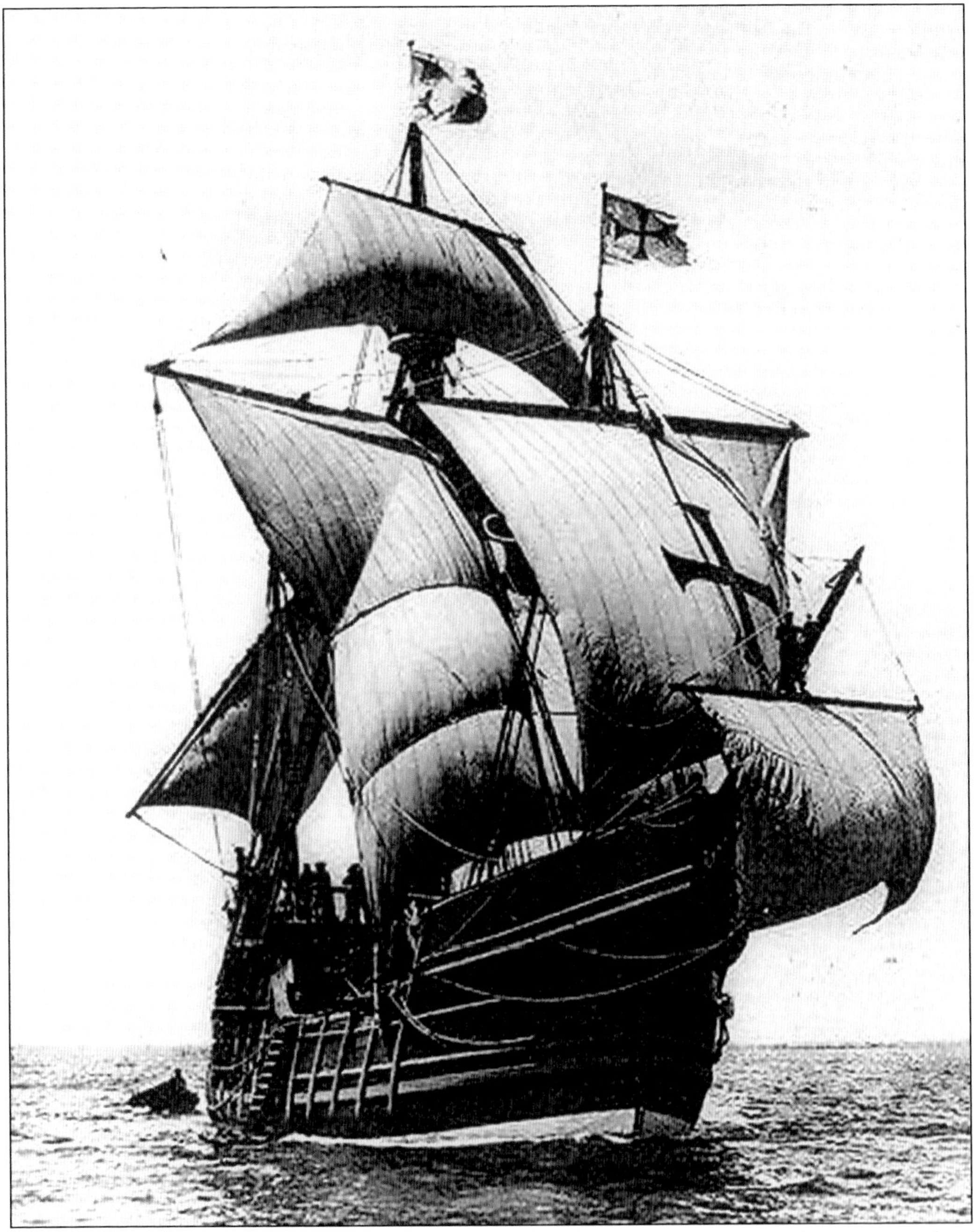

COLUMBUS'S FLAGSHIP, THE SANTA MARIA. The *Santa Maria*, under the command of Christopher Columbus, weighed about 100 tons and carried approximately 39 crew members. The flagship led the *Niña* and the *Pinta* on their designated voyage of discovery and exploration to find a shorter route to the Indies in 1492. The crew consisted mostly of experienced seamen from Palos, Spain, which was the port of departure on August 3, 1492. The *Santa Maria* wrecked on a reef off Hispaniola, an island in the Caribbean, on Christmas Day, December 25, 1492, and was destroyed. Columbus returned to Palos in March 1493 aboard the *Niña*, which was his favorite ship. (Courtesy of the Library of Congress.)

One

SANTA MARIA

On August 22, 1897, Mother Mary Blanche Davis, superior of the Sisters of Charity of Cincinnati, requested that Sr. Blandina Segale, S.C., and her sister, Sr. Justina Segale, S.C., begin to assist the poor Italian immigrants living within the community of Cincinnati. They began by creating the Santa Maria Institute, which allowed them a place to care for, along with other Sisters of Charity and lay social workers, every need of the Italian immigrants, as well as other nationalities. With $5 in her pocket, Sister Blandina established the organization that was incorporated on December 8, 1897, under the name of the Santa Maria Italian Educational and Industrial Home, first located at 510 East Third Street (Third and Lytle Streets) in the home of Sarah Peter, which became known as the Convent of St. Clara. As the Italians moved away from the urban environment of the city, two more welfare centers were founded. They were the Kenton Welfare Center in Walnut Hills and the St. Anthony (San Antonio) Welfare Center in South Fairmount.

Sister Blandina and Sister Justina filled their days visiting Italian families living in tenement houses within the city. They established St. Vincent Apartments and provided temporary and permanent homes for needy immigrants when they had no other place to live. They began teaching English to the Italians, helped them with the Americanization process, and created sewing circles for the women. Culinary skills were also taught, and day care was provided for infants and children. Parochial kindergartens and elementary schools, along with Sunday school, were established, and instruction of the Catholic faith was taught at all levels. The children were prepared for the sacraments of Holy Communion, penance, and confirmation. Various societies and sodalities were established for men and boys and for women and girls. All of this was accomplished while Sister Blandina was dependent upon the goodness of the church, other religious orders, and the aid society of the Santa Maria Institute known as the Willing Workers League for financial support and help at the institute.

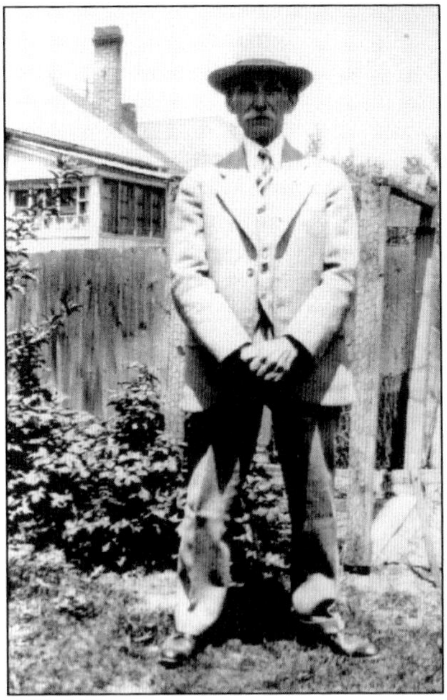

FRANCESCO SEGALE. Francesco Segale and his wife, Giovanna, along with their five children, sons Bartolomeo and Andrea (later changed to Henry) and daughters Rosa, Maria, and Catterina, traveled to America, arriving in New Orleans on March 6, 1854. They settled in the Ohio River basin where Francesco became a fruit peddler and later owned his own store. Giovanna, a homemaker, saw to the education of their children. (Courtesy of Roland and Nancy Becker.)

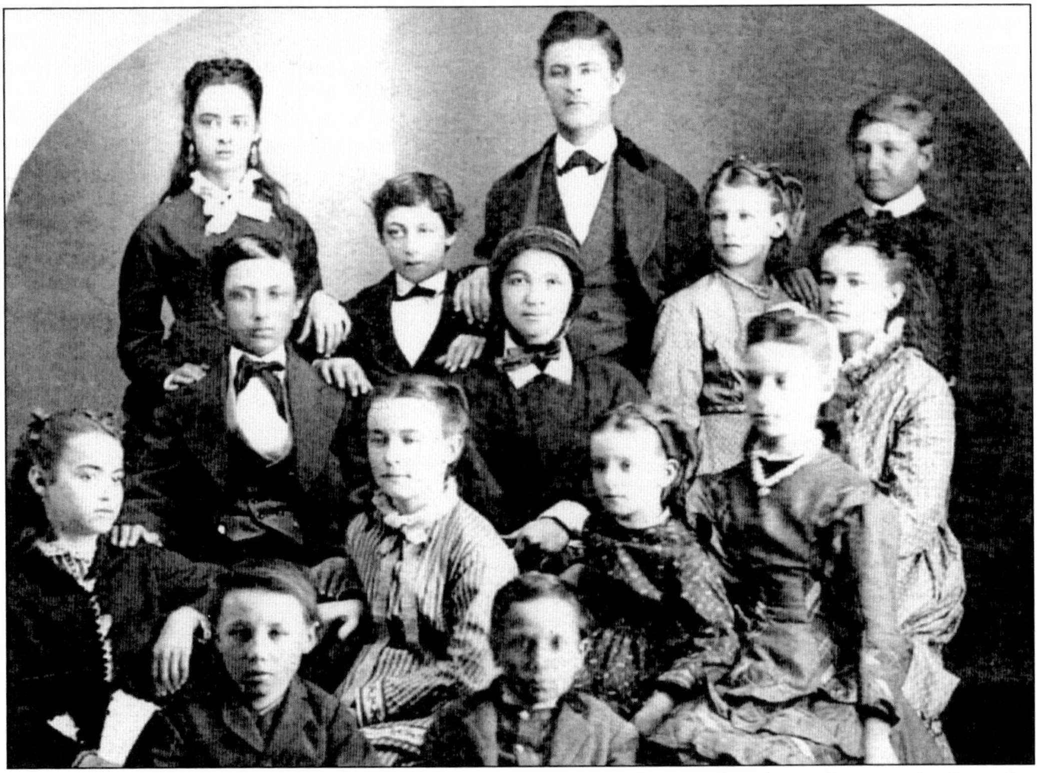

SR. JUSTINA SEGALE AND FAMILY MEMBERS, C. 1866. Sr. Justina Segale is photographed on the occasion of her joining the Sisters of Charity on September 27, 1866. Sister Justina taught in Trinidad, Colorado, and Albuquerque, New Mexico, for 15 years. She spoke English, Italian, and Spanish. She learned braille while working in Lansing, Michigan, so she would be able to educate the blind in their religion. (Courtesy of the Archives of the Sisters of Charity of Cincinnati and SMCS.)

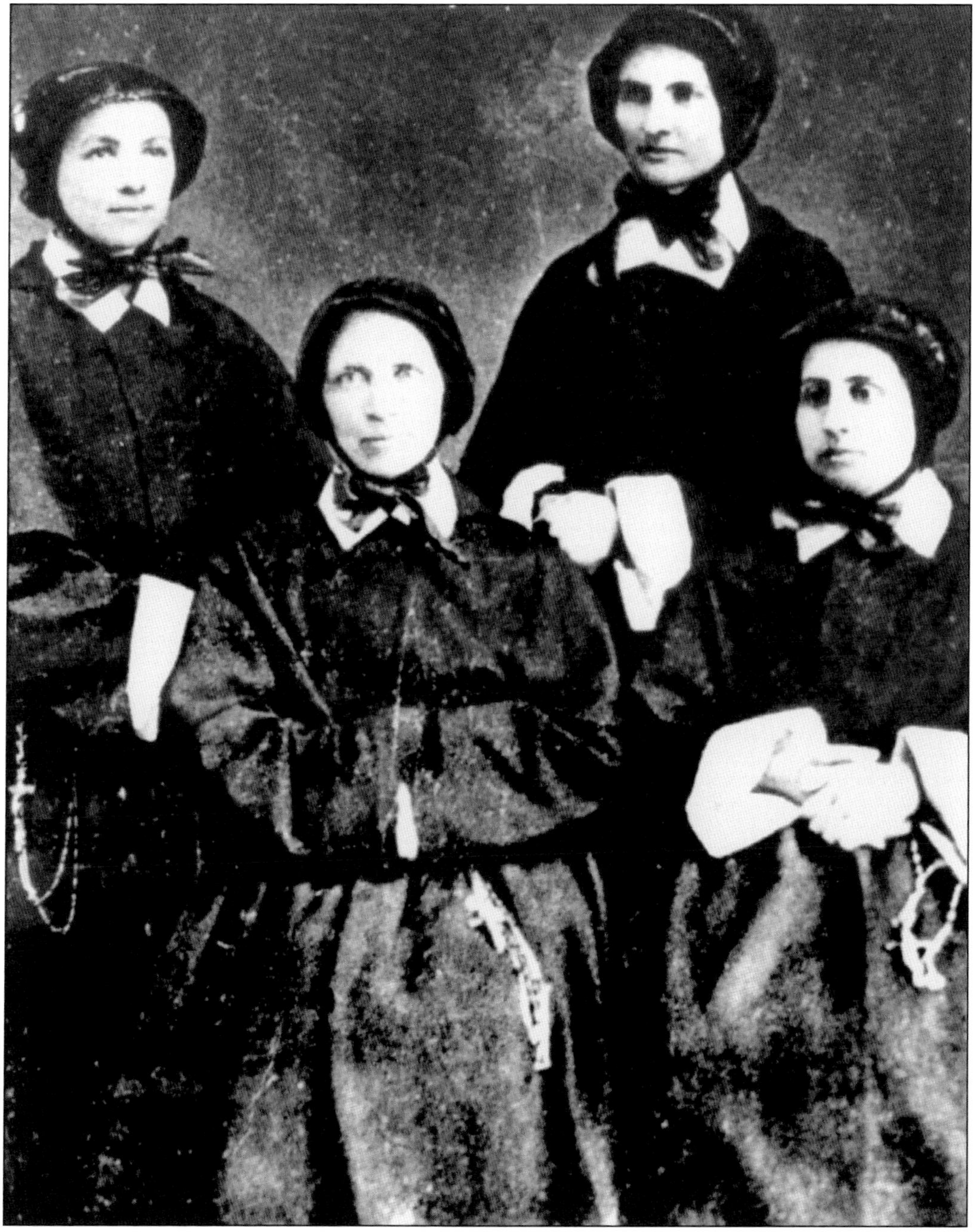

SISTERS OF CHARITY, TRINIDAD, COLORADO, C. 1872. At the age of 22, Sr. Blandina Segale traveled alone to Trinidad, Colorado, where the Sisters of Charity taught. Pictured are, from left to right, (first row) Sr. Eulalia Whitty and Sr. Marcella Huller; (second row) Sr. Blandina Segale and Sr. Fidelis McCarthy. Sister Blandina then moved to New Mexico where she began her work among the Native Americans, including establishing a trade school for them. She also built a hospital for the workmen building the Santa Fe Railroad. Sister Blandina spent over 20 years on missions in Colorado and New Mexico. (Courtesy of the Archives of the Sisters of Charity of Cincinnati and SMCS.)

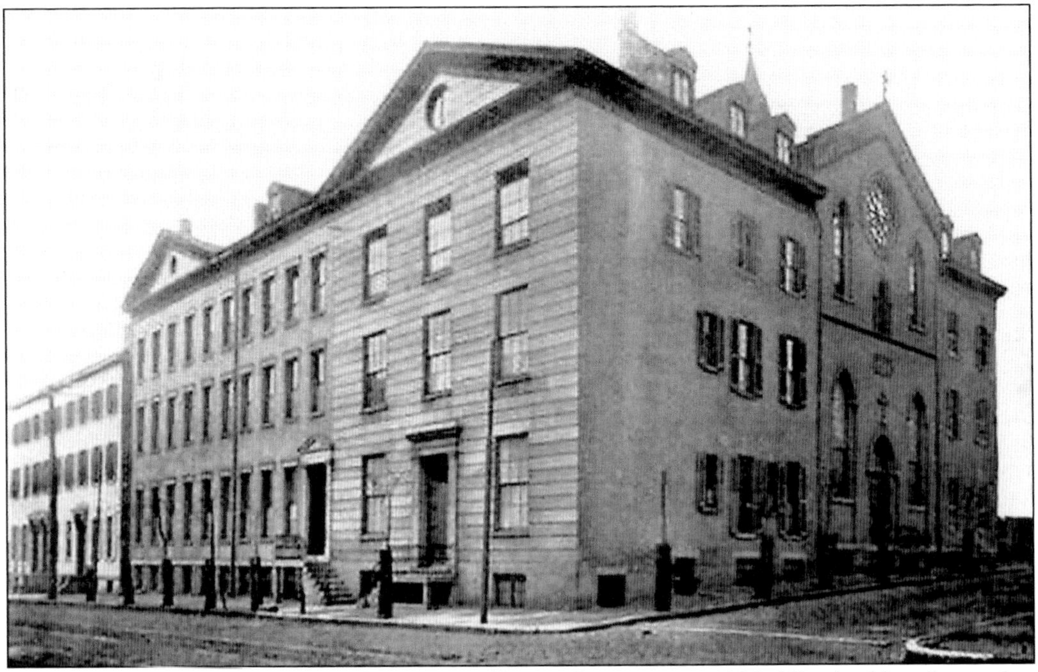

THE SANTA MARIA INSTITUTE, THIRD AND LYTLE STREETS, C. 1899. This building located at 510 Lytle Street was the original residence of Sarah Peter, who turned over the building in 1861 to the Sisters of the Poor of St. Francis. They, in turn, allowed the Sisters of Charity to use it for their institute. Sarah Peter continued to live there in private quarters until her death in 1877. (Courtesy of the Athenaeum of Ohio, Mount St. Mary Seminary.)

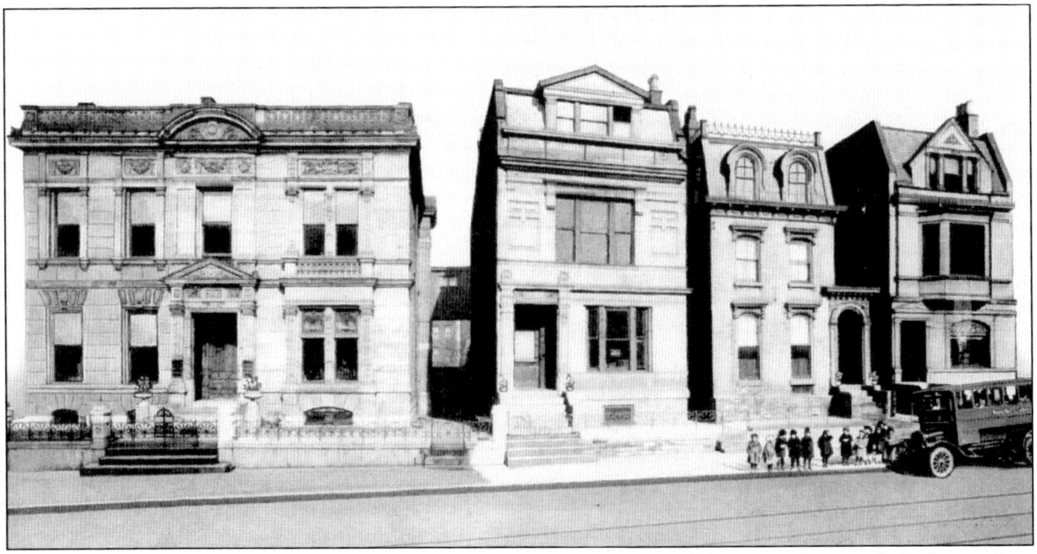

NO. 640 WEST EIGHTH STREET, C. 1912–1926. This row of houses ultimately belonged to the Santa Maria Institute. The administration building is at the left, followed by the nursery, St. Vincent Apartments, the welfare center, and the neighborhood house. In later years, many of the Italian immigrants who received help from the institute volunteered at the center and supported the institute as donors. (Courtesy of the Archives of the Sisters of Charity of Cincinnati and SMCS.)

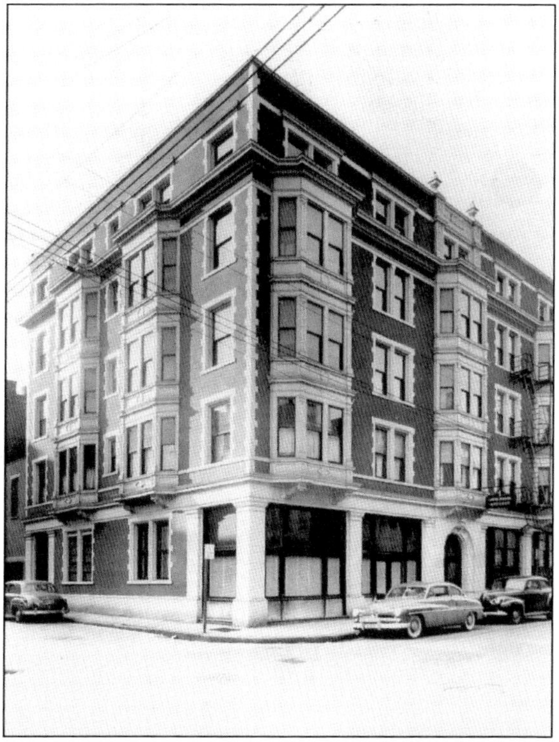

THIRTEENTH AND REPUBLIC STREETS, 1926. The last and most recognizable building of the Santa Maria Institute was located at Thirteenth and Republic Streets. In 1972, the Sisters of Charity of Cincinnati turned over the institute to the board of trustees, which renamed the institute Santa Maria Community Services (SMCS), an independent, nonprofit agency serving the needs of the community. On December 8, 2007, the agency celebrated its 110th anniversary. (Courtesy of the Archives of the Sisters of Charity of Cincinnati and SMCS.)

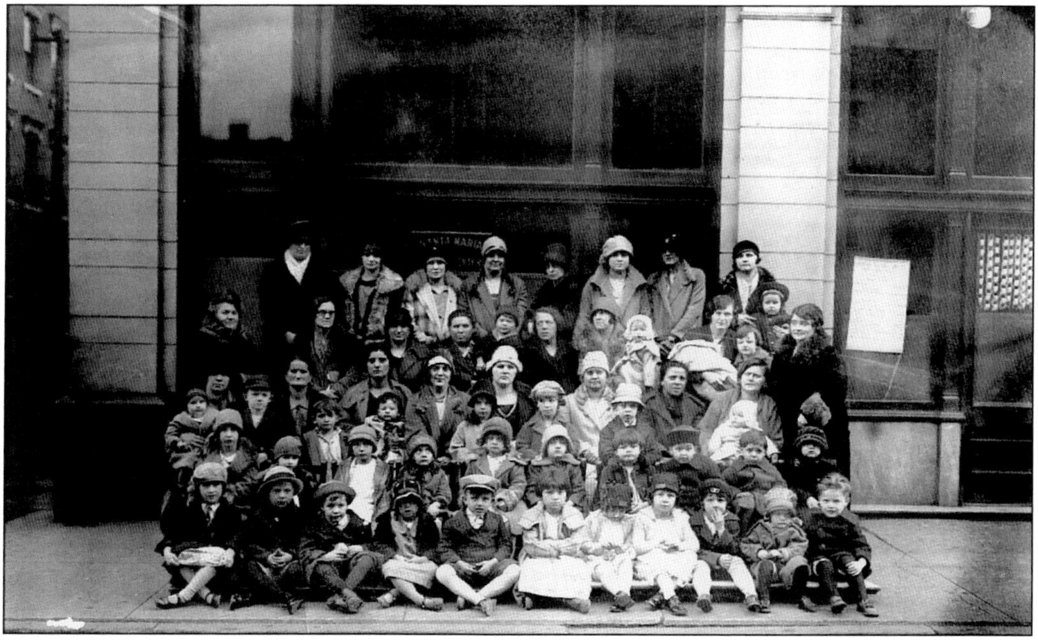

MOTHERS AND CHILDREN OUTSIDE THE SANTA MARIA, C. 1926. In 1897, the institute was first established as a center of social activity for the Italians while at the same time providing for the protection of their Catholic faith. Its mission was also to provide a safe gathering place for women to come and learn how to provide for their families while trying to establish themselves in America. (Courtesy of the Archives of the Sisters of Charity of Cincinnati and SMCS.)

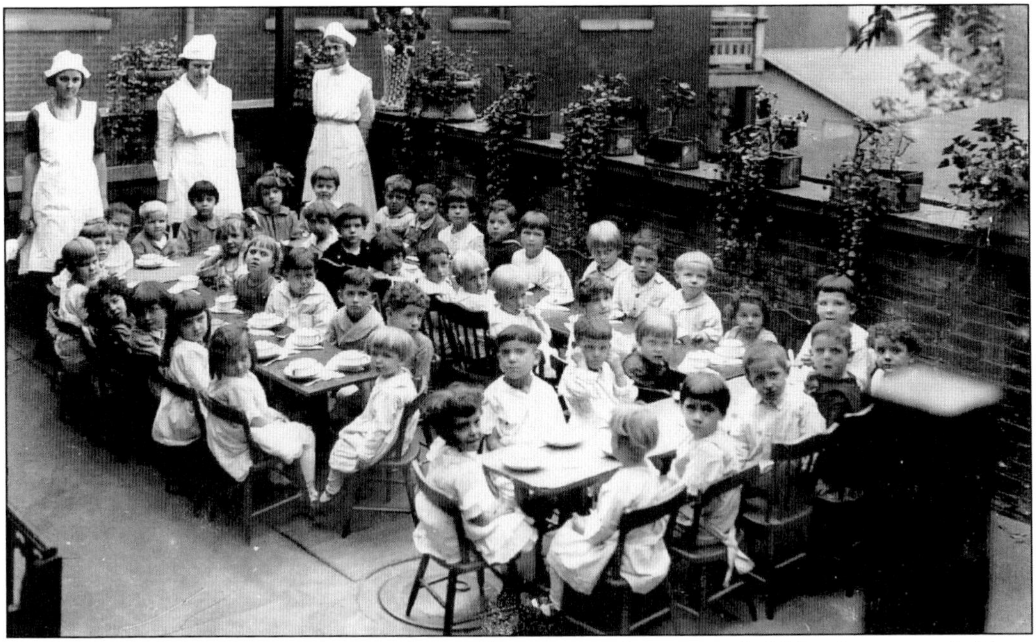

SANTA BAMBINO DAY NURSERY, c. 1920. This open-air dinner was held for the young children at the Santa Maria Institute. The day nursery was first opened on May 21, 1918, and was blessed by the Most Reverend Henry Moeller, D.D. Shown below is the infant nursery that opened at the same time. (Courtesy of the Archives of the Sisters of Charity of Cincinnati and SMCS.)

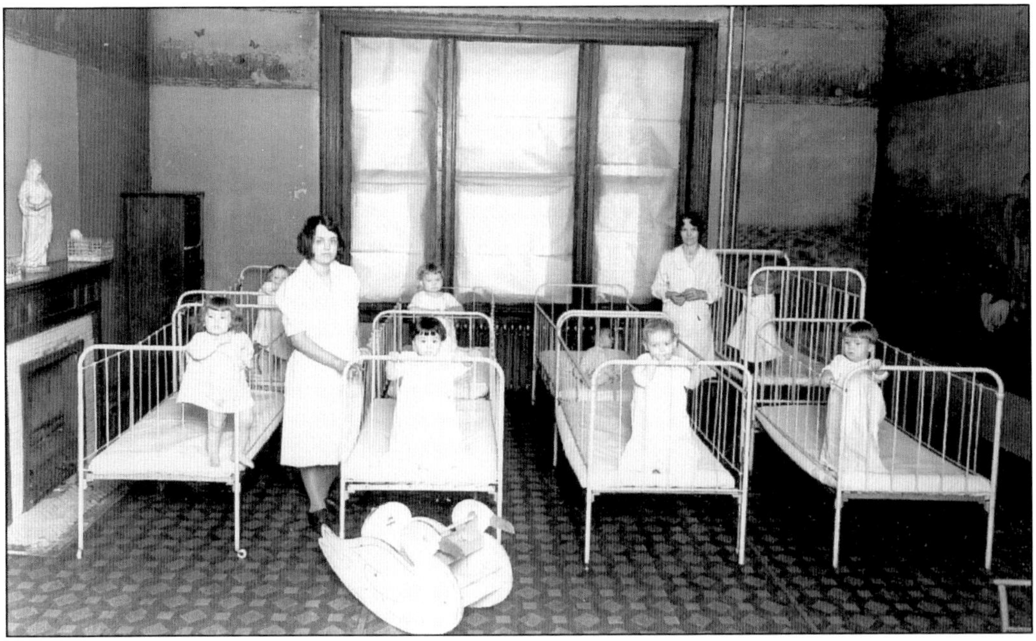

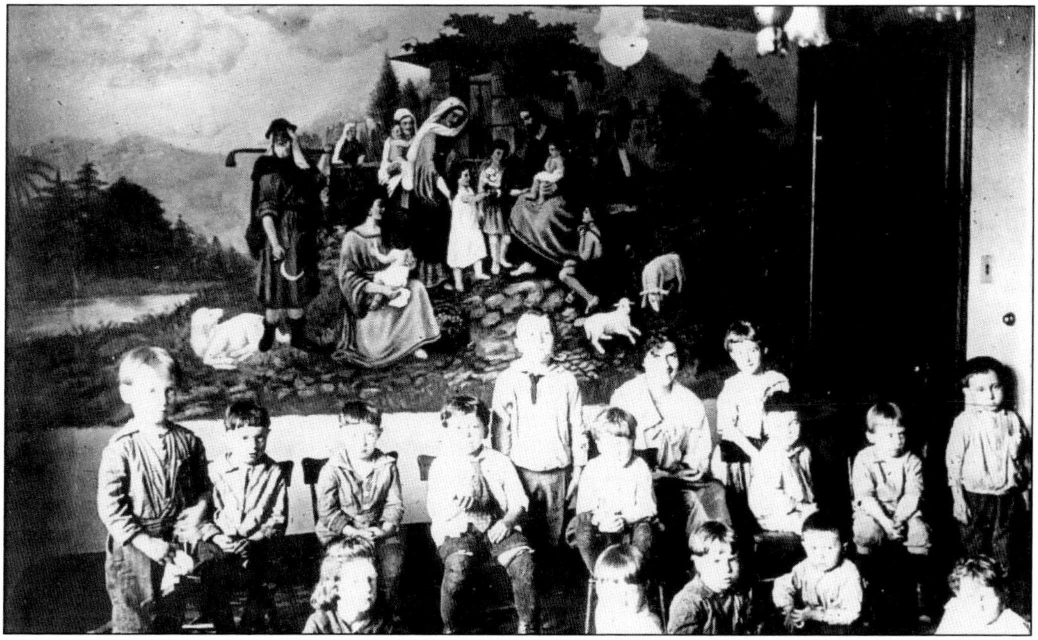

Santa Maria Day Care. The Santa Maria Institute opened its doors to provide day care on December 10, 1914. Sewing classes for children (shown below) began on December 3, 1899. The children were given embroidery and crocheting lessons. The institute supplied all the materials, and the children kept whatever they made. (Courtesy of the Archives of the Sisters of Charity of Cincinnati and SMCS.)

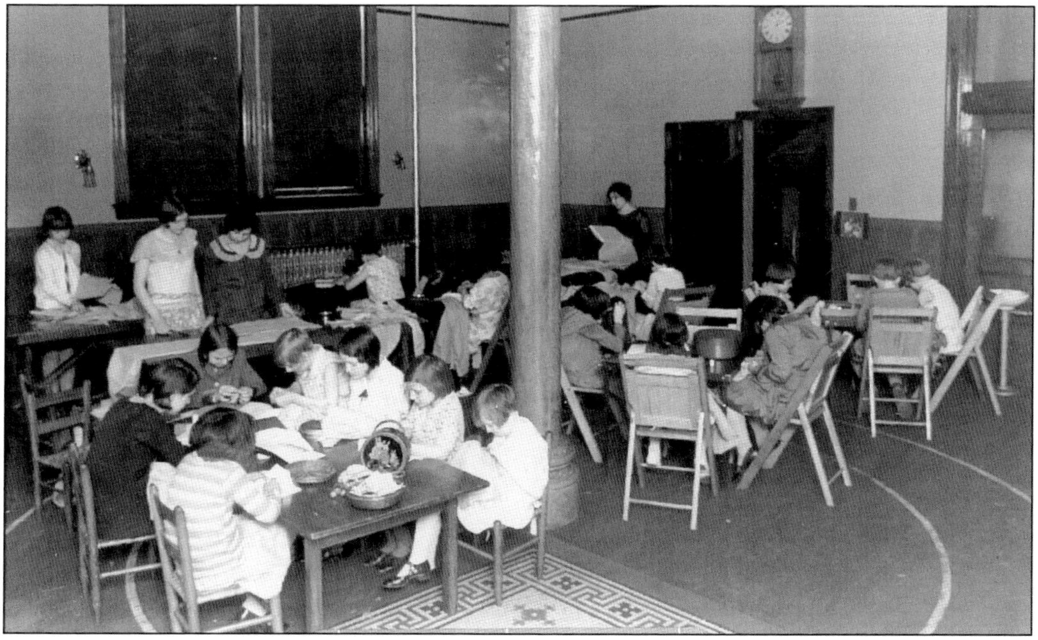

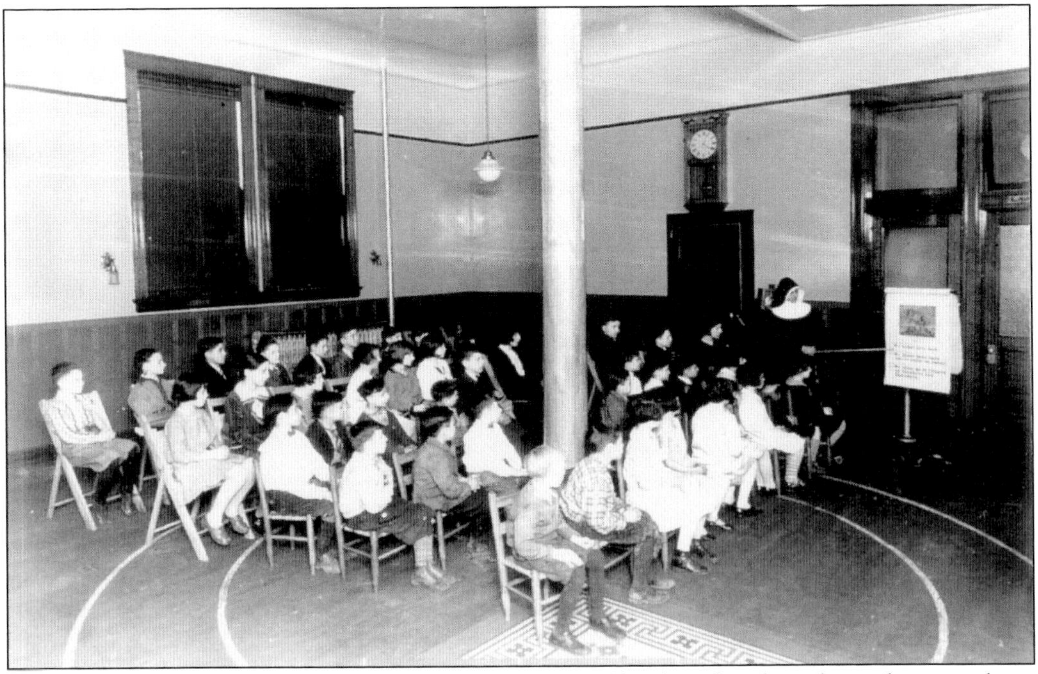

SISTER BLANDINA GIVING INSTRUCTIONS, 1930S. Sr. Blandina Segale is shown here teaching the Ten Commandments in religion class to a group of 10- and 11-year-old children. The children seem to be paying very close attention to what the sister is teaching. Shown below, the tiny Sister Blandina is standing next to Cecil B. DeMille. She met the director while attending a conference in California. DeMille directed nearly 80 films, two of which were *The Ten Commandments*, made in 1923 and 1956. (Courtesy of the Archives of the Sisters of Charity of Cincinnati and SMCS.)

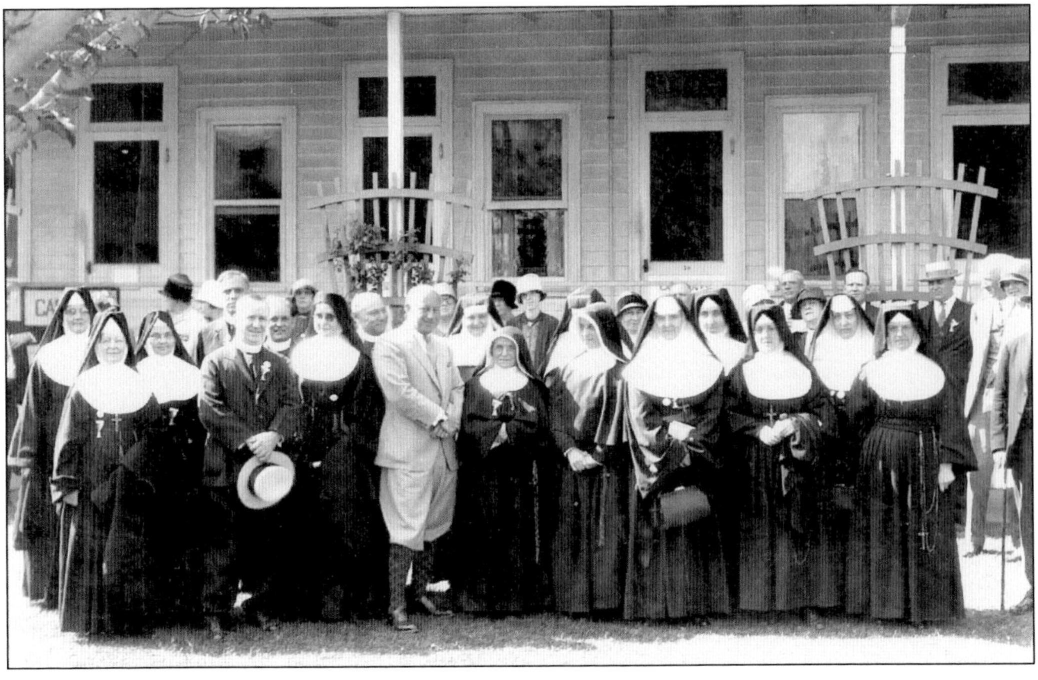

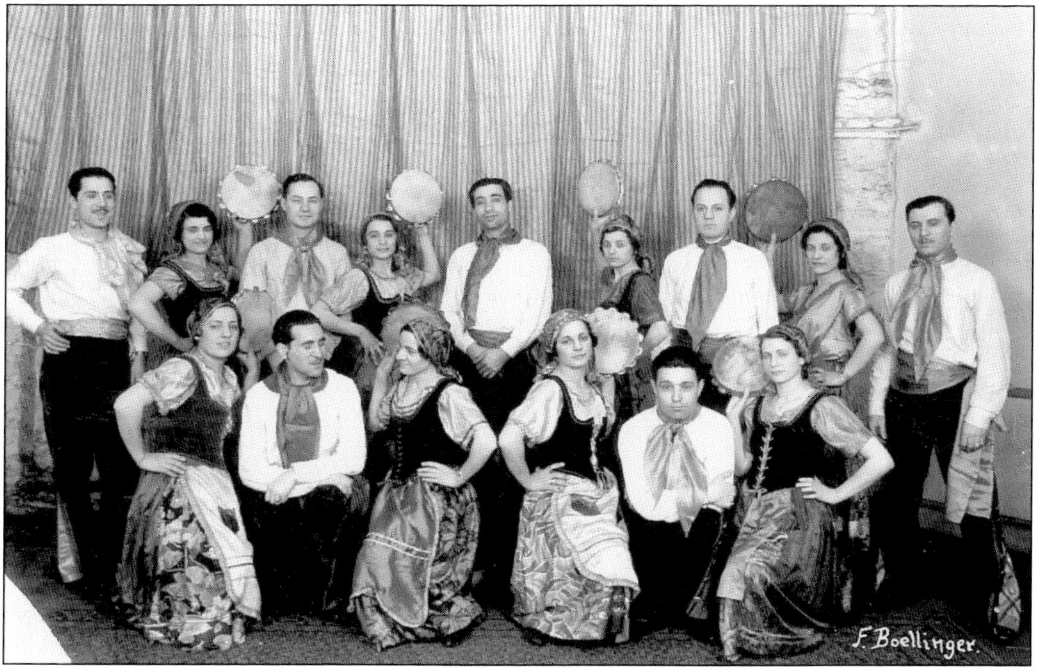

ITALIAN DAY, C. 1932. Performers are pictured here as they prepare to take part in Italian Day, celebrated on April 11 at All Nations Festival Hall. Two of the performers are Rosa Ciafardini DiPilla (standing fourth from the left) and her husband, Albert DiPilla (standing third from the right). The young women (shown below) are in their native dress of Italy. The different dresses indicate the region in Italy where they came from. (Courtesy of the Archives of the Sisters of Charity of Cincinnati and SMCS.)

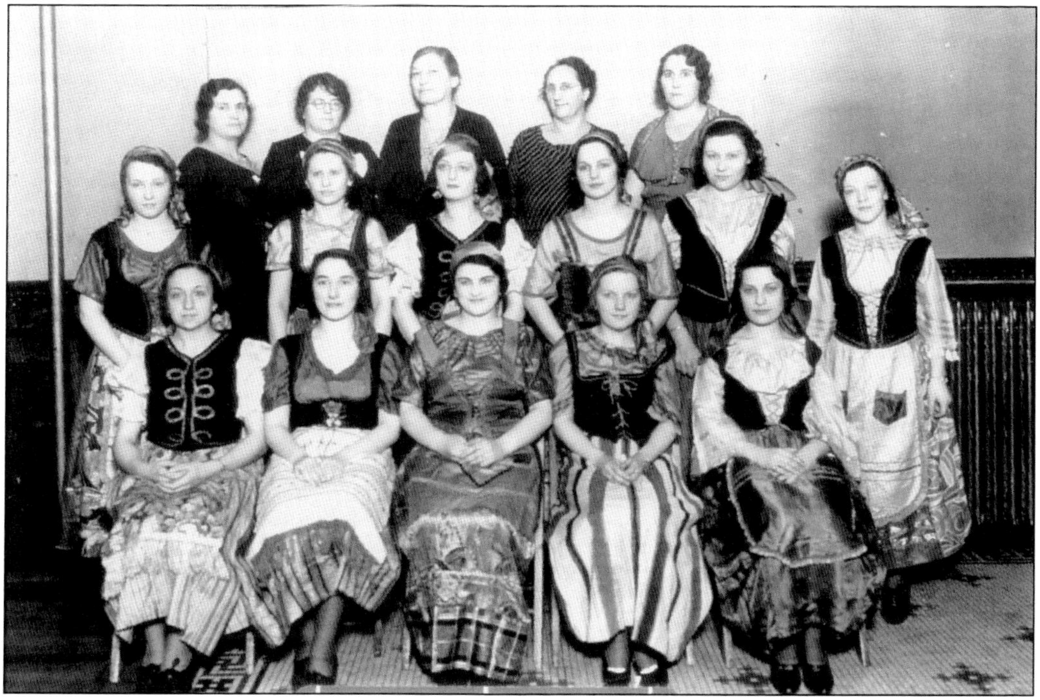

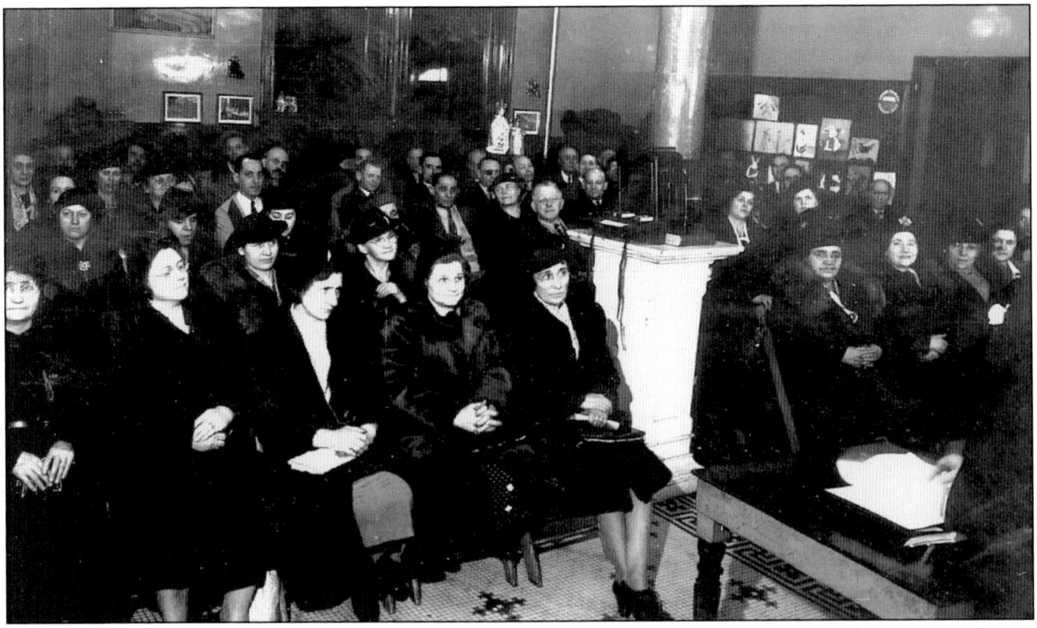

ENGLISH CLASSES, 1930S. Teaching the English language began in 1911 and was a daunting task from the beginning due to the various dialects spoken by the Italian immigrants. Specific classes were held for English instruction and reinforced within the social circles and sodalities formed by the sisters at the Santa Maria Institute as early as 1911. (Courtesy of the Archives of the Sisters of Charity of Cincinnati and SMCS.)

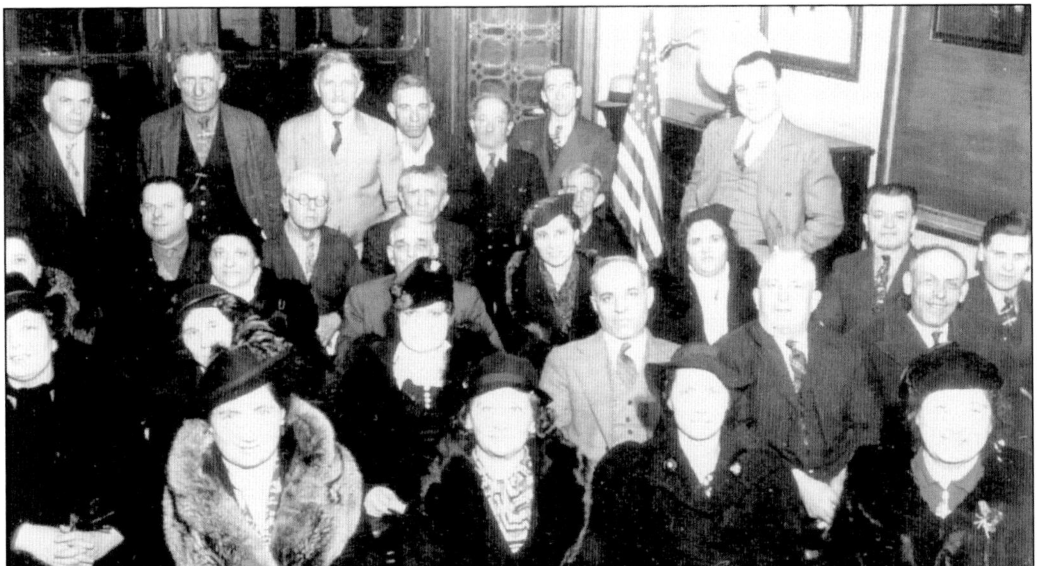

CITIZENSHIP CLASSES, C. 1939. The early immigrants of all nationalities in Greater Cincinnati did not readily apply for citizenship. During World War I, they were heavily criticized for not becoming citizens in a timely manner even though many had lived in Cincinnati for many years. During that time, renewed focus was placed on citizenship, and after the war, the push continued for all immigrants to become citizens. (Courtesy of the Archives of the Sisters of Charity of Cincinnati and SMCS.)

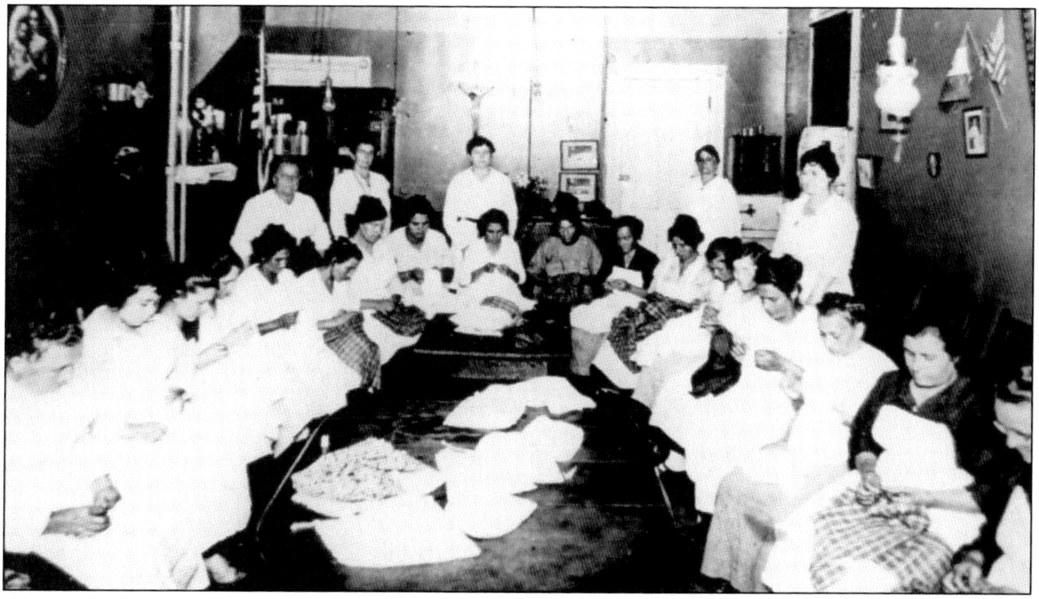

WOMEN'S SEWING CIRCLE, 1920S. It is believed that this photograph was taken at the Santa Maria Institute, which began offering sewing classes for immigrant women on January 25, 1900. There they learned to make children's clothes and to remake their own dresses as well as make new ones. The women were permitted to keep what they made or donate the articles to the St. Vincent de Paul Society. (Courtesy of the Cincinnati Museum Center, Cincinnati Historical Society Library.)

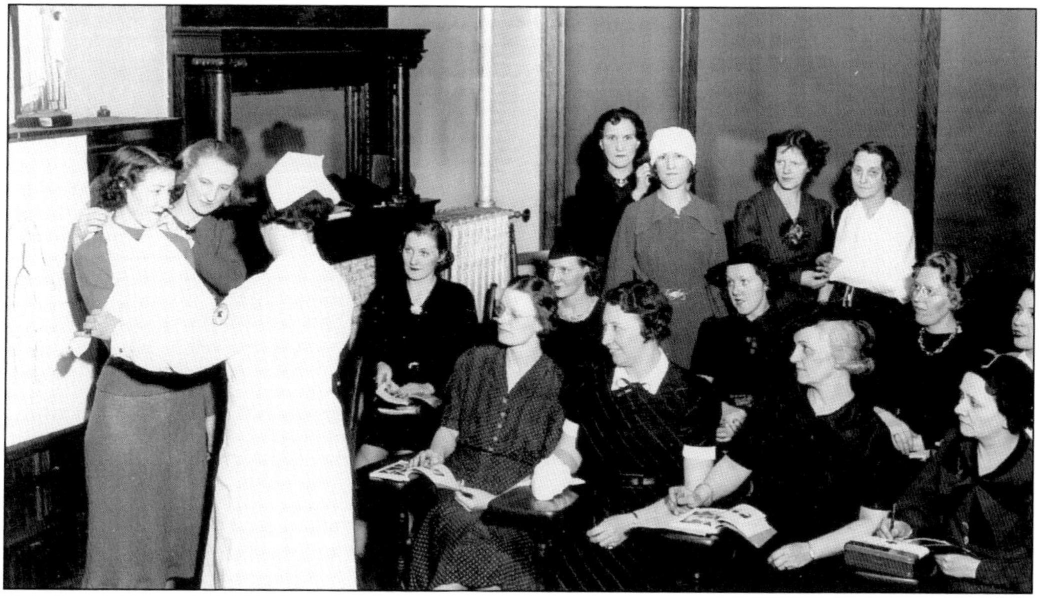

RED CROSS HOME NURSING, C. 1935. Beginning as early as World War I, women were taught how to care for others. In 1918, female members of Sacred Heart Italian Church met in the church's rectory hall to make items for the military. During the Spanish flu pandemic, the workers made stockings and sweaters at home since the church was closed for seven weeks to prevent the spread of the deadly influenza. (Courtesy of the Archives of the Sisters of Charity of Cincinnati and SMCS.)

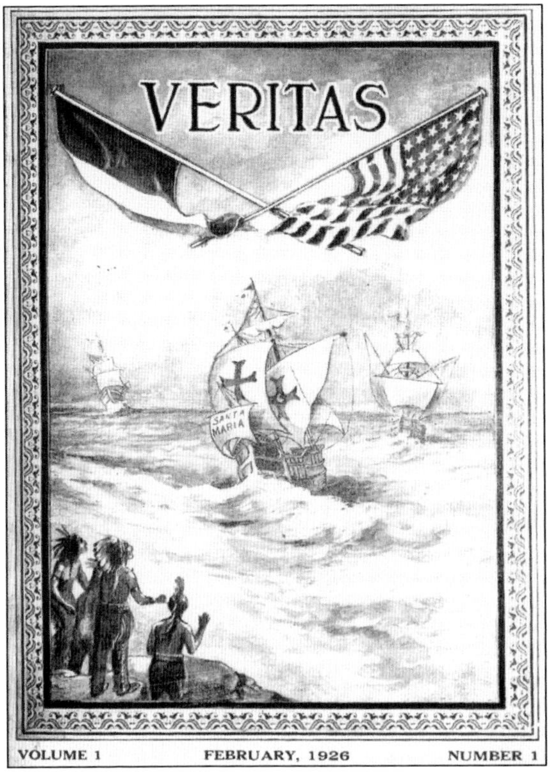

VERITAS. In 1926, the sisters created a publication called *Veritas*, meaning "truth," which was written for Italian American Catholics. Recipes and helpful hints about marriage, raising children, and caring for the home were a focus for instruction in a column titled "Women's Realm." Once it was determined that the magazine name was in use for another journal, the sisters changed the name to the *Santa Maria*. (Courtesy of the Archives of the Sisters of Charity of Cincinnati.)

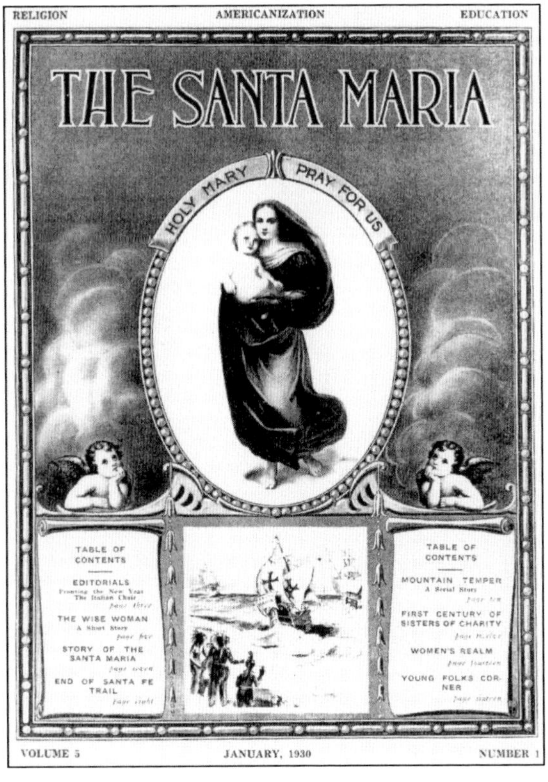

THE *SANTA MARIA*, 1930. The *Santa Maria* magazine began its fifth year under the patronage of the blessed mother while maintaining its connection with the Santa Maria Institute and the flagship of Christopher Columbus. It remained in publication until 1931. From its inception, the articles were written in both Italian and English. (Courtesy of the Archives of the Sisters of Charity of Cincinnati.)

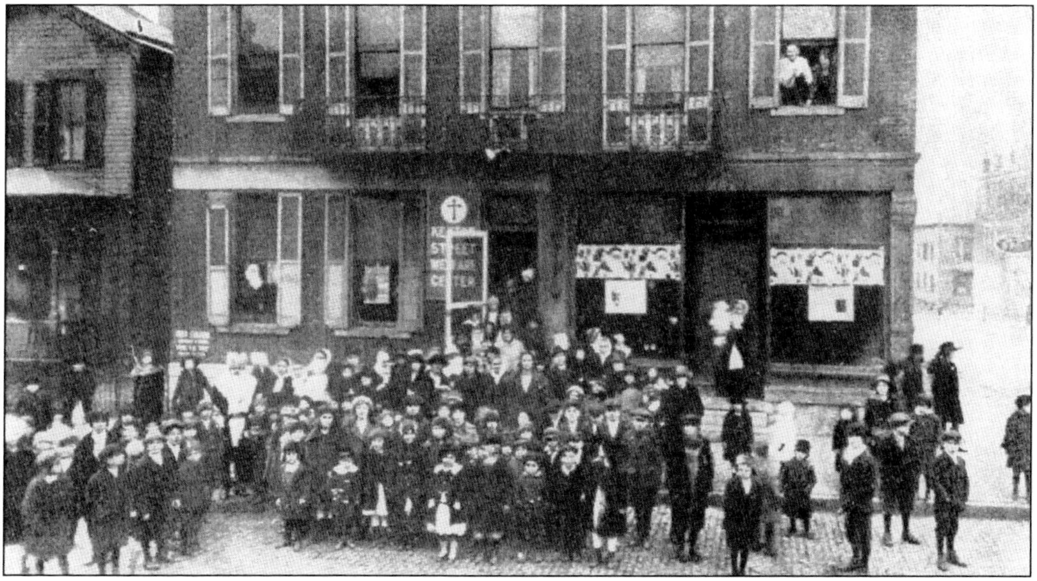

KENTON WELFARE CENTER, c. 1920. The Santa Maria Welfare Center in Walnut Hills was located at Symmes and Burbank Streets and formally opened on May 15, 1919. The following year, the center moved to Kenton Street, and the name was changed to reflect the move. By 1924, 700 Italians and Italian Americans lived in the area. (Courtesy of the Sisters of Charity of Cincinnati.)

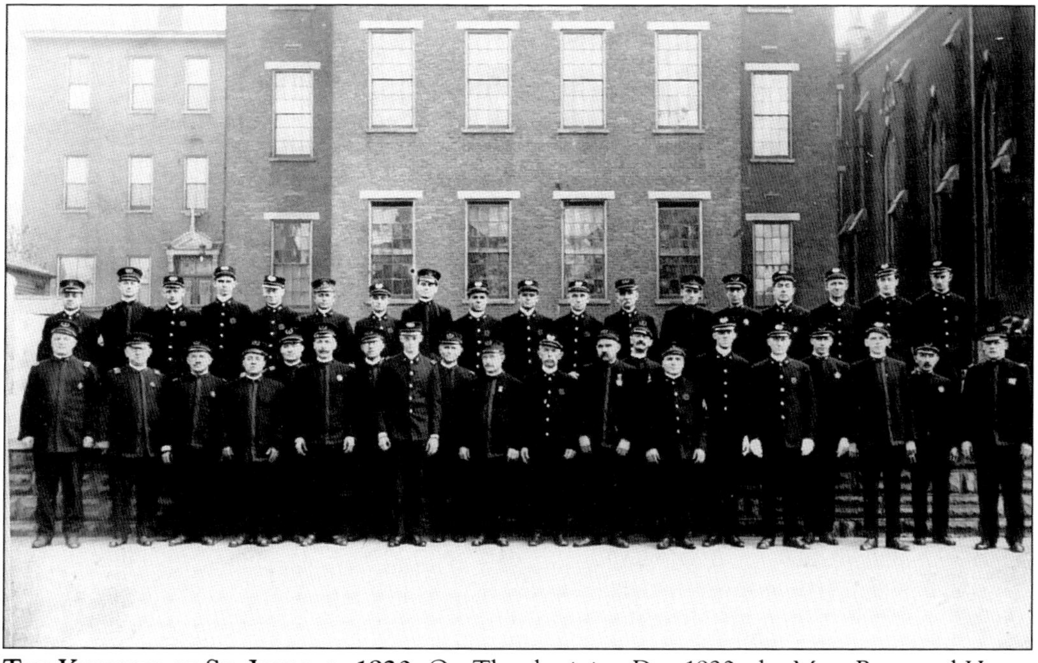

THE KNIGHTS OF ST. JOHN, c. 1920. On Thanksgiving Day 1920, the Most Reverend Henry Moeller, D.D., blessed the Kenton Welfare Center. The celebration featured music by the Knights of St. John Band of Covington, Kentucky, led by their bandmaster Eugene (Gene) Giancola (forefront). Giancola attended Holy Trinity School and was taught by the sisters of the Santa Maria Institute. (Courtesy of R. Toni Bungenstock.)

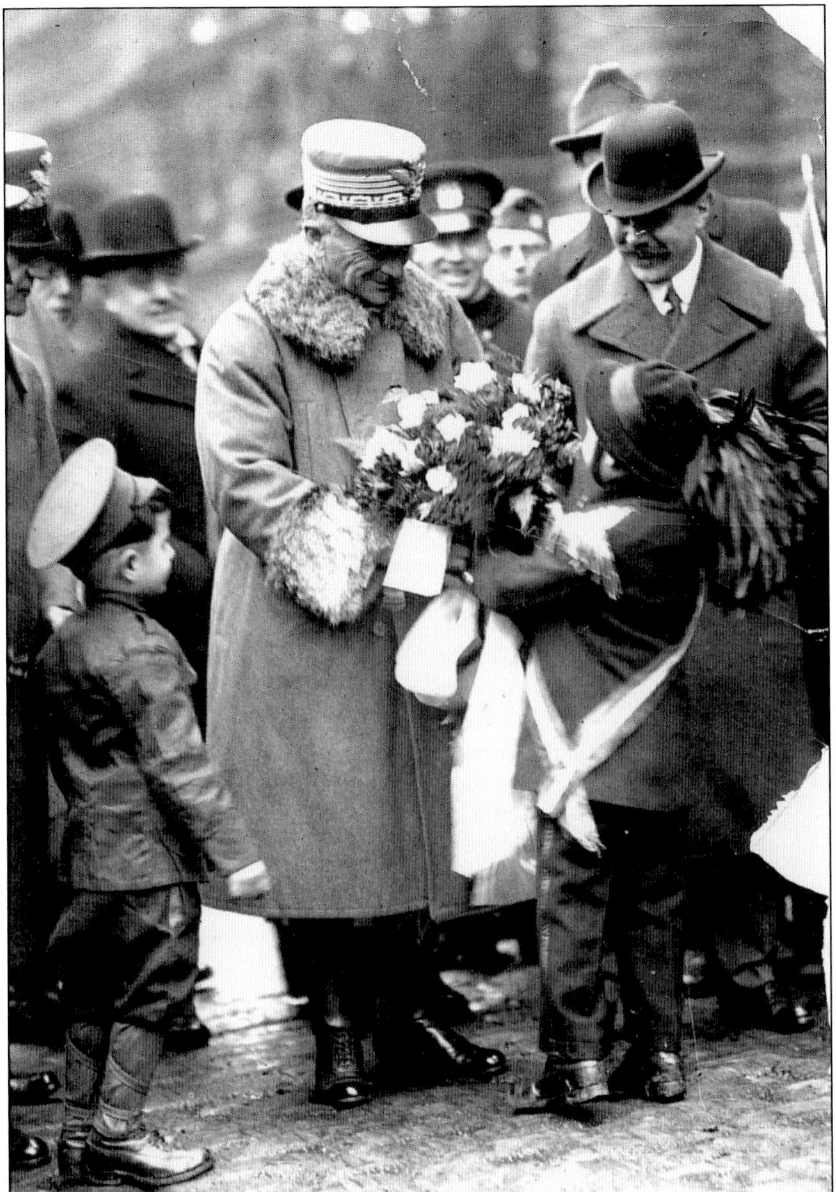

GEN. ARMANDO DIAZ, COMMANDER OF THE ITALIAN ARMY, WORLD WAR I. Gen. Armando Diaz served during the Italo-Turkish War (1911–1912) and was appointed major general in 1914. He became Italy's chief of staff during World War I and launched an offensive on October 23, 1918, at Vittorio Veneto, destroying the Austro-Hungarian army. He received the title of *duca della vittoria* (duke of victory) and became a senator in 1921. On December 5, 1921, General Diaz visited the Kenton Welfare Center and attended a solemn requiem mass for the Italian war dead at Sacred Heart Italian Church. After mass, two children, who represented the Santa Maria Institute, gave him a bouquet of flowers. The Italian people also presented him a check of 50,000 lire for the Italian war invalids. Later he became the Italian minister of war from 1922 to 1924. He retired in 1924 due to poor health, and on February 29, 1928, General Diaz died in Rome at the age of 66. (Courtesy of Gerardo "Curliy" DiTullio.)

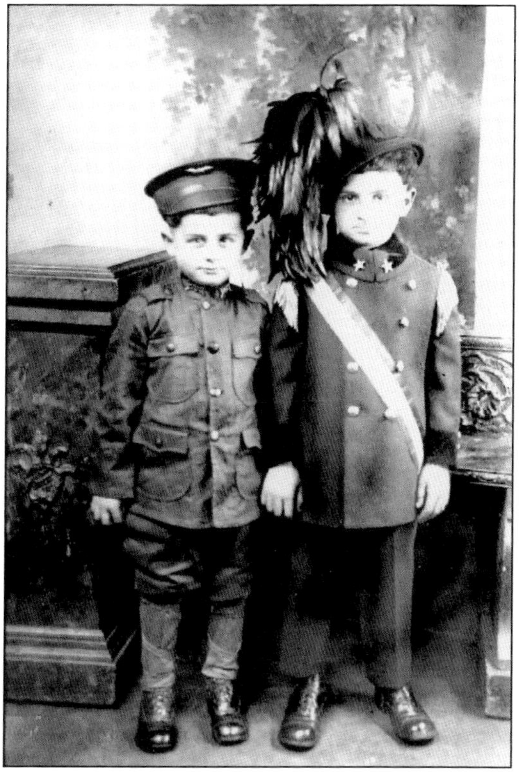

JOHN AND GERARDO DITULLIO, DECEMBER 5, 1921. John DiTullio (left) was four years old when he joined his older brother Gerardo "Curly" DiTullio, age eight, in presenting the bouquet of flowers to General Diaz. The two boys, dressed in Italian uniforms, represented the Santa Maria Institute. (Courtesy of Gerardo "Curly" DiTullio.)

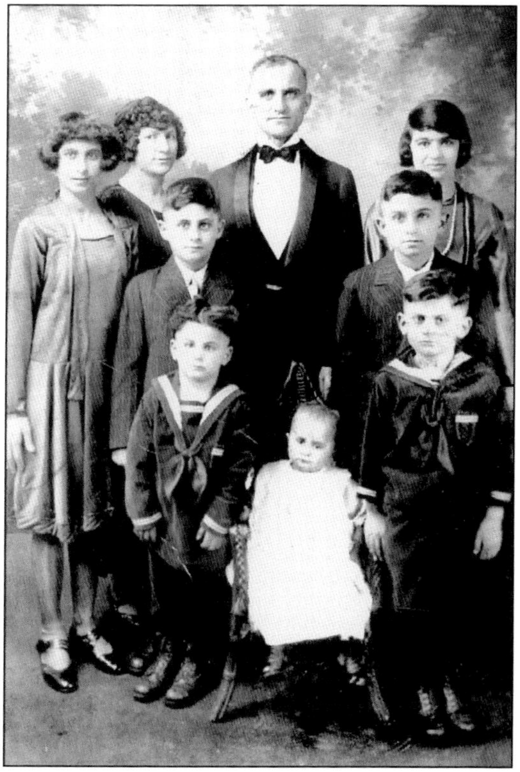

ALEXANDER AND ELLEN "LENA" DITULLIO FAMILY. Alexander DiTullio, originally from the province of Campobasso, Molise, Italy, married Lena Forney. Alexander made the sailor uniforms for his two small children, Eugene (left) and George (right). The DiTullios settled at 2032 Highland Avenue in Mount Auburn. All their nine children were born in America; their names are Gerardo, Eugene, Jeanette, Peggy, John, Anna, Malvina, Adeline, and George. (Courtesy of Gerardo "Curly" DiTullio.)

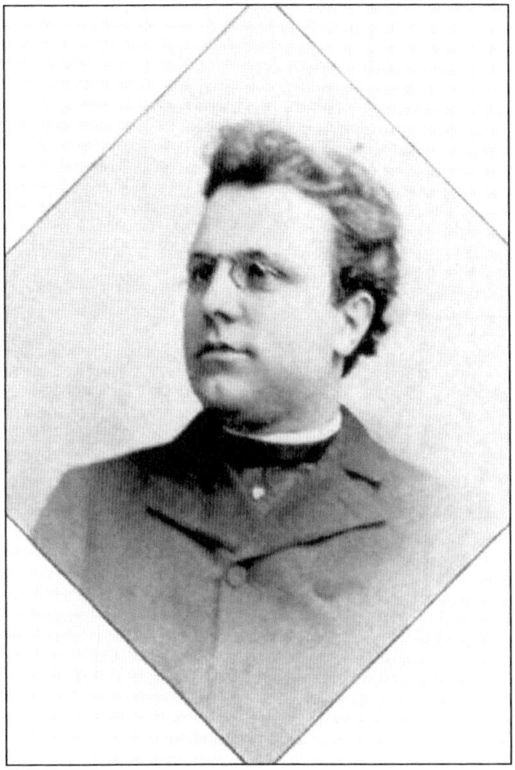

Fr. Peter Lotti, 1892–1897. As pastor of Sacred Heart Italian Church, Fr. Peter Lotti began and completed the building of the church. Father Lotti was born in Florence, Italy, on August 6, 1864, to Savino Lotti and Josephina Pieri Lotti and was educated at the Abbey of Ficsole in Florence, Italy. He came to America in 1890. After a short stay in Bridgeport, Connecticut, Father Lotti came to Cincinnati. (Courtesy of the Athenaeum of Ohio, Mount St. Mary Seminary.)

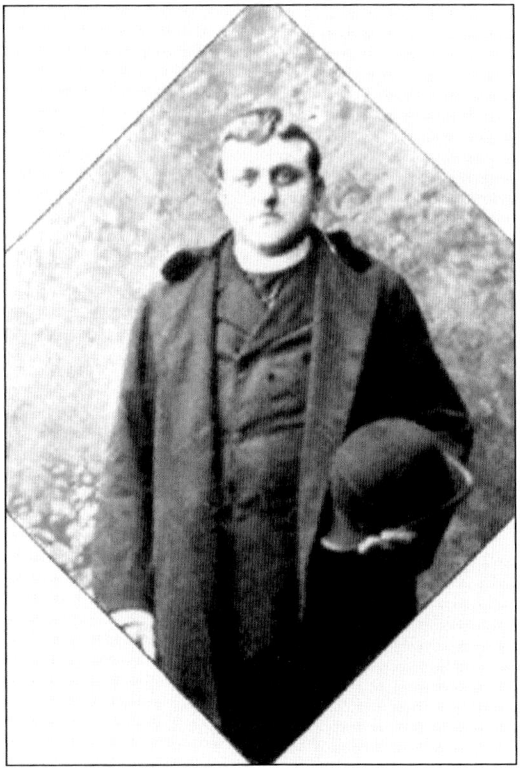

Fr. Joseph Quadranti, 1898–1903. As assistant pastor of Sacred Heart Italian Church, Fr. Joseph Quadranti had the greatest honor of receiving Bishop John Baptist Scalabrini, bishop of Piacenza, Italy, on October 5, 1901, to visit the Romanesque-style church and the Santa Maria Institute. (Courtesy of the Athenaeum of Ohio, Mount St. Mary Seminary.)

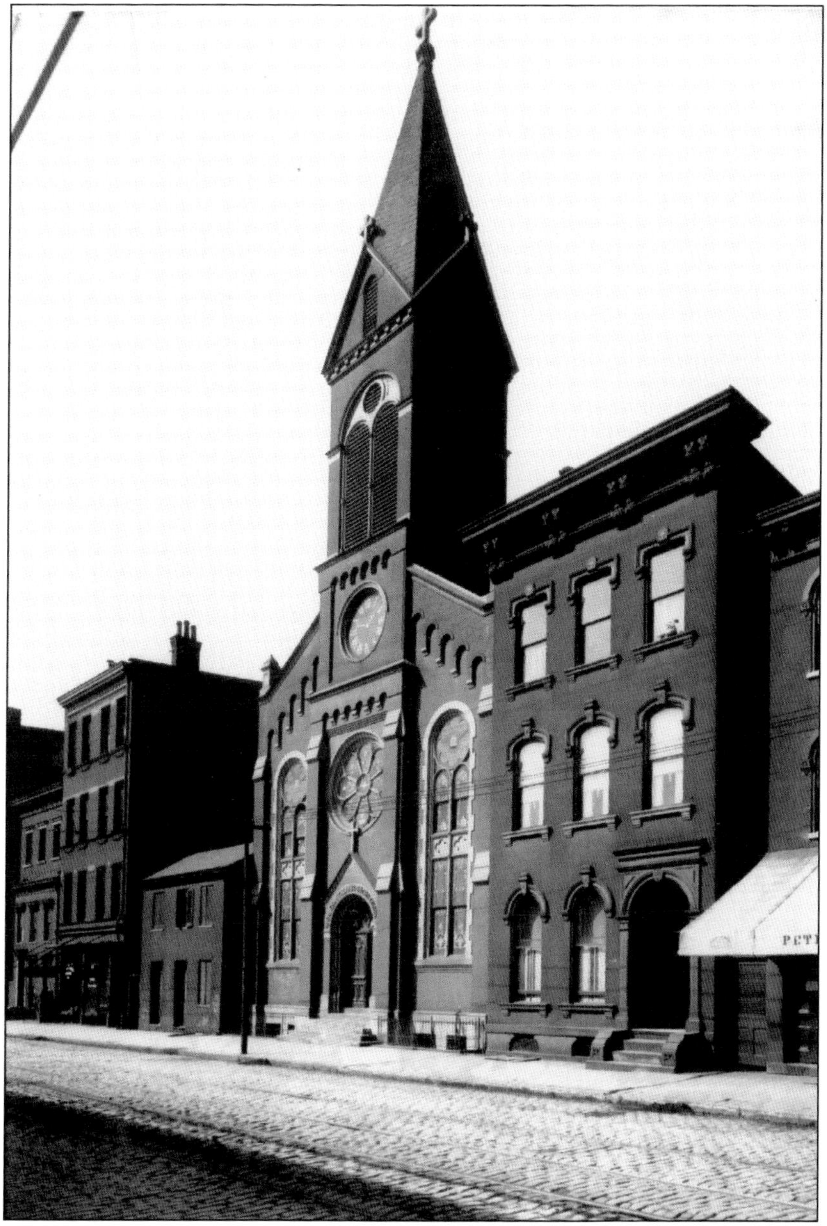

SACRED HEART ITALIAN CHURCH, C. 1969. This beautiful church was located at 527 Broadway Street in downtown Cincinnati. Above the arched front door was the inscription Chiesa Italiana Sacro Cuore, which translates to Sacred Heart Italian Church. Under the care of the Scalabrini Fathers, it served as the place of worship for many Italian immigrants beginning in the late 19th century. Since 1890, over 7,490 baptisms were performed, 1,670 marriages, and 2,692 funeral services. The church was razed in 1970 for the building of Proctor and Gamble corporate headquarters. The parishioners joined the parish of Sacred Heart Church in Camp Washington in 1970. Ultimately, Sacred Heart Italian Church would become the parent church in 1922 for San Antonio Church, located in South Fairmount, and Our Lady of Mount Carmel in 1925 in Walnut Hills. The Feast of the Sacred Heart of Jesus is June 21. (Courtesy of the Cincinnati Museum Center, Cincinnati Historical Society Library.)

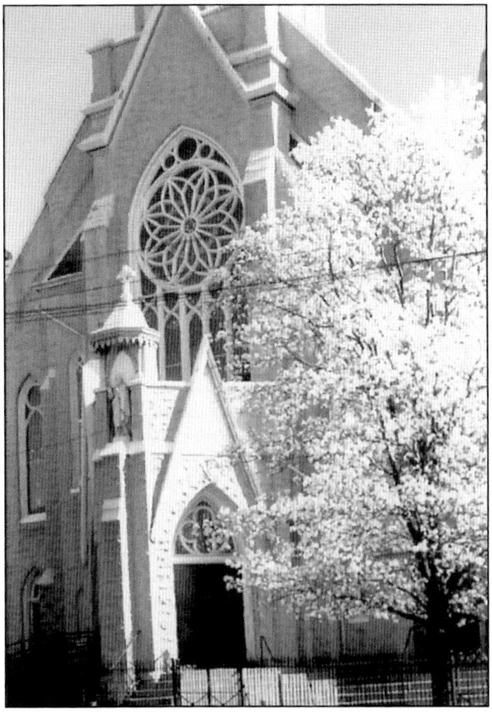

SACRED HEART CHURCH, CAMP WASHINGTON. Sacred Heart parish was established in 1870 and originally located at 2737 Colerain Avenue opposite Heywood Street. The current church, shown here, is located on the corner of Massachusetts and Marshall Avenues and was dedicated on June 30, 1889. It endured the flood of 1937 and underwent major renovation in July 1970. (Courtesy of Fr. Mario Rauzi, C.S.)

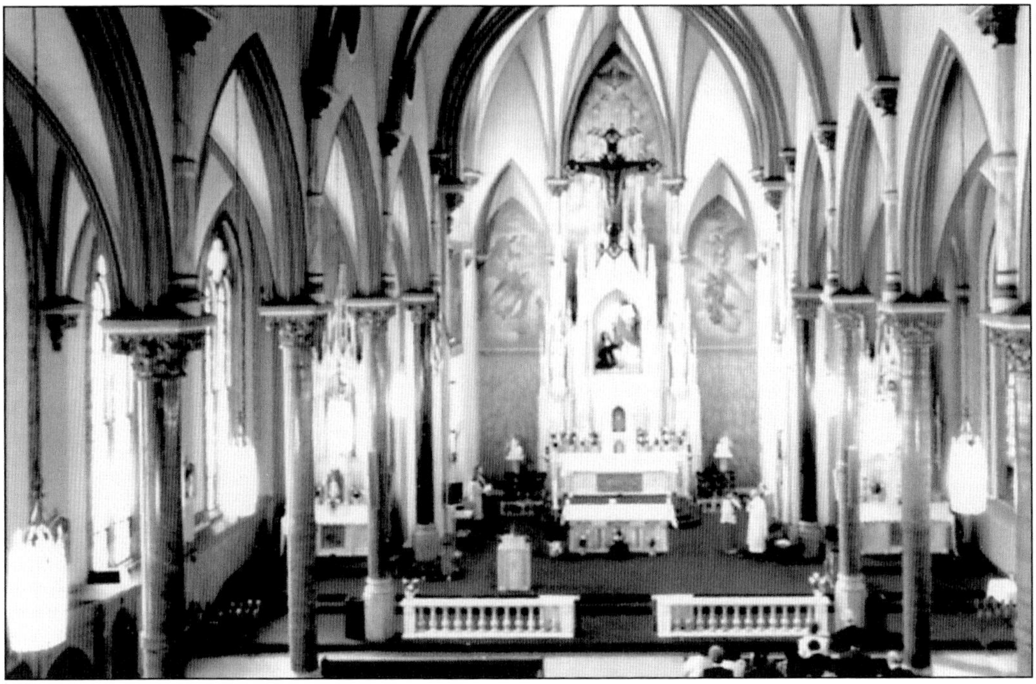

CHURCH ALTAR AND COMMUNION RAIL. The marble communion rail was purchased in 1927 at a cost of $1,800; the original Altar of Sacrifice (shown in the forefront) was bought with funds raised by the parish through fund-raising events and monies collected from donors. These items, in addition to the sanctuary and the baptismal font, were brought from Sacred Heart Italian Church in downtown Cincinnati to Sacred Heart Church. (Courtesy of Fr. Mario Rauzi, C.S.)

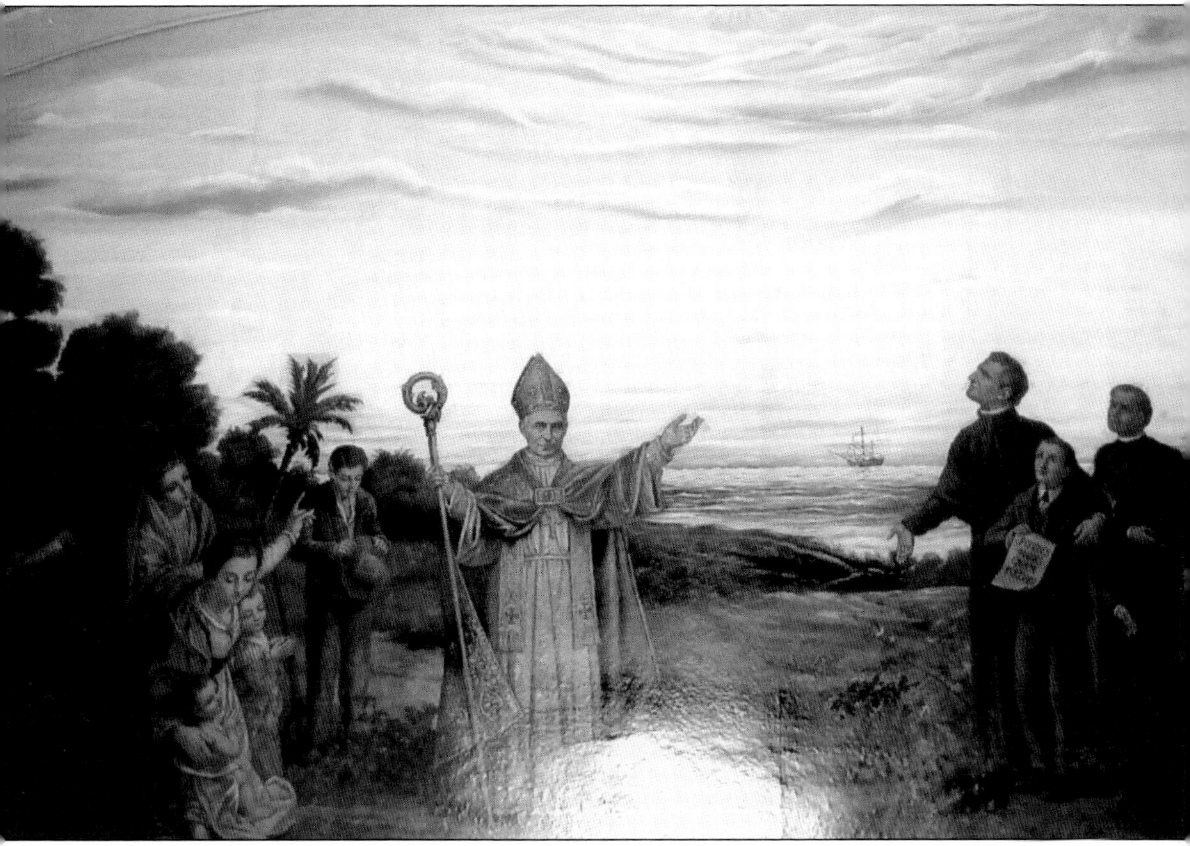

BISHOP SCALABRINI GROUP PAINTING ON CANVAS. Located on the back wall of the stage in the former school auditorium, now the Italian Center, on the church property of Sacred Heart, Camp Washington, is a wall mural taken from the sanctuary of Sacred Heart Italian Church. Shown in this mural is the horizon meeting the sea with a single ship sailing the sea. To the left of the seashore is Bishop Scalabrini, founder of the Missionaries of St. Charles, in his pontifical vestments. Beside him to the left are a group of Italian immigrants arriving in America. To the right is St. John Bosco, founder of the Salesian congregation, and next to him is depicted St. Dominic Savio. Also shown in the mural are Don Luigi Guanella, the founder of the Daughters of Providence, and St. Frances Cabrini (kneeling in the foreground), who established hospitals and educational institutions in the Americas. Next to her (but not shown) are a nun of the Daughters of Providence and a Scalabrinian priest. (Authors' collection.)

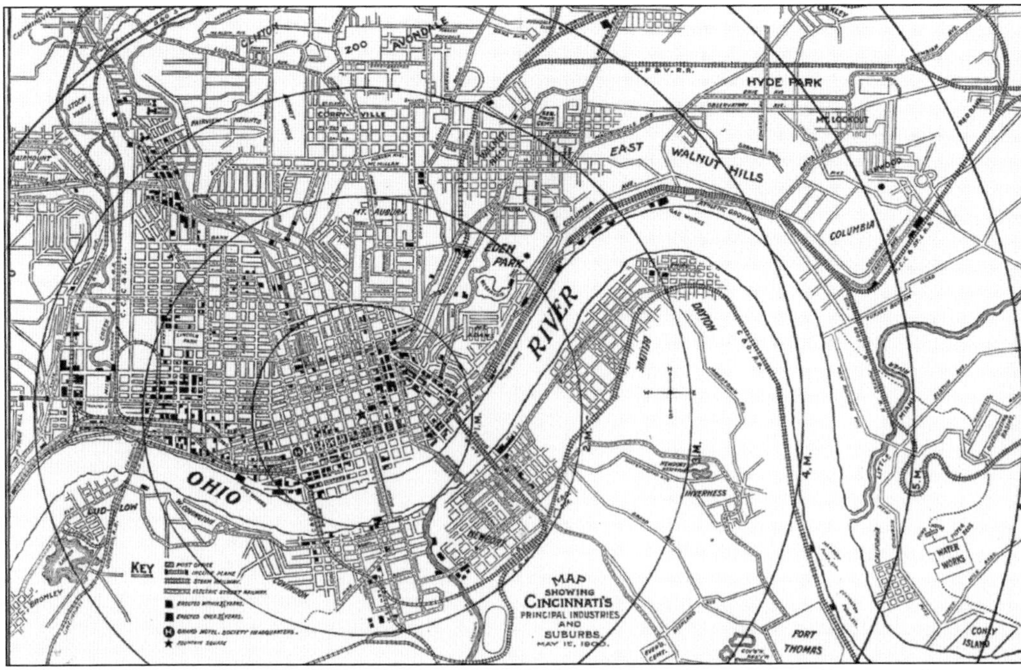

CINCINNATI AND VICINITY MAP, MAY 1, 1900. This map with its rings gives an indication of the territory originally occupied by the Italian immigrants and how far they initially moved out of the area. At first they resided within the center circle down to the riverbank, then migrated three miles out into Walnut Hills (at the right) and about four miles out to Fairmount (at the left). (Courtesy of the Cincinnati Museum Center, Cincinnati Historical Society Library.)

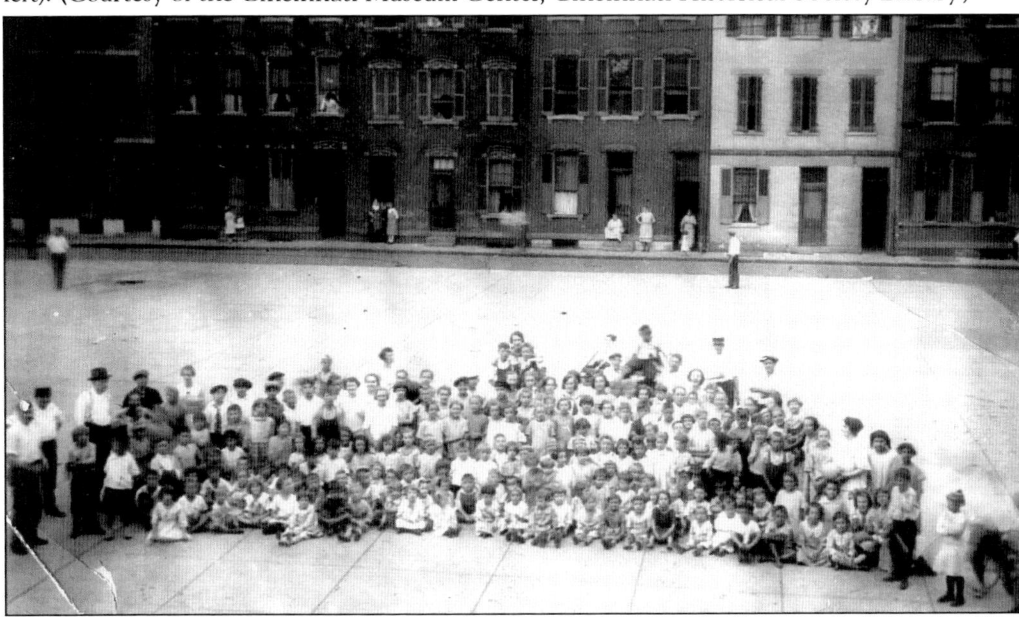

CHILDREN OUTSIDE THE TENEMENTS. Although the location of this photograph is unknown, it clearly depicts the gathering of people outside the tenement houses within the city. Children gather to play while parents and neighbors meet to talk and to catch up on the news of the day. (Courtesy of the Archives of the Sisters of Charity of Cincinnati and SMCS.)

Two

Italian Colonies

While the core of the Italian community started in the Ohio River basin area of downtown Cincinnati, Italian families later moved to the hilltop areas and suburbs as early as 1867. Immigrants heavily populated such streets as Broadway Street, Third Street through Sixth Street, the lower part of Plum and Race Streets, Water and Front Streets, and Central Avenue and Linn Street in the crowded downtown area. Most of the early immigrants lived in tenement housing in close, cramped quarters in a dirty city, which was a result of cows and pigs being driven through the downtown streets on their way to the slaughterhouses. Coal contributed to the pollution as it was used to heat not only the tenements but also the factories within the city. By 1900, the automobile made its contribution to polluting the air. This living environment was difficult for the Italians who were not used to urban living.

Most of the Italian population clustered in fairly large numbers within multicultural neighborhoods. For example, the Genoese and northern Italians lived in the lower West End, while the Sicilians and southern Italians lived in the lower East End of Cincinnati. This division seemed to follow the regions of Italy where they came from and the time they arrived from Italy. For example, on the eastern side of the city, Little Italys reached into Walnut Hills along the streets of Kenton, Burbank, May, and Boone, and on the western side of the city into Fairmount especially along Queen City Avenue.

As the population moved into these areas, so did the need for social welfare centers. No records exist indicating where the Italian population worshipped prior to 1890 when the parish was formed for Sacred Heart Italian Church. With the establishment of the Kenton Welfare Center in 1920 and St. Anthony Welfare Center in 1922, the centers became the gathering place for worship and neighborhood activity, just as the core within downtown Cincinnati had become active with the Santa Maria Institute and Sacred Heart Italian Church. Out of these welfare centers, they would eventually build their own churches, namely San Antonio di Padova and Our Lady of Mount Carmel.

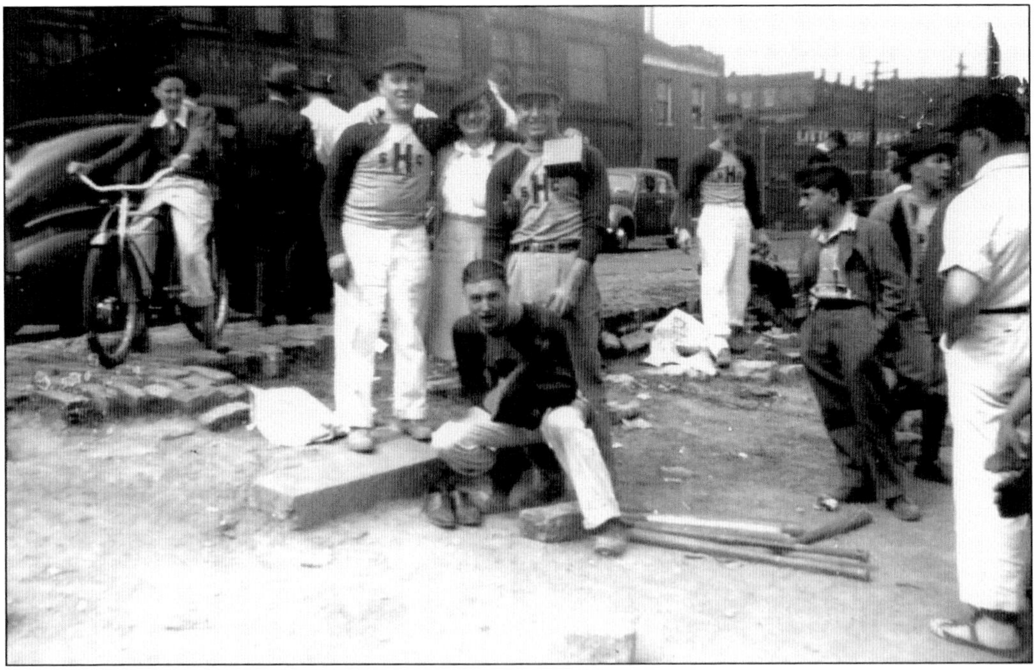

SACRED HEART ITALIAN CHURCH BASEBALL TEAM, MAY 11, 1941. This was the only baseball team Sacred Heart Italian Church ever had. Four of the players, from left to right, are Geno Pierani, Dick Aielli, Steve Sciamanna, and Johnny Pierani. Standing between Geno and Dick is Eva Contadino. In the photograph below, the team is shown playing on the Cincinnati riverfront between the Central and Louisville and Nashville (L&N) Bridges. Geno Pierani is rounding the base. (Courtesy of Tony Pierani.)

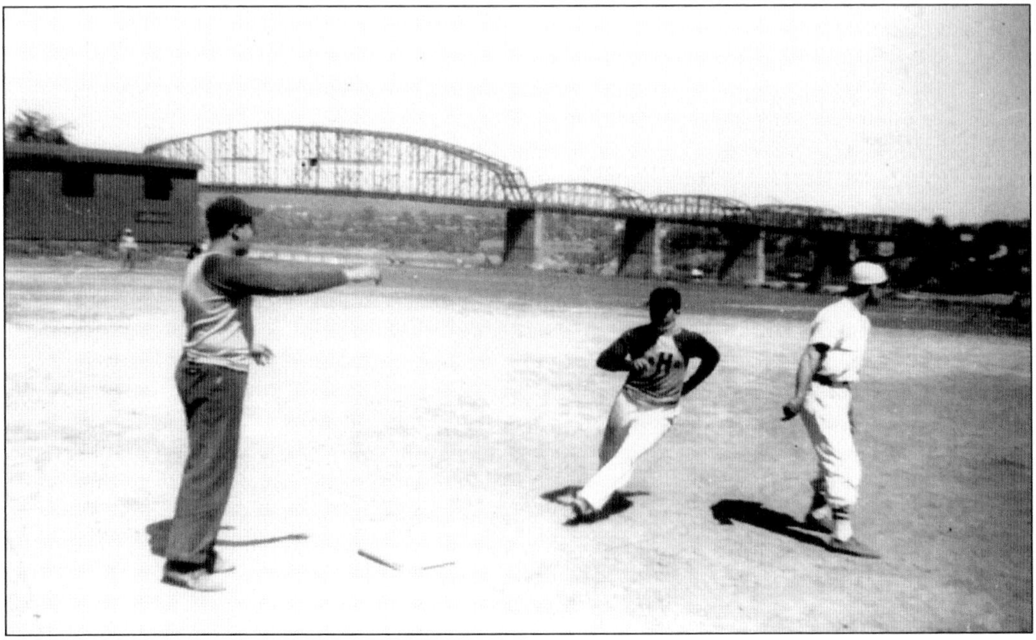

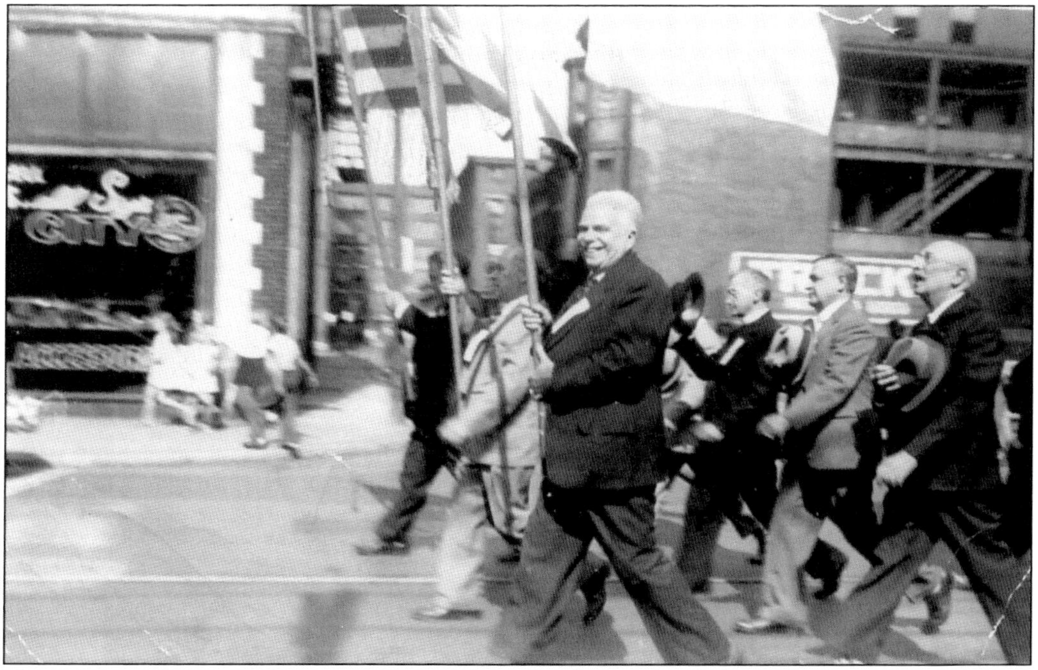

HOLY NAME PARADE, OCTOBER 11, 1942. Official records of the Holy Name Society state the first rally began in 1907. By 1913, over 30,000 members from all area parishes marched in the west side of Cincinnati to the ball field for solemn benediction. In the photograph above, Holy Name members are parading down Sixth and North Streets, and in the photograph below, they are marching into Crosley Field. For many years, the parade coincided with the celebration of Columbus Day. (Courtesy of Tony Pierani.)

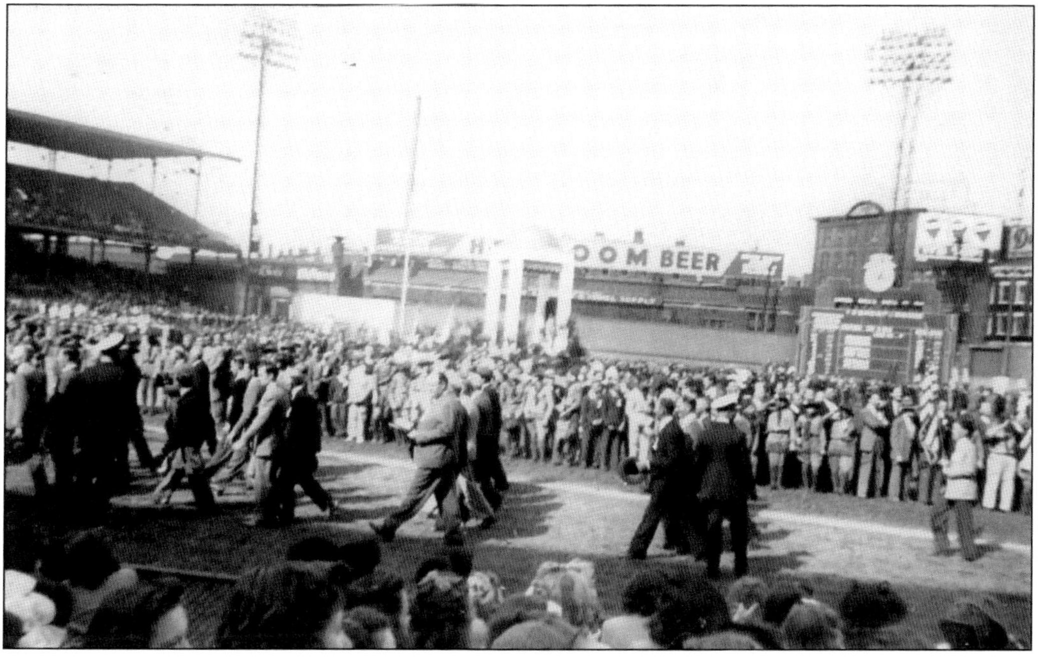

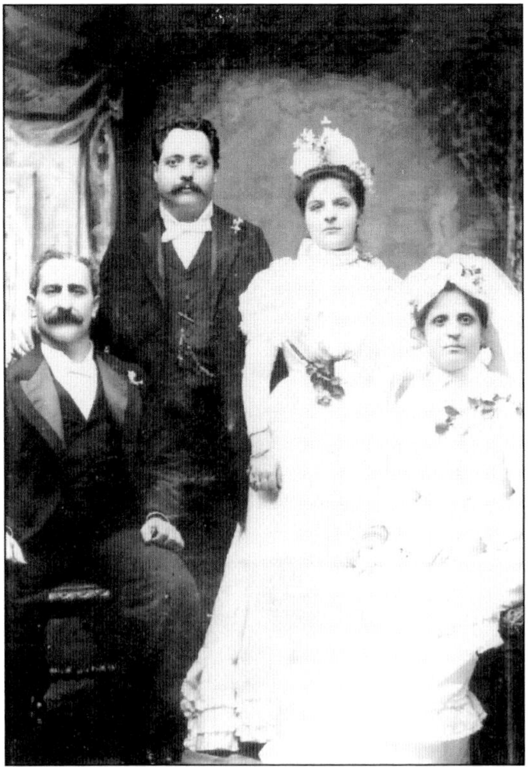

WEDDING OF PIETRO (PETER) CETRULO AND STELLA GAGLIARDI, MAY 7, 1899. Married at Sacred Heart Italian Church, Stella Gagliardi and Pietro (Peter) Cetrulo (seated) pose for their formal wedding photograph with their witnesses, Antonio Delvecchio and Maria Passafiume. Peter Cetrulo emigrated from Caposele, Italy, a small mountain village near the city of Avellino, province of Avellino, Campania, and became a naturalized citizen in 1889. (Courtesy of Robert C. Cetrulo, J.D.)

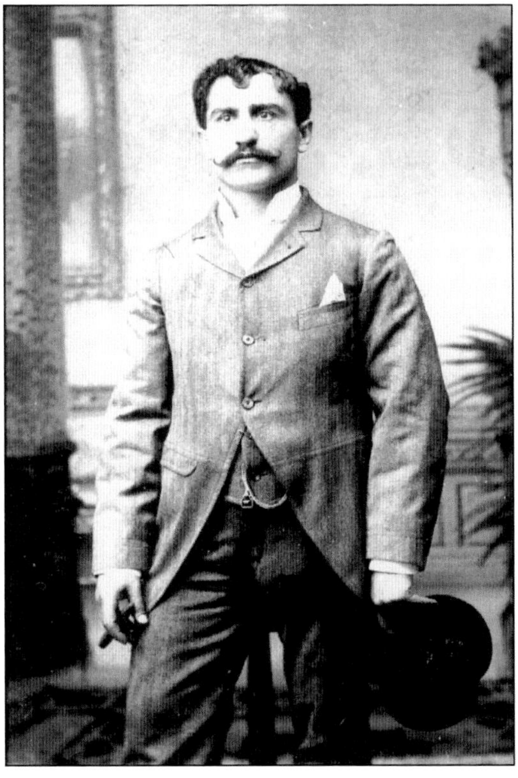

PETER CETRULO. Peter and Stella Cetrulo first settled in Covington, where Peter operated the Covington Barbershop on Court Street. They later moved to Cincinnati, and Peter opened a barbershop at 527 Elm Street, which is now the location of the Cincinnati Convention Center. Peter would sing operatic arias while he cut his customers' hair. The Cetrulos lived above the barbershop and raised three children, Frank, Camillo, and Rose. (Courtesy of Robert C. Cetrulo, J.D.)

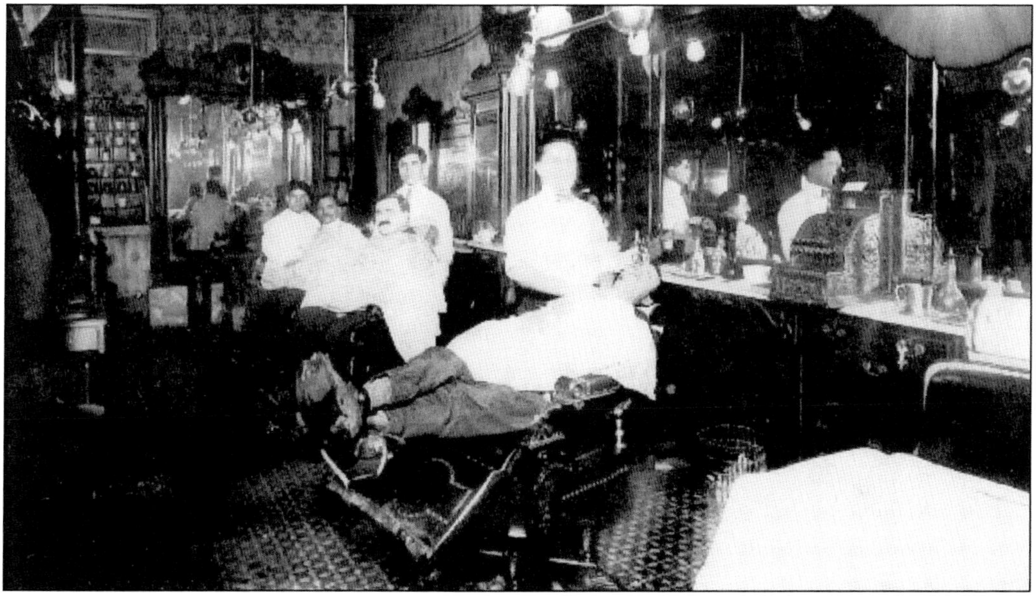

VILLARI'S BARBER SHOP, C. 1913. Having emigrated from Sicily, Italy, in the early 20th century, Pietro (Pete) Villari opened a barbershop on Central Avenue and provided a shave and haircut to his patrons for 25¢. The barbers' wives would wash and boil the towels they used. The barbershop later moved to DeSales Corner in the mid-1930s where Dominick Villari ran the shop alone. The three barbers shown in the photograph are Pete (far left), Dominick (center), and Nick Abitico. (Courtesy of Josephine Ottaviani.)

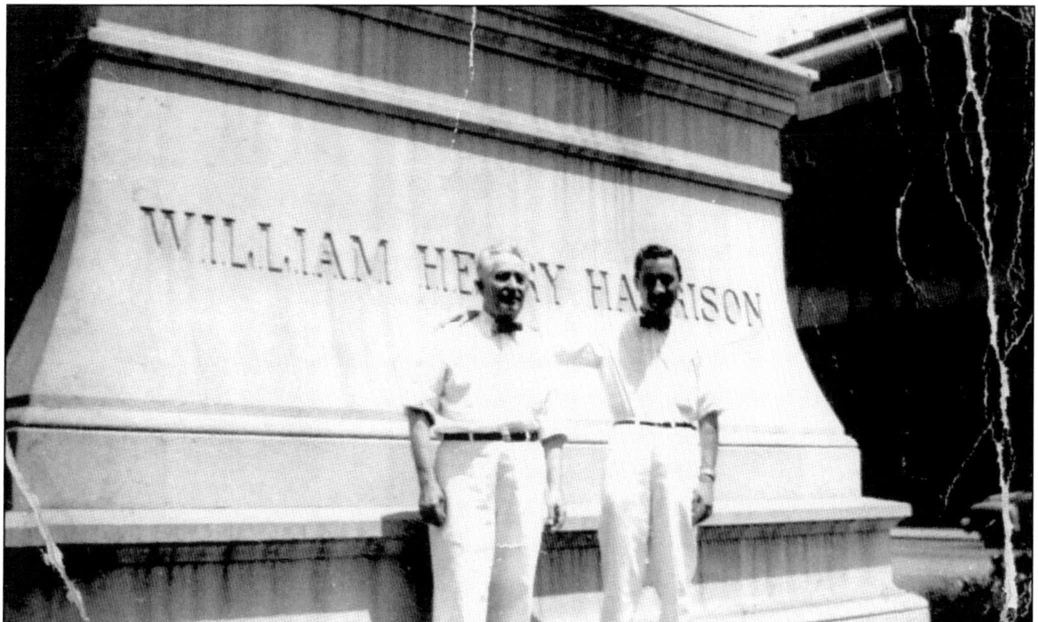

ANGELO BRUNO. Angelo Bruno (left), who emigrated from Ena, Sicily, bought the barbershop located at 5 Garfield Place in 1931. He operated it for 36 years, selling it to Fausto Ferrari in 1967. In this photograph, they are standing in front of the William Henry Harrison memorial located in Piatt Park, Garfield Place at Elm Street. (Courtesy of Fausto Ferrari.)

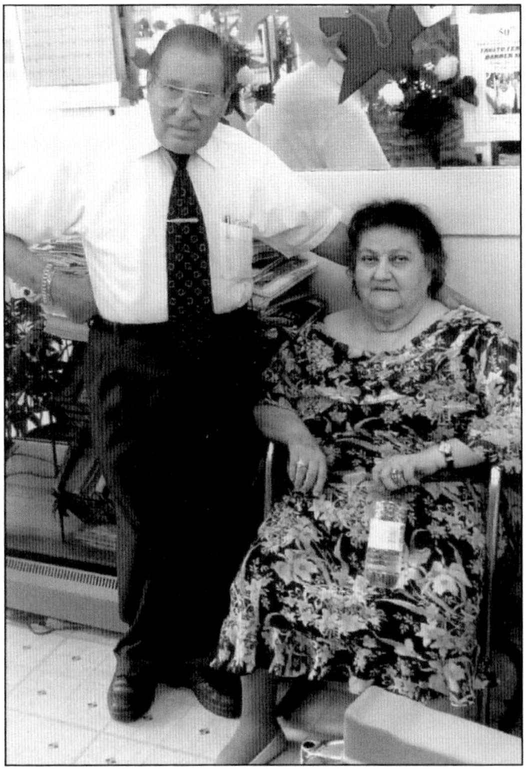

FAUSTO FERRARI AND LENA ALLAVATO FERRARI. Fausto and Lena Ferrari, now married over 40 years, emigrated from Fuscaldo, Italy, in March 1957. Upon arrival in Cincinnati, Fausto went to work for Angelo Bruno as a barber. He became a naturalized citizen in 1964. Fausto's brother Emilio joined him in Cincinnati in 1969. (Courtesy of Fausto Ferrari.)

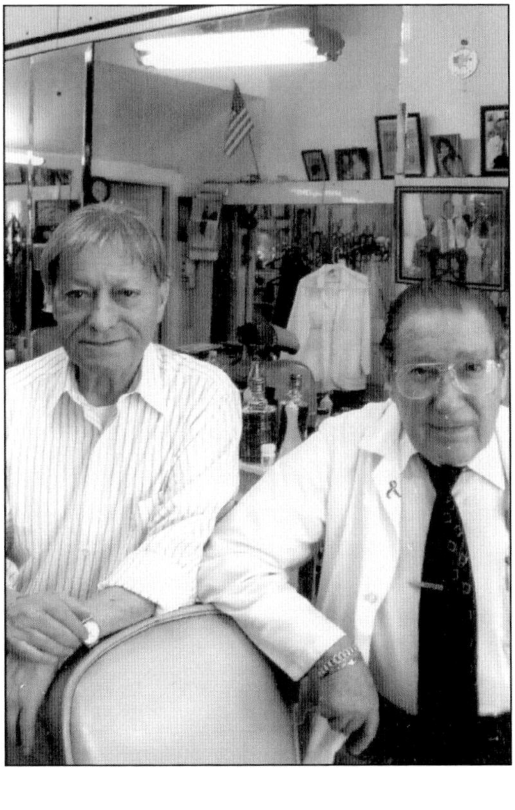

FAUSTO FERRARI BARBER SHOP. Fausto "the Barber of Garfield Place" and Emilio Ferrari operate the shop and continue to cut hair with a scissors while using a straight razor on the back of the neck. The back counter holds a collection of vintage bottles filled with various aftershave lotions, making the entire room smell wonderful. Scattered among the bottles are prayer cards and postcards from Fausto's town of Fuscaldo. (Courtesy of Fausto Ferrari.)

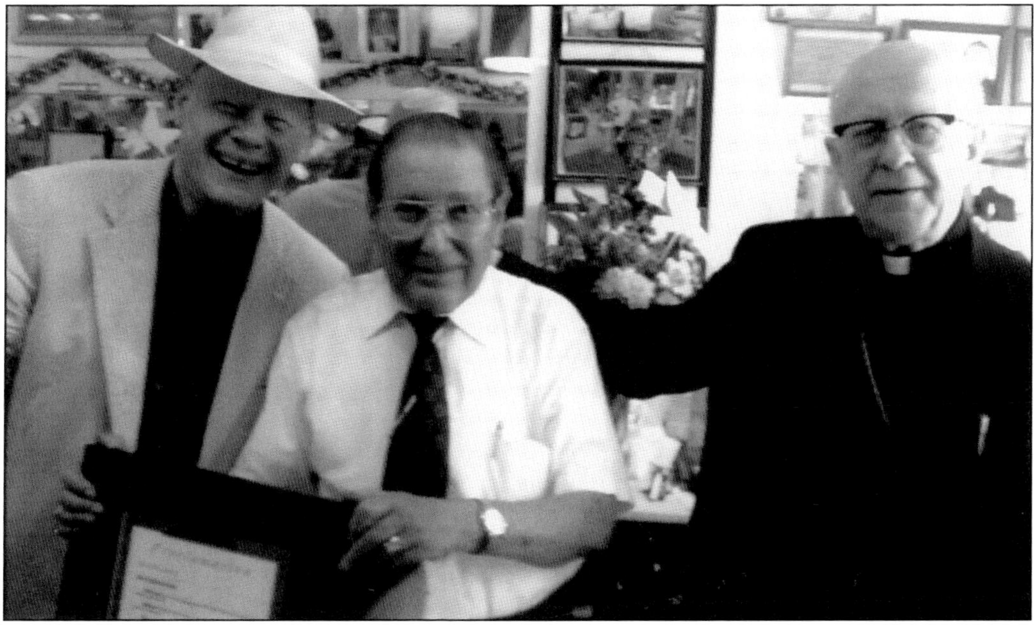

Fausto Ferrari Barber Shop Day, July 7, 2007. Cincinnati mayor Mark Mallory issued a proclamation from the City of Cincinnati in honor of Fausto Ferrari's 50th anniversary in the barber business. Celebrating with him are, from left to right, the former vice mayor Jim Tarbell and Archbishop Daniel Pilarczyk, one of his loyal customers. (Courtesy of Fausto Ferrari.)

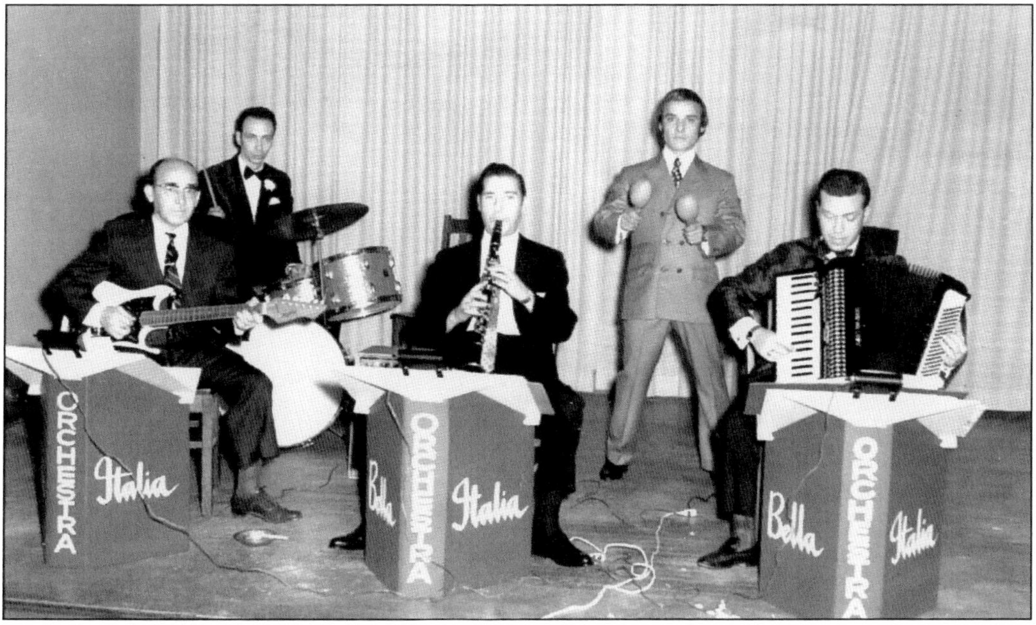

Bella Italia Orchestra, 1969. Fausto Ferrari began playing musical instruments when he was 13 years old. He gathered some friends together, and they began playing at Coney Island and for weddings and various events held at the downtown hotels. In addition to playing the clarinet, he played the accordion, guitar, and mandolin. Band members are, from left to right, Elia Santoro (guitar), Enricho Lanza (drummer), Fausto Ferrari (clarinet), and Frank Santoro (accordion). (Courtesy of Fausto Ferrari.)

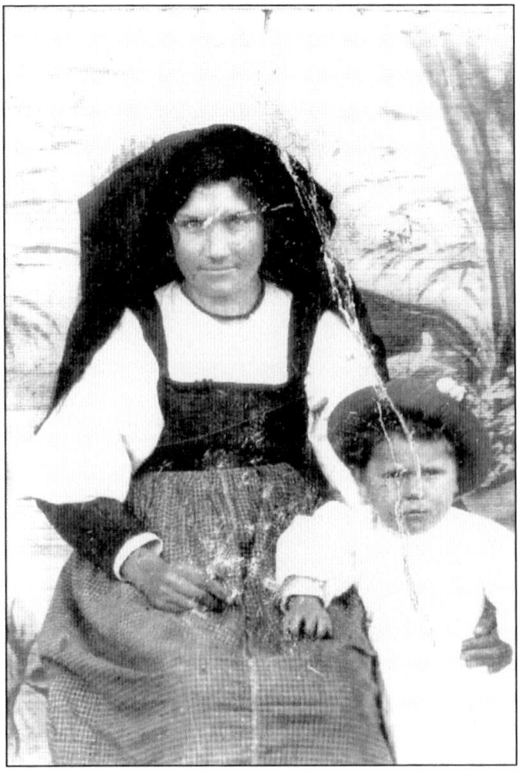

MARIA DUCA POLICASTRO WITH SON ANGELO. Maria Duca Policastro, age 20, and son Angelo, age 4, sailed from Naples, Italy, on June 18, 1913, arriving at Ellis Island on July 1, 1913, aboard the *Canada*. According to the ship manifest, their passage was paid for by her husband Guiseppe (Joseph). Maria arrived with $60, and Angelo arrived with $57. They were to join Joseph at 1127–1129 Vine Street in Cincinnati. (Courtesy of Joe Policastro.)

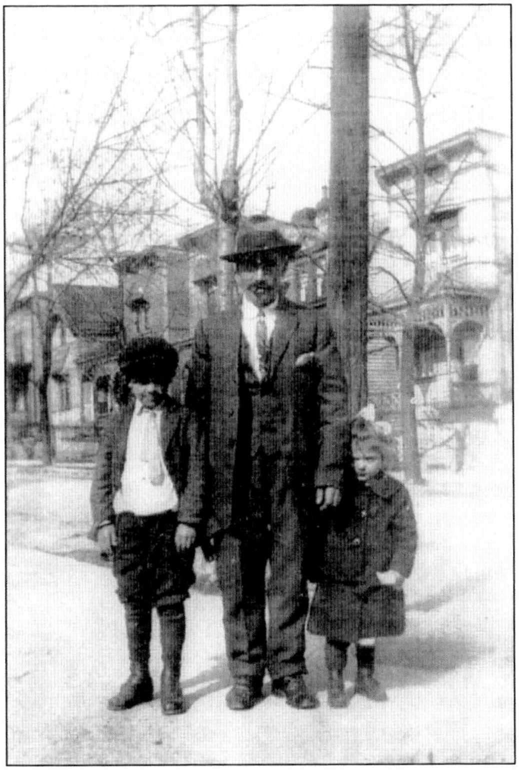

JOSEPH PEPINO POLICASTRO. The Policastro family resided at 2217 Symmes Street, where Joseph's uncle Gregorio (Gregory) Tozzi, a produce dealer and grocery store operator, had purchased several pieces of property. Tozzi had emigrated from the town of San Gregorio Magno, located in the province of Salerno, in the region of Campania, Italy, around 1889. He then sent for Joseph around 1911. Standing next to Joseph are his children Angelo and Philomena. (Courtesy of Joe Policastro.)

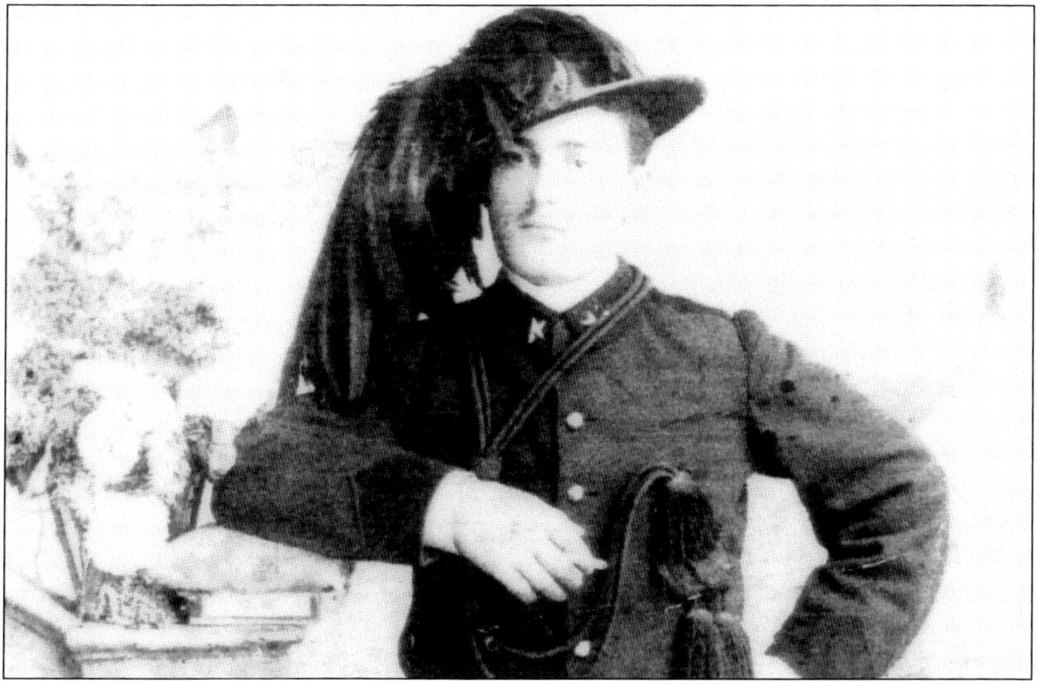

INFANTRY SOLDIER, C. 1904. Joseph Policastro served in the Italian army in 1904. Once he arrived in America in 1911, he worked for Proctor and Gamble as a general laborer and later owned and operated Joe's Café at 2217 Symmes Street. His son Paul (shown at right) served in the U.S. Marine Corps during World War II. He was severely wounded in the stomach and honorably discharged after serving over three years with the marines. After the war, he began his career as an electrician and taught electrical engineering at the college level. Standing next to him are his sister Angela and niece Mary Ann. (Courtesy of Joe Policastro.)

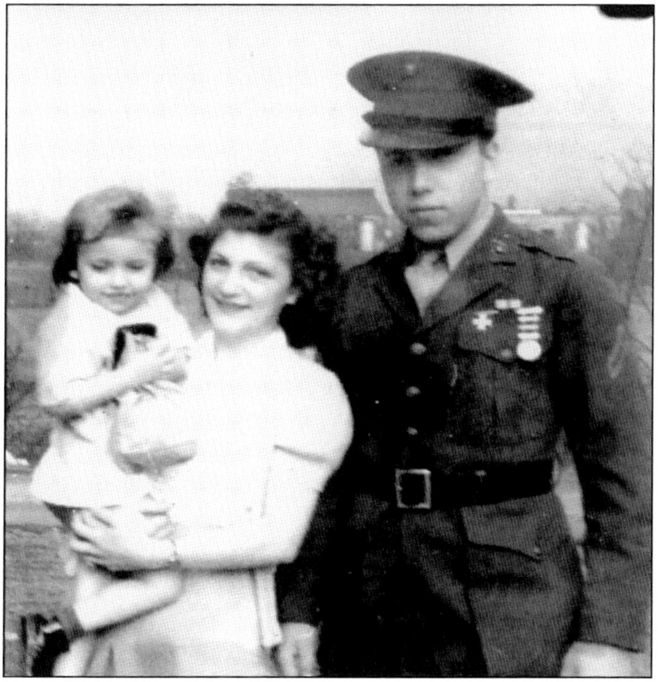

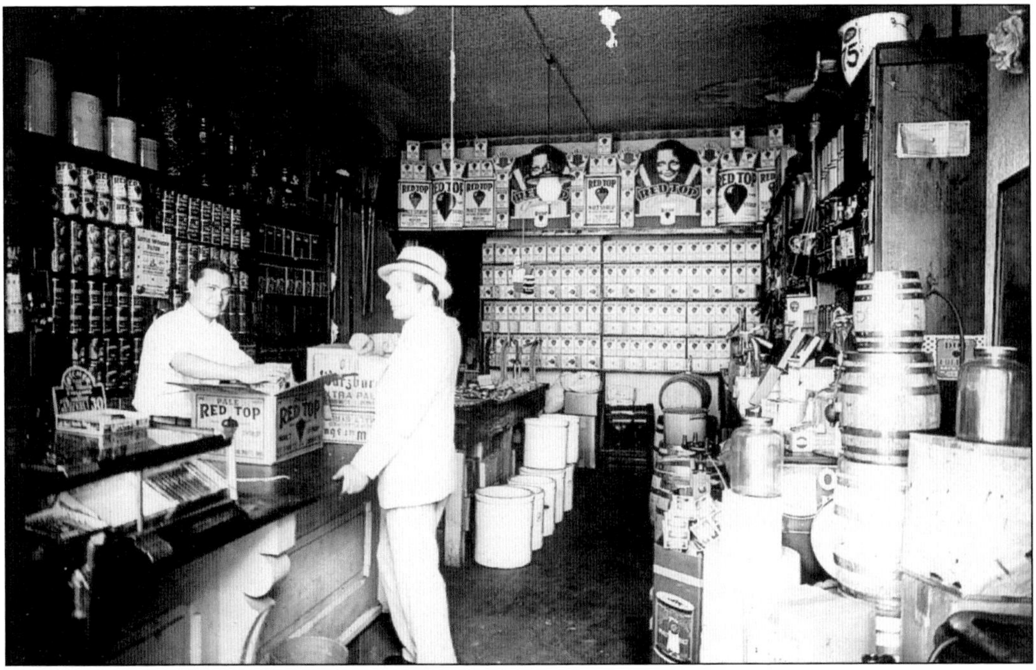

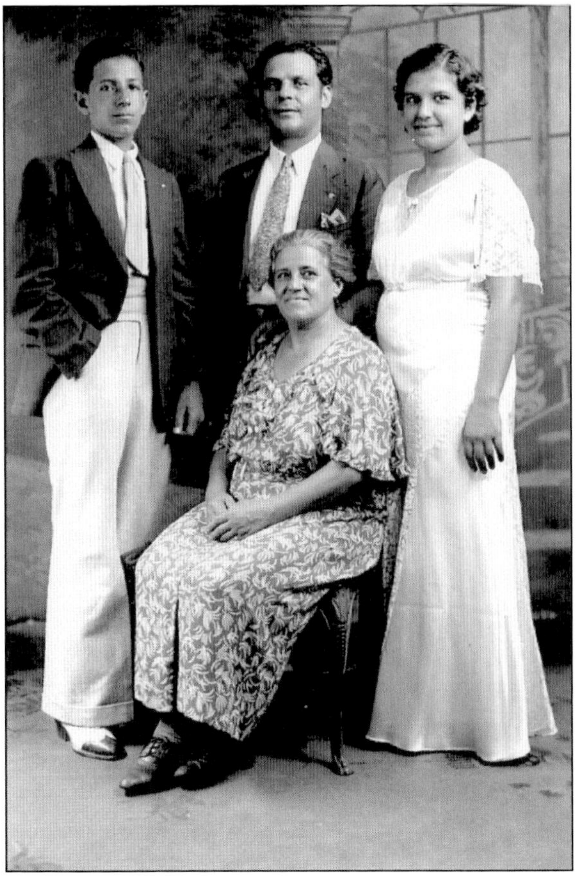

MAZZEI/ARGENTO FAMILY. Carmine Mazzei (pictured above wearing a hat) was born in Fuscaldo, Italy. He came to America after World War II by way of South America. In Italy, he was an accomplished musician and shoemaker. When he arrived in Cincinnati, he was employed in the tailoring business as a cutter and presser. Teresa Argento is seated at left with her son Carmen, husband Albert, and daughter Rose Argento Mazzei. The Argentos emigrated from Fuscaldo, and Teresa owned a small Italian American grocery store at Thirteenth and Walnut Streets in downtown Cincinnati. That was the family's first contact with the food industry. In January 1960, Carmine, Rose, and Frank Mazzei bought their first pizza store. As years passed, Carmen Argento and Pete Mazzei joined the company to operate three pizza stores, the Fireside Ristorante, Pfc. Harrisons, and ultimately Pompilios, located in Newport, Kentucky, in 1982. (Courtesy of Frank Mazzei.)

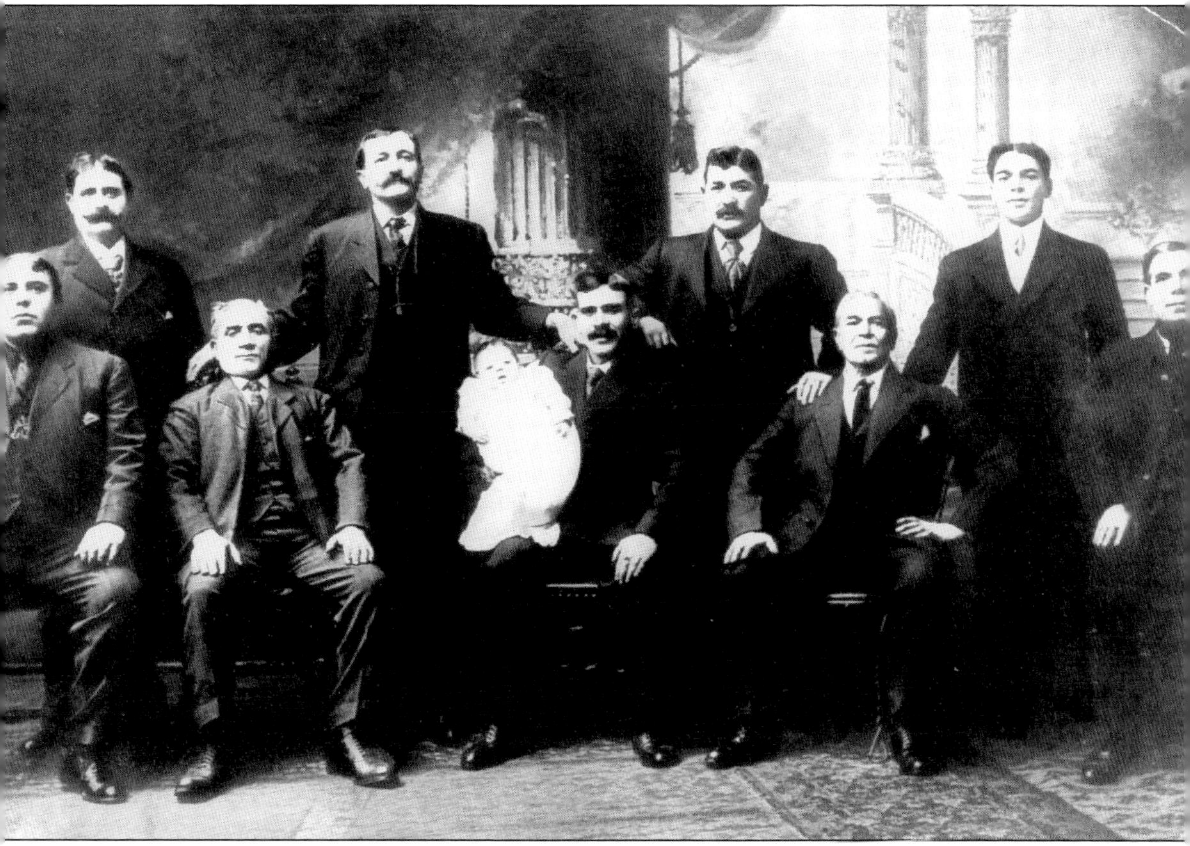

BAPTISM OF FRANK ANTHONY SANSONE, 1908. The Sansone family poses for this portrait in celebration of the birth and baptism of Frank Anthony Sansone. Pictured are, from left to right, (first row) Frank Pusateri, husband of Rosie Sansone; John Sansone, brother of Carl; baby Frank Anthony Sansone; Fabiano Sansone, father of baby Frank; Carl Sansone, father of Fabiano; and Frank Sansone, brother of Carl; (second row) Joe Geraci, husband of Mary Sansone; Joe Bova, husband of Marina Sansone; John Sansone, brother of Fabiano; and Peter Sansone, brother of Fabiano. The Sansone and Geraci families were from Palermo, Sicily. (Courtesy of Joe Geraci.)

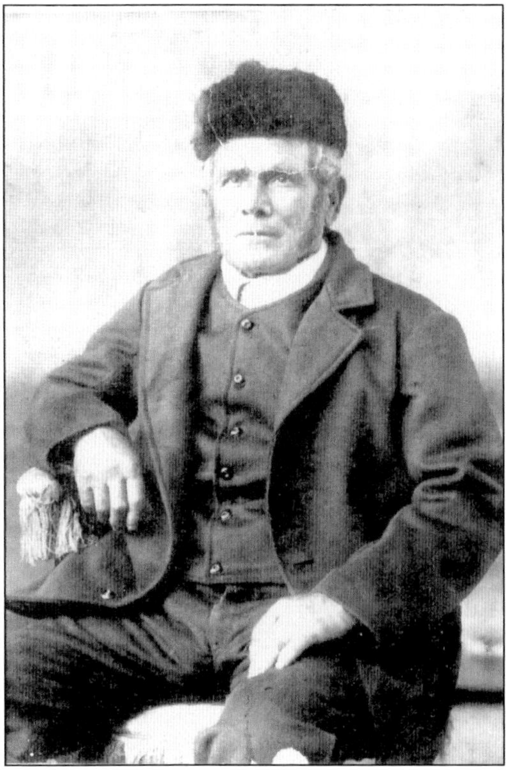

MICHAELANGELO SALAMONE AND ANNA GENTILE SALAMONE. Michaelangelo Salamone was born in 1828. He was a deep-sea fisherman in Italy. Anna Gentile Salamone was born in 1835. She was a seamstress. They emigrated in 1903 from Termini Imerese, in the province of Palermo, Sicily. They raised a family of five children, Antonino, Maria, Providenza, Vincenzo, and Anna. Michaelangelo and Anna came to America after their children arrived here. They lived with family at 545 West Sixth Street in downtown Cincinnati. (Courtesy of the Salamone family.)

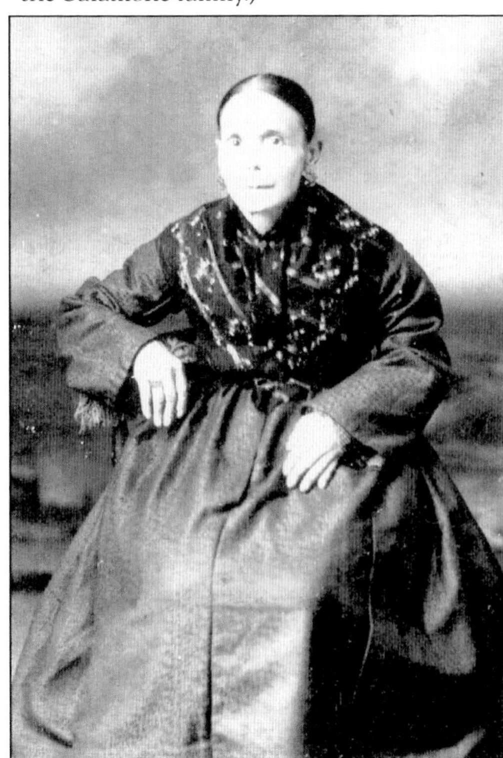

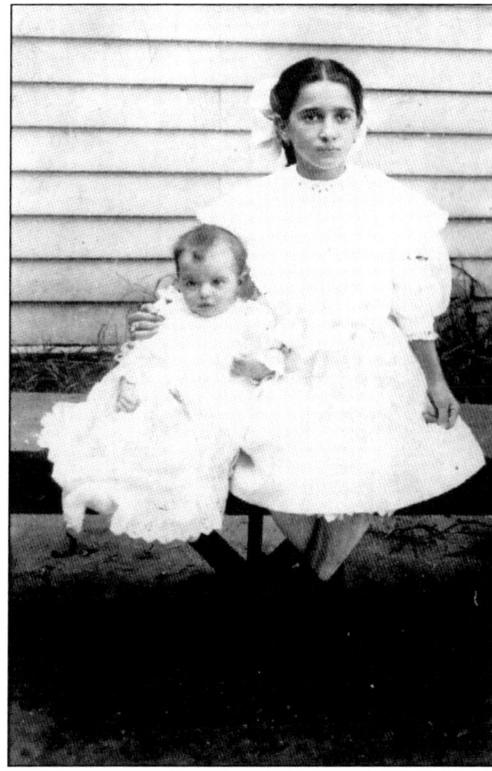

Salamone Children and Grandchildren. Shown at right are Anna and baby Lorenza, daughters of Antonino Salamone and Salvatora Cacicia Salamone. Antonino, at the age of 34, immigrated to America through Castle Garden, New York, on August 30, 1889. He traveled with members of the Rizzo and Mascari families, all from the town of Termini Imerese in the province of Palermo, Sicily. He later went back to Italy and married Salvatora Cacicia and returned to America with their two-year-old son Michaelangelo (Ang) around 1893. Antonino and Salvatora had a total of nine children (two girls and seven boys), Ang, Guiseppe, Anna, Vincenzo and Ignazio (twins who died as infants), another Vincenzo and Ignazio, Cosimo, and Lorenza. Below are Antonino, Ang, and Salvatora Salamone. (Courtesy of the Salamone family.)

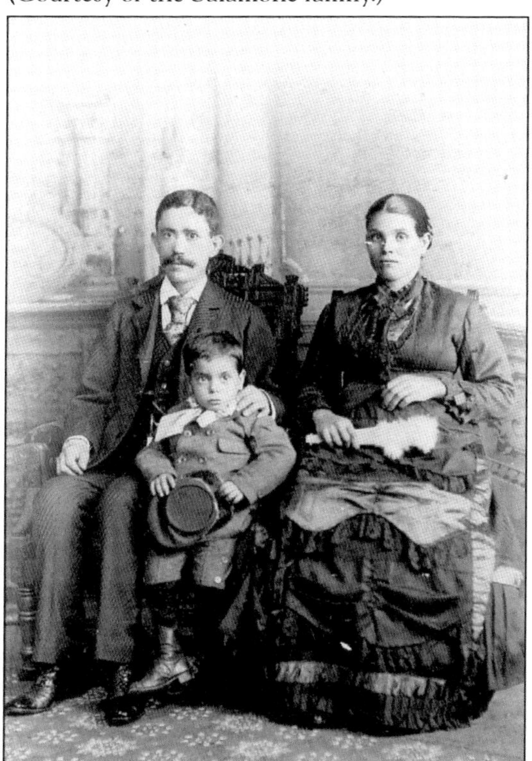

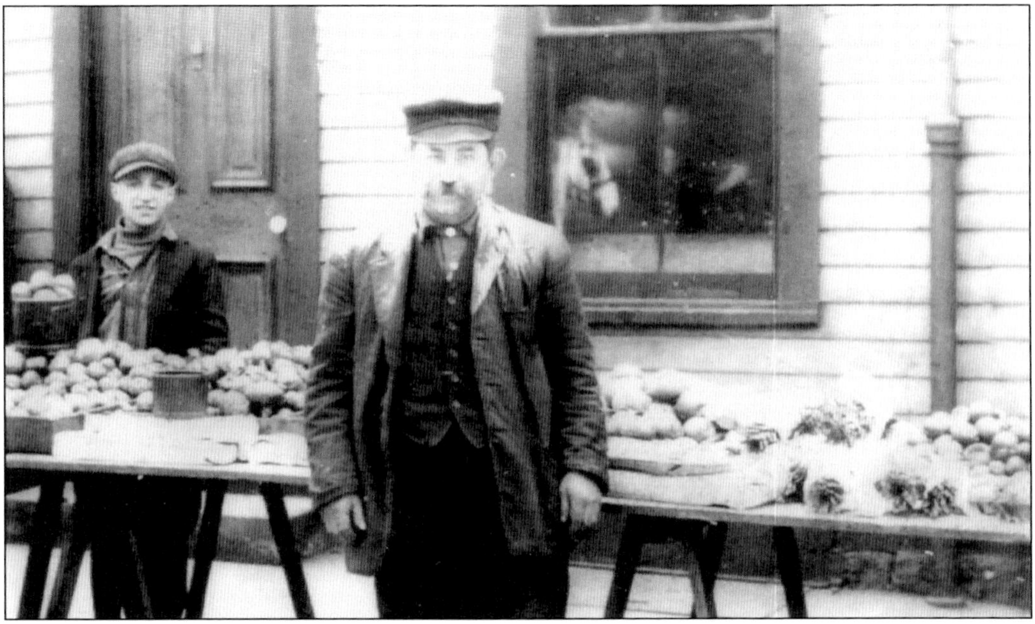

A. SALAMONE PRODUCE AND FRUIT STAND. Antonino Salamone is shown above in front of his fruit market at 737 Court Street along with his nephew Henry Rizzo. In Italy, Antonino had been trained in English and bookkeeping. Antonino first began his business as a pushcart stage. Antonino's son Ang is shown below with his younger brother Ignazio "Pat." After Antonino's death in 1930, Ang became like the "godfather" of the family. He made all the decisions for the family, including where they would live, and all important life events had to be approved by him first. In 1964, the business ceased operations with the construction of Interstate 75. Queensgate playfield is now on the former site of A. Salamone Produce. Pat went on to handle the accounts at Caruso and Cirisi Produce. (Courtesy of the Salamone family.)

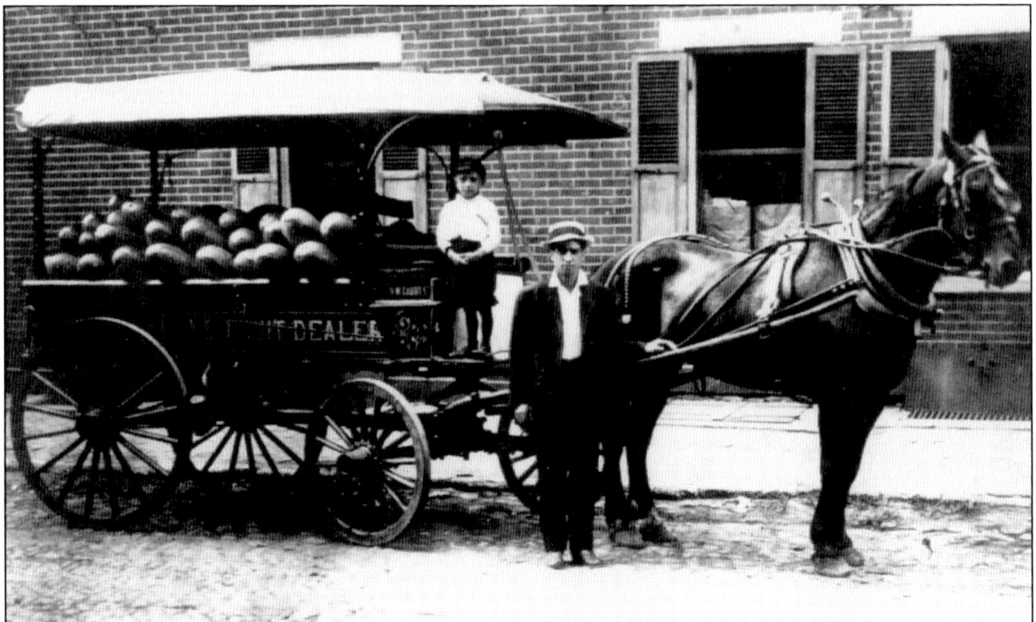

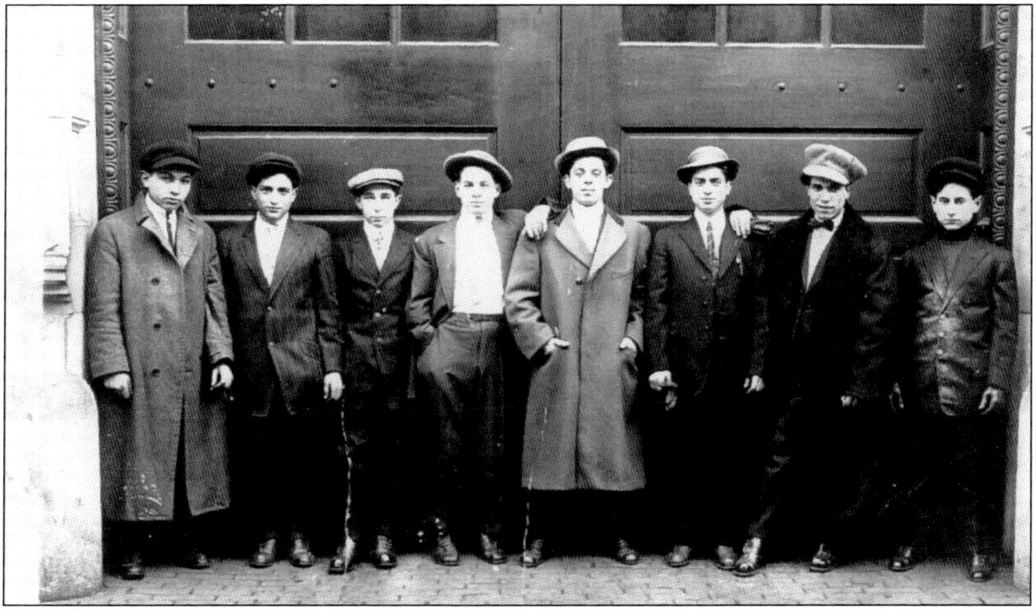

ITALIAN LINEUP. Standing in front of Engine Company No. 45, located at 315 West Court Street, are, from left to right, unidentified, Pino Salamone, two unidentified, Carlo Geraci, Ang Salamone, Charlie Catanzaro, and Paul Pusatari. The firehouse was located across the street from where Italian society social meetings were held. The firehouse now houses the Cincinnati Fire Museum. (Courtesy of the Salamone family.)

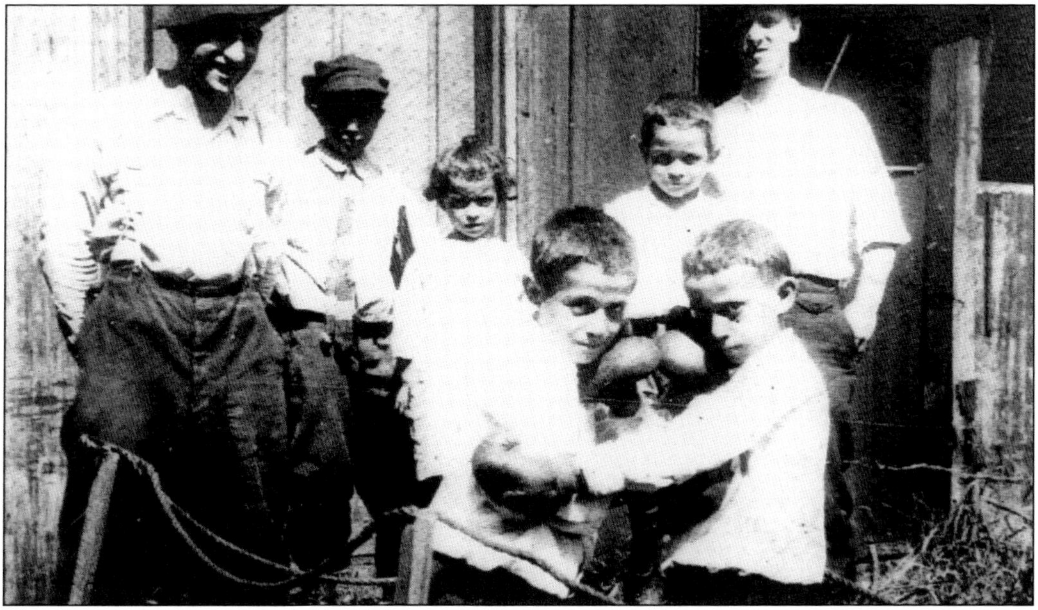

SALAMONE CHILDREN BOXING. In the backyard of 737 Court Street, Pat Salamone and cousin Angelo duke it out in the ring as uncle Pino Salamone (left), Vincenzo Salamone, Lorenza Salamone, Cosimo Salamone, and Willie Muench watch. The reason why Ignazio became known as "Pat" started on one St. Patrick's Day when he colored his hair green and everyone started calling him Pat. The name stuck, and he was called Pat the rest of his life. (Courtesy of the Salamone family.)

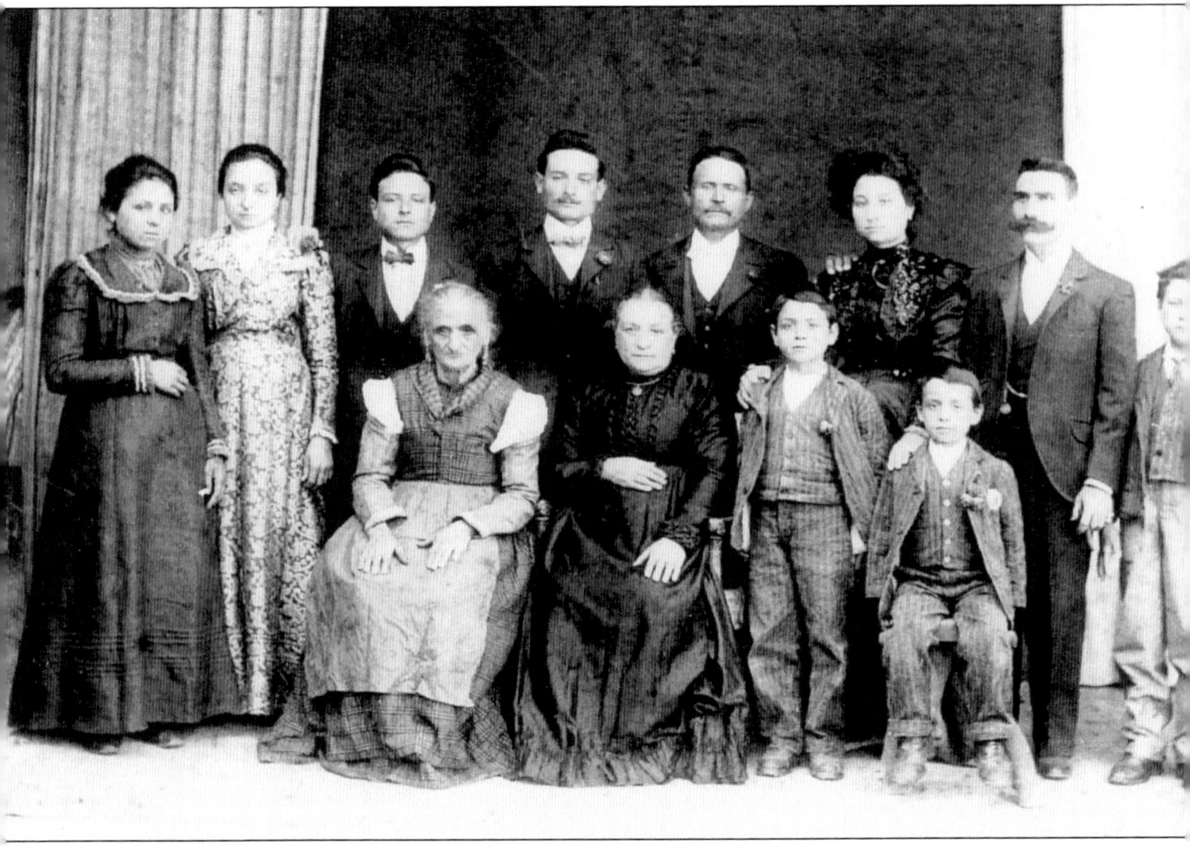

THE SANTORO FAMILY. The three boys of Nicola Santoro and Concetta Seta Santoro, shown at the right, came to America along with an older brother Raffaele. Eugenio was the first to arrive at the age of 17 on the ship *Verona*, arriving at Ellis Island on April 8, 1914. He was listed as a shoemaker according to the ship's manifest and was going to visit a Seta cousin at 726 Main Street in Cincinnati. The second to arrive was Salvatore at the age of 24 on April 19, 1921, aboard the ship *Canada*. He had $40 in his pocket and was going to visit his brother Eugenio at 510 Lock Street in Cincinnati. The third to arrive was Ernesto at the age of 23 aboard the ship *Conte Rosso*, and he was going to visit his brother Eugenio. Raffaele, the fourth brother, age 31, accompanied him. (Courtesy of Joe and Rose Santoro.)

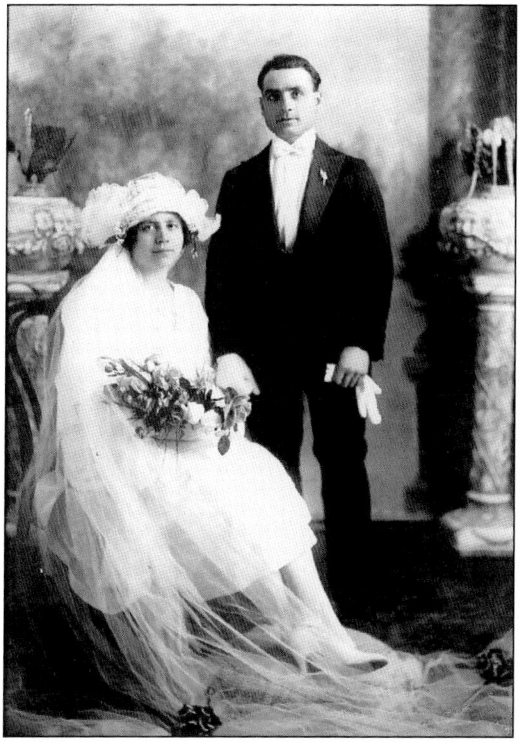

SALVATORE SANTORO AND TERESINA SETA SANTORO. Salvatore and Teresina Santoro were married on February 1, 1927, in Fuscaldo, Consenza, Calabria, Italy. Teresina traveled to America with Concetta Santoro, age one, aboard the *Saturnia*, arriving at Ellis Island on November 2, 1928. They joined Salvatore at 510 Lock Street in Cincinnati. Salvatore utilized his skills as a stonecutter and later became a tailor. Teresina was employed as a stitch marker and did alterations at Globe Tailoring Company in Cincinnati. (Courtesy of Carmela Iacullo.)

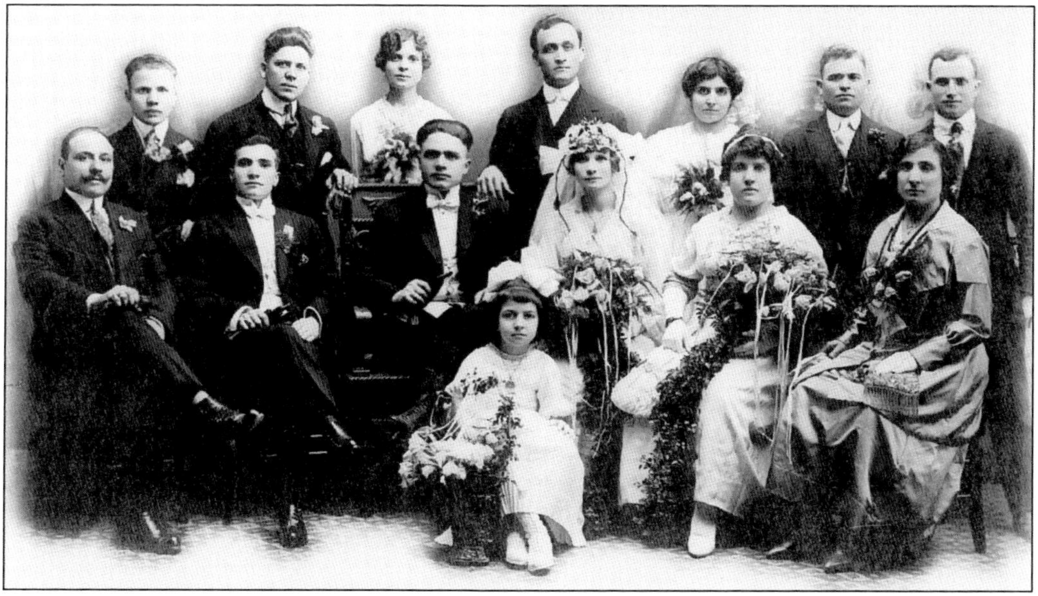

MICHELE IACULLO AND GRAZIA VELLA IACULLO WEDDING. Grazia Vella immigrated to America aboard the *Italia*, arriving on December 22, 1916. She and Michele (Mike) Iacullo were married on January 18, 1919, with the reception at the Gaetano Gambino home located at 921 Freeman Avenue in Cincinnati. Members of the bridal party are, from left to right, (first row) unidentified flower girl; (second row) unidentified, Vince Pubimo, Mike and Grazia, unidentified, and Concetta Vella Gambino; (third row) Sam Gambino, Guy Gambino, Anna Vella Gambino, and four unidentified people. (Courtesy of Carmela Iacullo.)

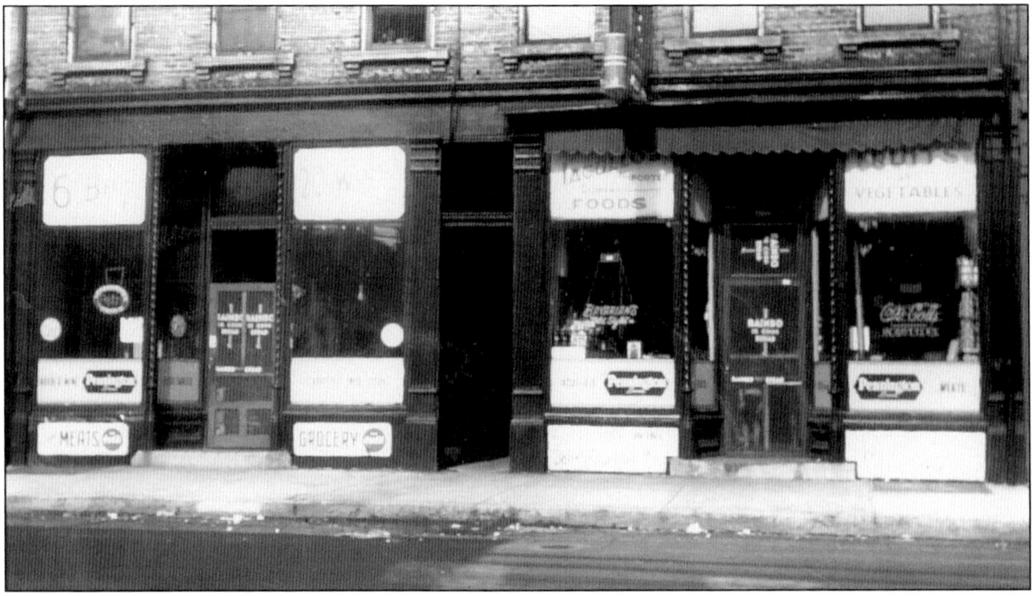

IACULLO FOOD MARKET. Mike Iacullo and his sons owned and operated this food market located at 1418 Walnut Street until 1974. They specialized in Italian foods, meats, and produce. (Courtesy of Carmela Iacullo.)

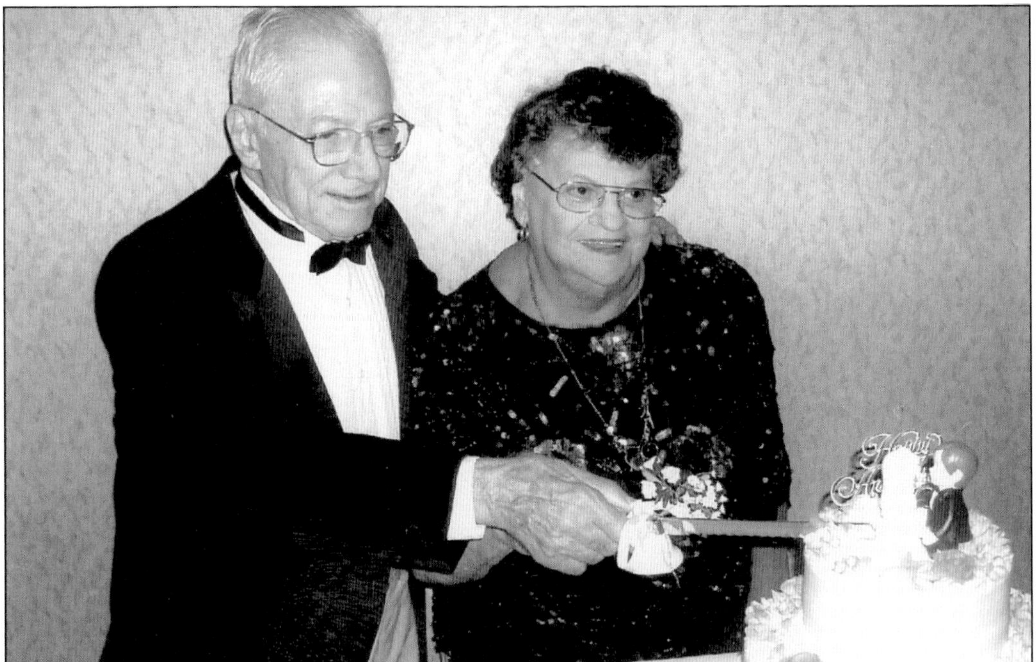

VINCENT IACULLO AND CARMELA SANTORO IACULLO'S 55TH WEDDING ANNIVERSARY. Vincent Iacullo and Carmela Santoro were married at Holy Name Church on Auburn Avenue on December 16, 1950, and together they raised three children, Grace Ann, Theresa Marie, and Janet Marie. After they were married, Vincent continued to work at the grocery store and at the Hamilton County Court House as an assignment clerk. He worked there for 30 years. (Courtesy of Carmela Iacullo.)

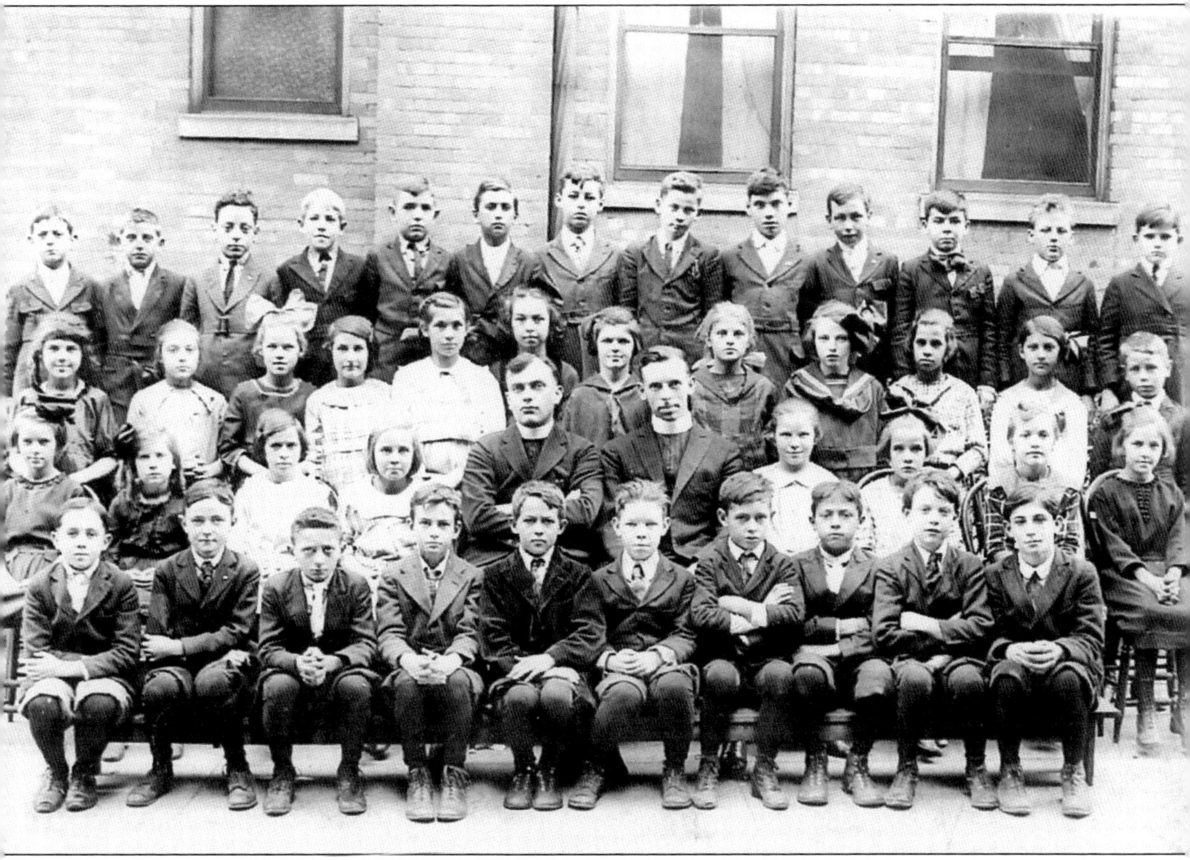

ASSUMPTION SCHOOL IN WALNUT HILLS, 1919. Shown here are, from left to right, (first row) Bob Meldon, Jim McFadden, Frank DiPuccio, Bill Cook, Frank ?, Bob Madden, Frank Miller, Carl Scardina, John Donnellon, and Mel Lynch; (second row) Clare Bowling, ? Schawnike, Ann Conklin, unidentified, Father Connor, Father McDevitt, Ann Woods, ? McNair, Lina Pagano, and unidentified; (third row) Kelly Lovella, ? French, Margaret Curran, ? Flynn, Bob Somehorest, Margaret Glenn, Dutch Marmion, Theresa Foos, Gertrude Kelly, Dorothy Jacobs, Margaret Ruhl, and Bob Daughtery; (fourth row) Tach Janzen, Tony Puella, Al Simone, Art McKenna, John Boniface, Tom Denterlein, unidentified, Eddie McGinnis, Tom Devans, Gene Woerst, Leonard Benz, Carl Gable, and Louis Grenninger. (Courtesy of John DiPuccio.)

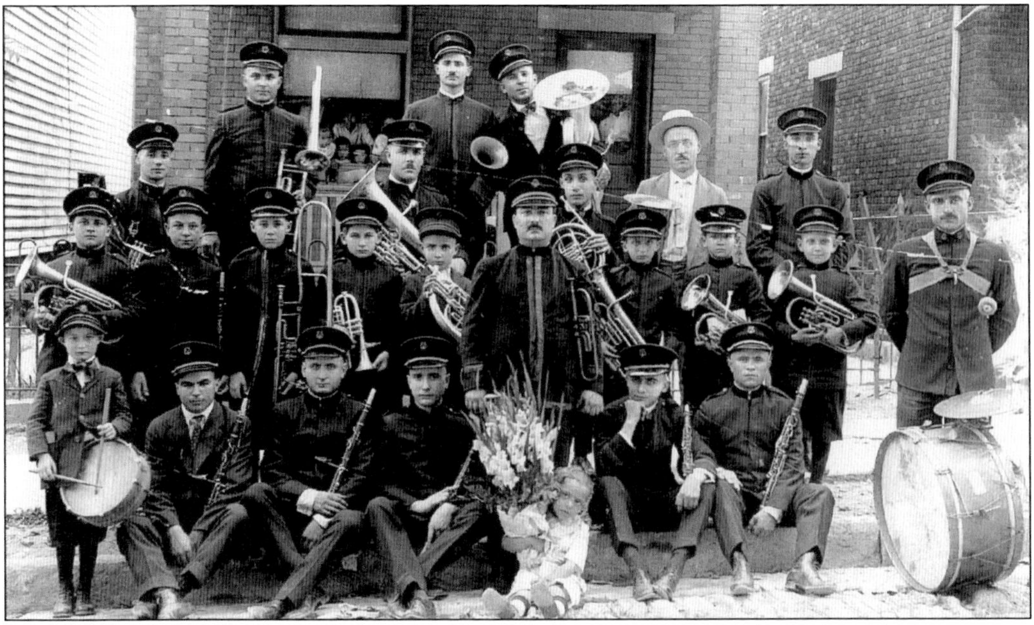

BOONE STREET BAND, JULY 17, 1921. Some of the Boone Street Band members shown here are as follows: John Delatore, Carmen Iacobucci, Roy DiPuccio, John Pompilio, Sylvia DeNuccio, Ruby Renaldi, Art Lupelli, Mike Fusaro, Joe Federico, Roy Federico, Guy Berraterri, Mr. Delatore (teacher), Frank DiPuccio, Nick Piccirillo, Tony Pompilio, Joe DeNuzzio, John Daraterri, John Muzzo, Joe ?, Tony DeNuccio, and Ralph DeNuzio. (Courtesy of John DiPuccio.)

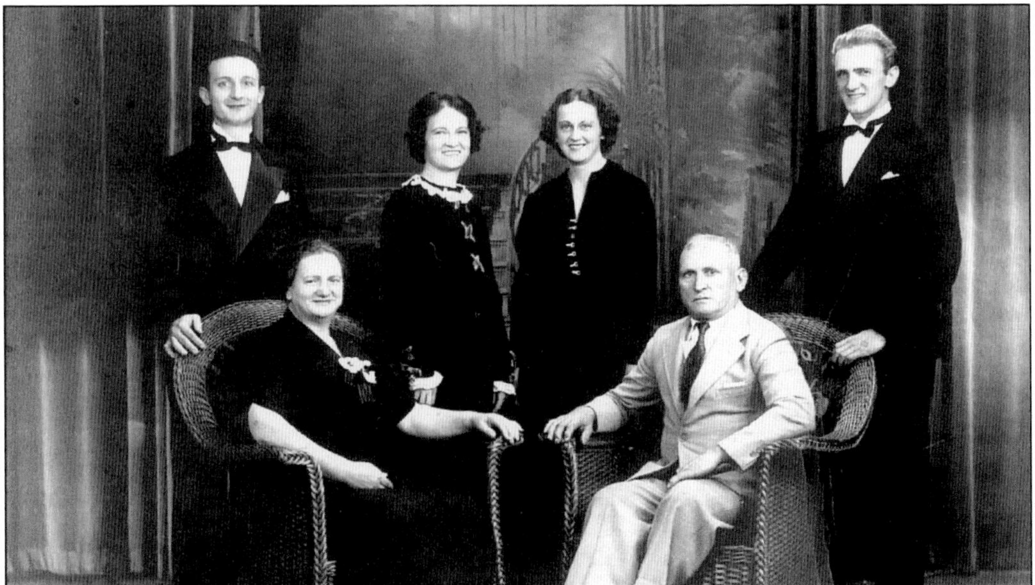

PHILOMENA AND JOHN DIPUCCIO FAMILY. Seated are Philomena and John DiPuccio, and standing are, from left to right, their children, Frank, Angela, Marie, and Anthony. The family resided at 2330 Kemper Lane. John immigrated to America first, and Philomena arrived with their daughter Angela in 1909. (Courtesy of John DiPuccio.)

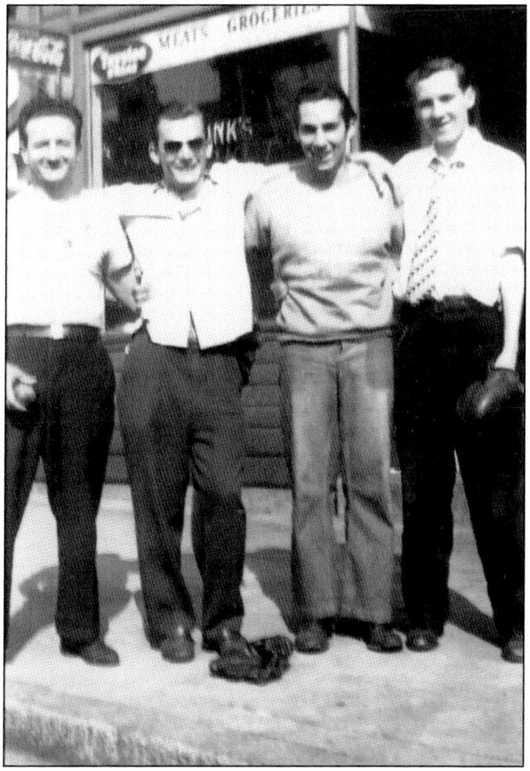

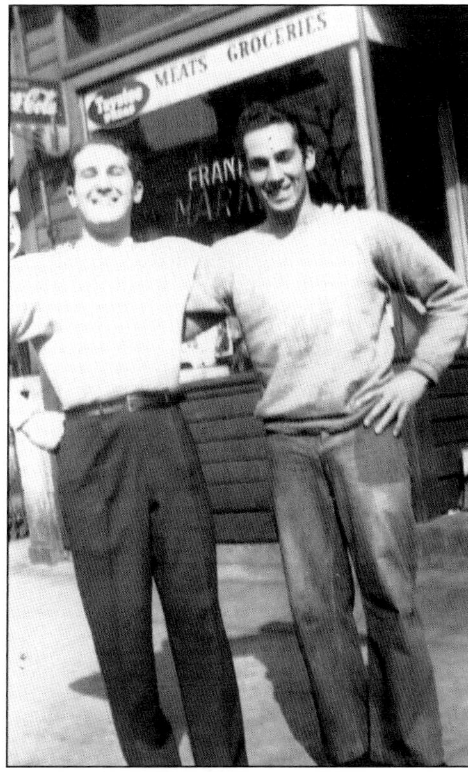

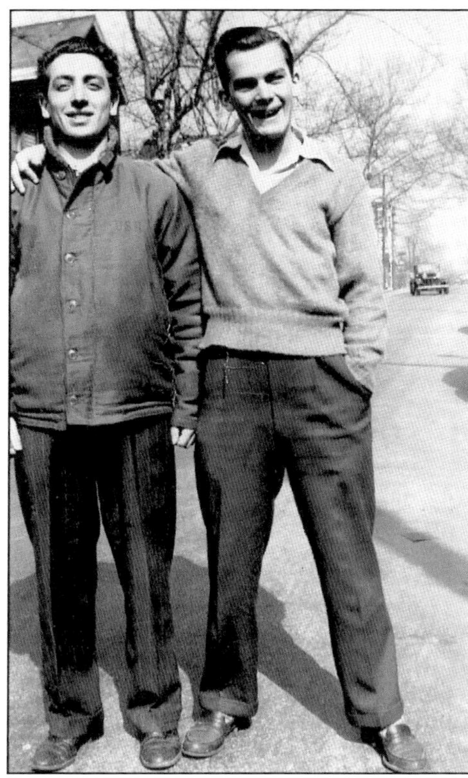

DiPuccio Grocery Store on May Street. Frank DiPuccio (above left) owned the grocery store located at 2408 May Street in the late 1930s–1940s. Shown next to him are friends Joe Provident, John DeNuccio, and Remmit Kinkley. The store served as a place for friends to gather and to toss a baseball when they were not busy with customers. Fred DeNuccio (above right), with his brother John, and Tony Provident (shown below at the left), along with his brother Joe, were like many neighborhood friends. In their spare time, they would weight lift, canoe, and swim in the Ohio River. (Courtesy of John DiPuccio.)

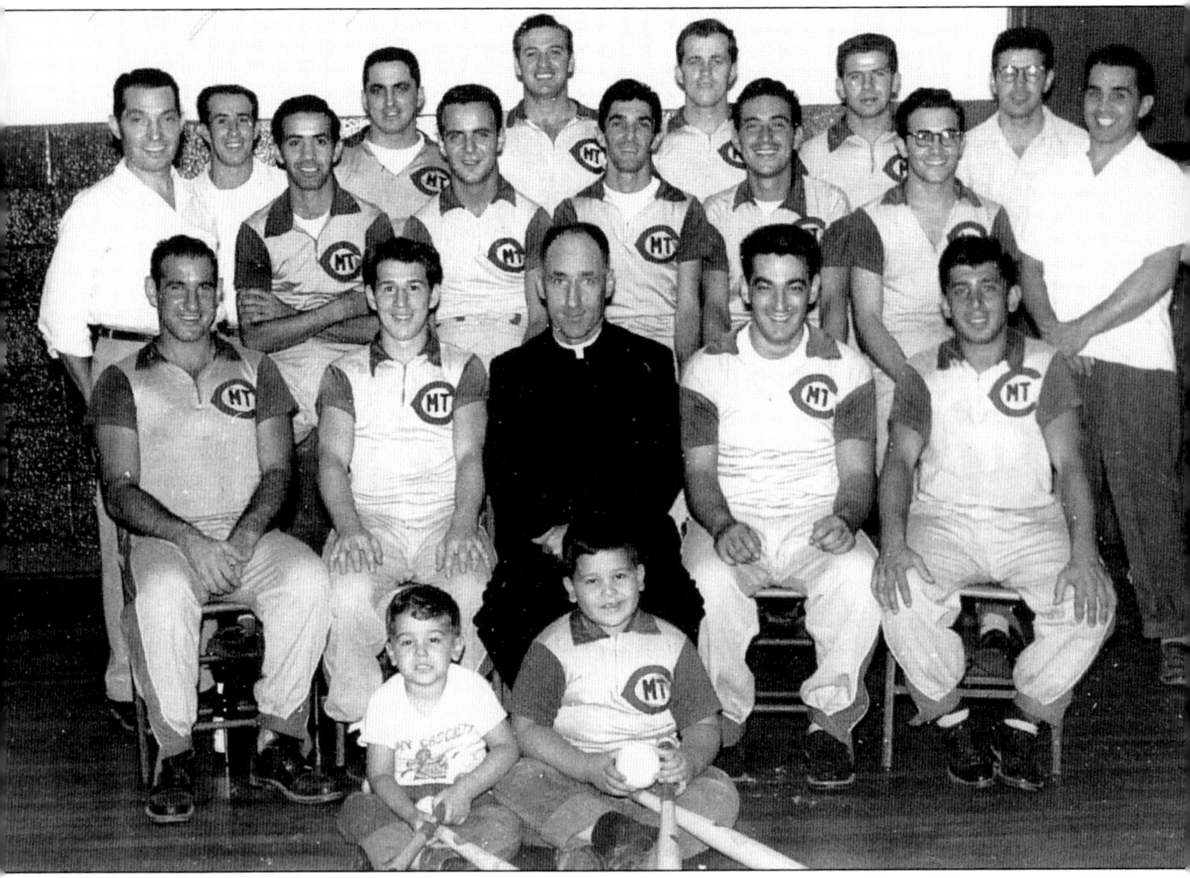

OUR LADY OF MOUNT CARMEL CATHOLIC YOUTH ORGANIZATION CITY CHAMPIONS, 1955. This young men's softball team had a record of 11 wins and one loss in the league competition and took the play-offs with a clean sweep of three victories. From left to right are (first row) Tony Balzano, Nick Pitocco, Fr. Anthony Migoni, C.P.P.S., Pastor Tony Fazio, and Jerry DeNuzio; (second row) Larry Lavatori, manager, Anthony Pirraglia, Steve Stephens, Dominic Daniele, Mike Vaccariello, Anthony Perrino, and Mike Pitocco, coach; (third row) Phil Pitocco, equipment, Bill Anaruma, Pat Cioffi, Jim Anaruma, John Belperio Jr., and Joe Pirraglia, transportation. Batboys seated on the floor are, from left to right, Joe "JoJo" and Mickey Pitocco. Team members not shown are George Belperio, Jim Hicks, and Martin Hines. Last year's players Mario Pitocco and Eddie Lavatori were serving overseas with the army. (Courtesy of Mike and Mary Pitocco.)

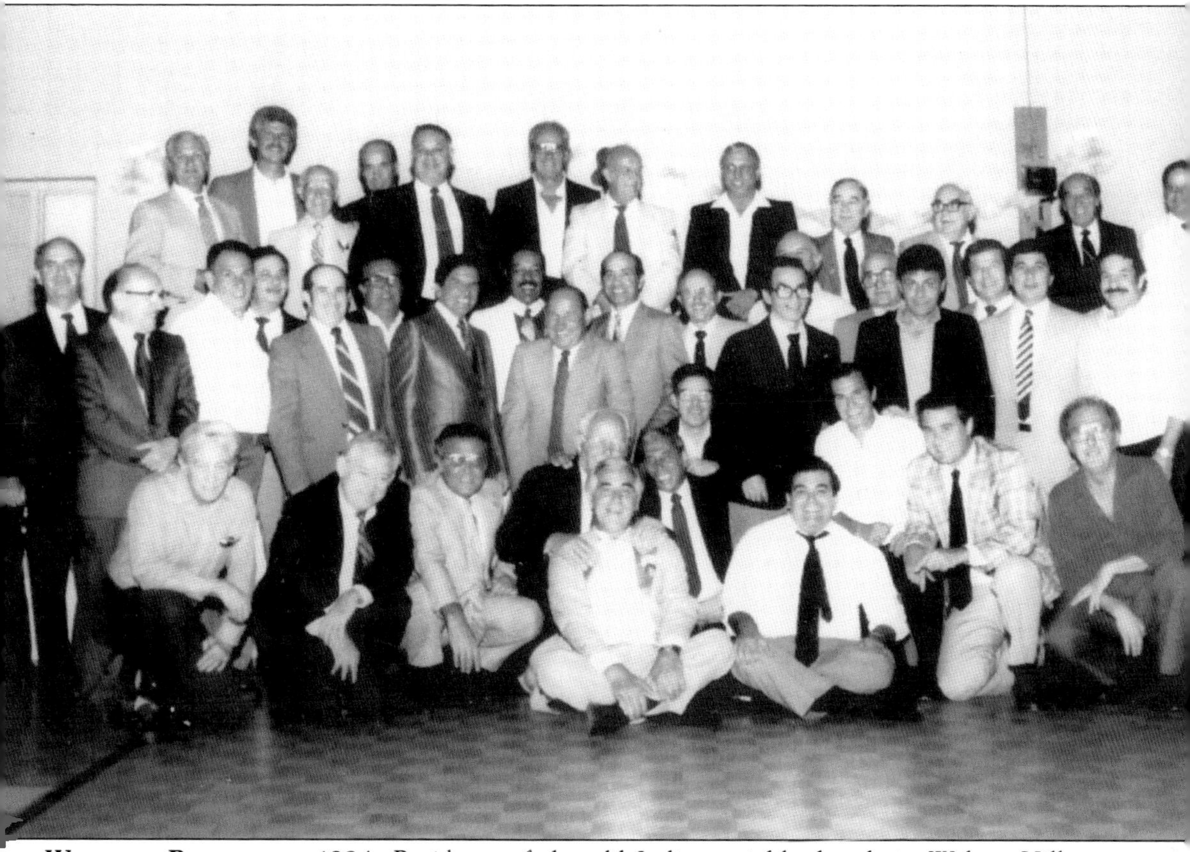

Wedding Reception, 1984. Residents of the old Italian neighborhoods in Walnut Hills gathered for this group photograph at the wedding of Mike Vaccariello's daughter Lisa. Shown are, from left to right, (first row) Al Paganelli, Pat Taylor, Anthony Perrino, John Vaccariello, Mike Vaccariello, Jerry DeNuzio, Joe Pirraglia, Joe Pitocco, Ed Lavatori, Dominic Perrino, and Jerry Hicks; (second row) Joe Paganelli, Steve Stephens, Leonard Pizzo, Lou DelNegro, Frank Perrino, Phil Pitocco, Vic Como, Willie Bizzari, Sonny Webb, Tony Balzano, Anthony Pirraglia, Angelo Paganelli, Mike Pitocco, Tony Pierani (behind Mike), Carl Lariccia, Paul DiPetriantonio, John Belperio, Nick Perrino, Angelo Cucinotta, and Tony Fazio (not pictured); (third row) Lefty Longano, Nick Longano, Roy Vaccariello, Lou Iorfida, Vince Cerchio, Jim Hicks, Angelo Daniele, Harold Ketz, Lou Vaccariello, Roy Vaccariello, Tony Daniele, and Guy Liber (partially shown). (Courtesy of Mike and Mary Pitocco.)

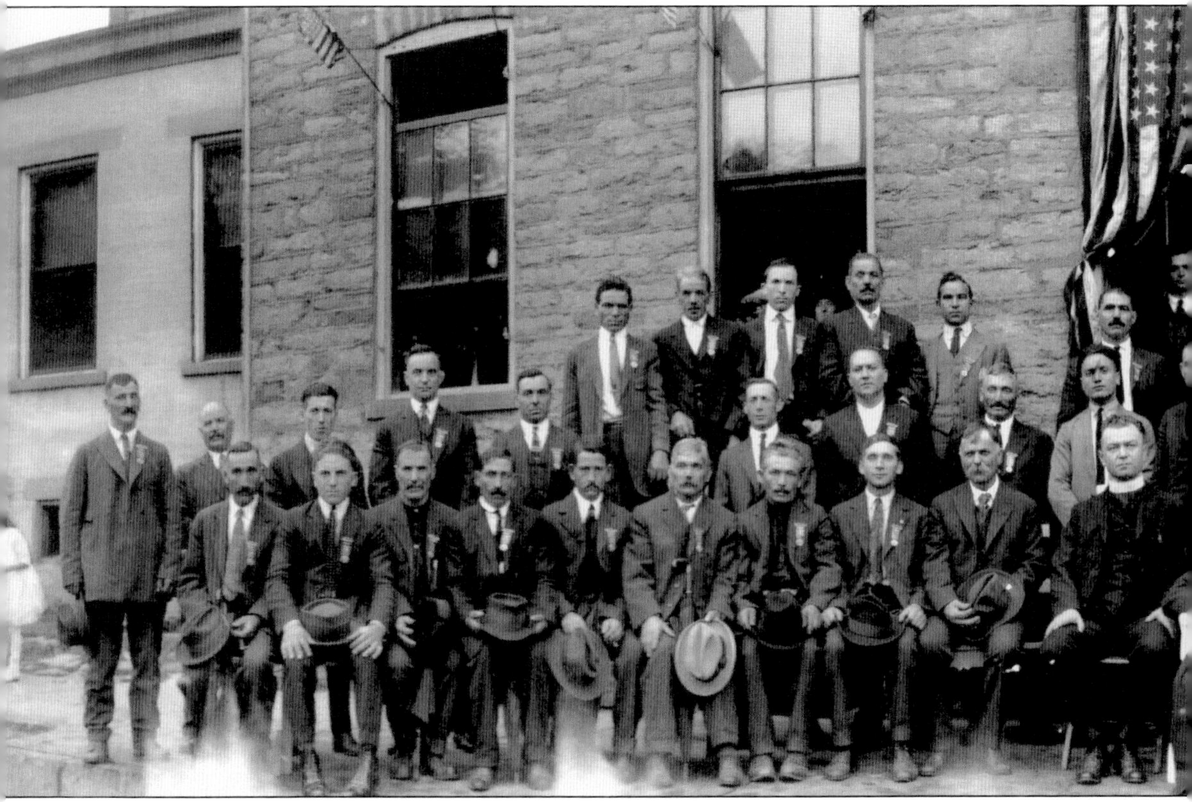

St. Anthony's Welfare Center and Neighborhood House. Members of the congregation and visitors seated from left to right are (first row) Anthony Mazzaro, unidentified, Dominic Acito, Dominic Stevens, unidentified, Joseph Roberto, Joseph Schiavo, Carmine Ventre, Vito Floria, Fr. Antonio Bainotti, Most Reverend Henry Moeller, D.D., Charles Ginocchio (Italian consul in Cincinnati), Pasquale Marchesano, Rosario Augustine, Frank Gargano, Joe Guerrera, Pasquale de Carro, Tony Augustine, Joe Ventre, Gennaro Palmire, Bobbie Prinzo (small boy), Vito Prinzo, and Pat Gallardo; (second row) Antonio Roberto, Frank Andriacco, Anthony

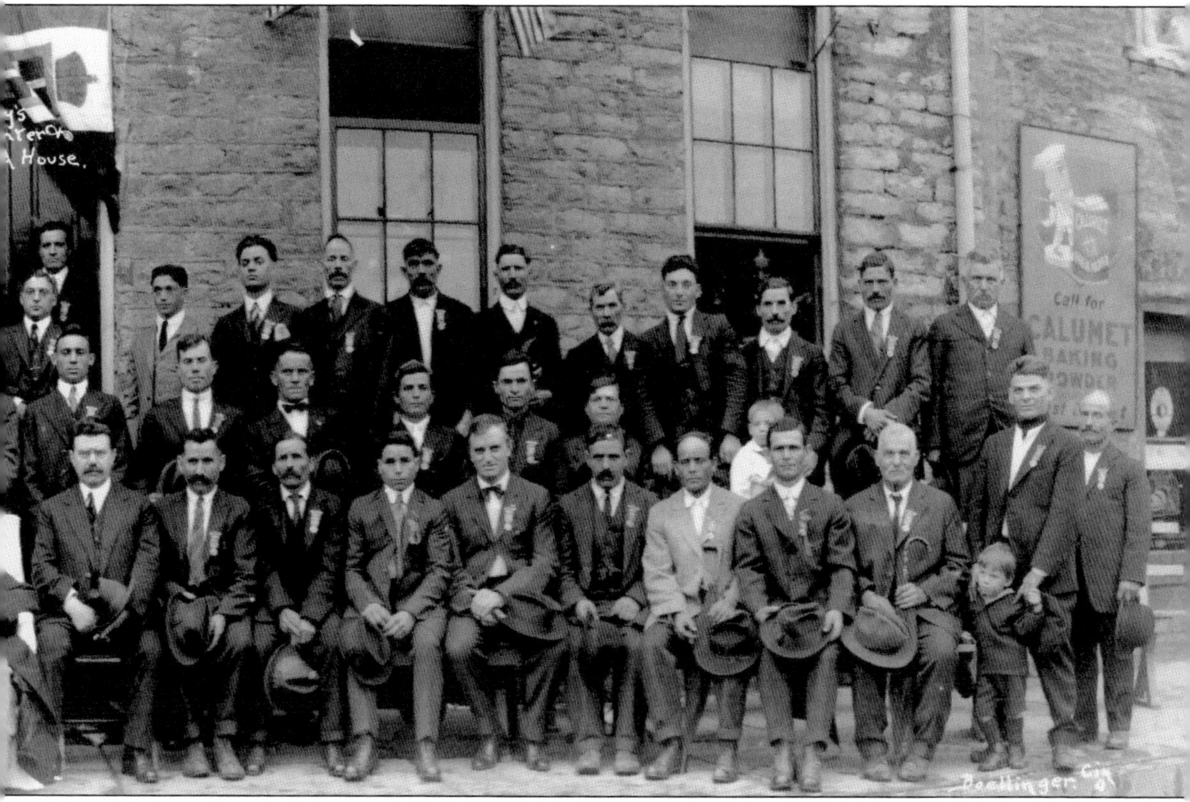

Mazzaro, Rosario Fariello, Pete Mazzaro, Vito Ventre, Silvano Minella, Pasquale Schiavo, Nick Cuiccio, Vito Guilarmo, Pat Roberto, Vito Grammaglia, Mike Scoritzell, Angelo Fariello, Frank Sheppe, Lugi LaCortiglia, Nobile Esposito, and unidentified boy; (third row) Sebastian Gargano, Tony (Herman) DiStasi, Guy Cavallo, Joe Powell, Dominic Faygo, Lorenzo Panaro, Joe Guerrera, Anthony Palmire, John Panaro, Joe Grieco, Tony Grieco, Angelo Delseno, unidentified, Nobile Schare, Louie Moore, Rosario DiStasi, unidentified, and Joe ?; (fourth row) Louie Ventre, Dominic Daleassandro, and Tony Cuptio. (Courtesy of John Fariello.)

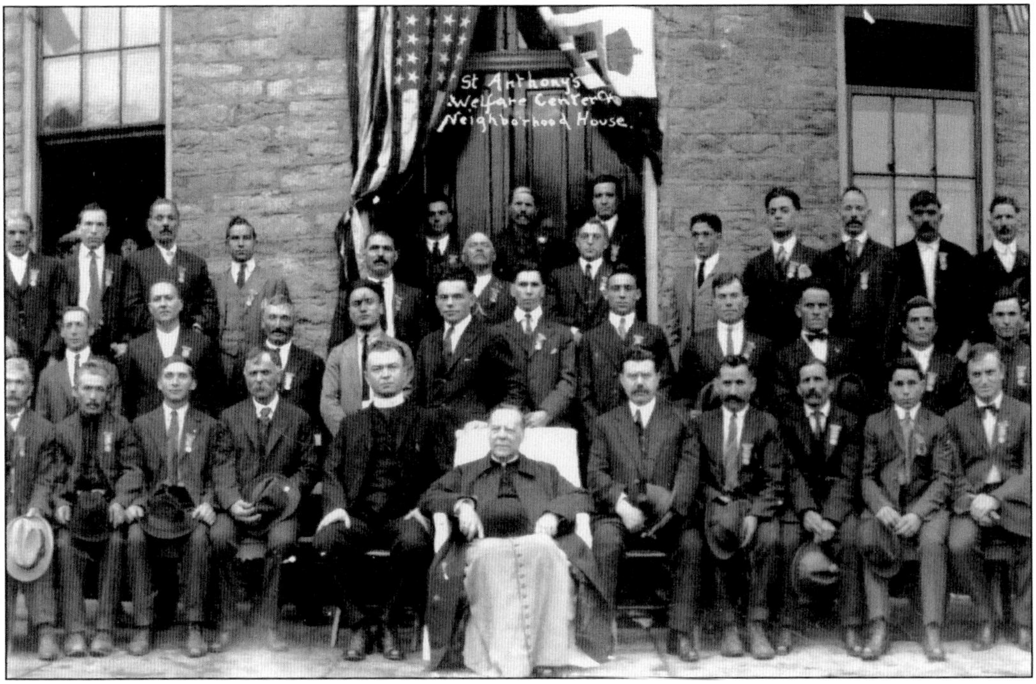

ENTRANCE OF ST. ANTHONY WELFARE CENTER. Three Sisters of Charity, Sr. Blandina Segale, Sr. Justina Segale, and Sr. Euphrasia Hartman, raised $3,400 from the Italians and bought a building located at 1946 Queen City Avenue to establish a Catholic church for the Italians of South Fairmount. Fr. Antonio Bainotti dedicated the original church on October 8, 1922. Shown in the center of this photograph is the Most Reverend Henry Moeller, D.D. (Courtesy of John Fariello.)

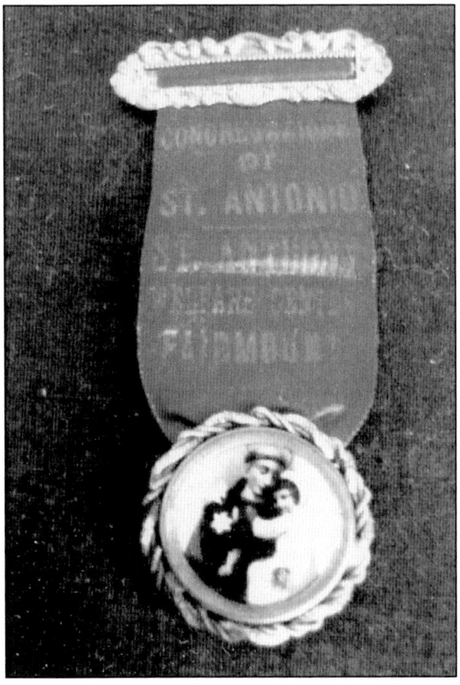

THE MEDAL OF ST. ANTHONY OF PADUA AND THE INFANT JESUS. Members of the congregation wore the medal of St. Anthony of Padua holding a lily and the infant Jesus beneath the ribbon that stated Congregazione Di St. Antonio–St. Anthony Welfare Center Fairmount. This ribbon belonged to Rosario Fariello. (Courtesy of John Fariello.)

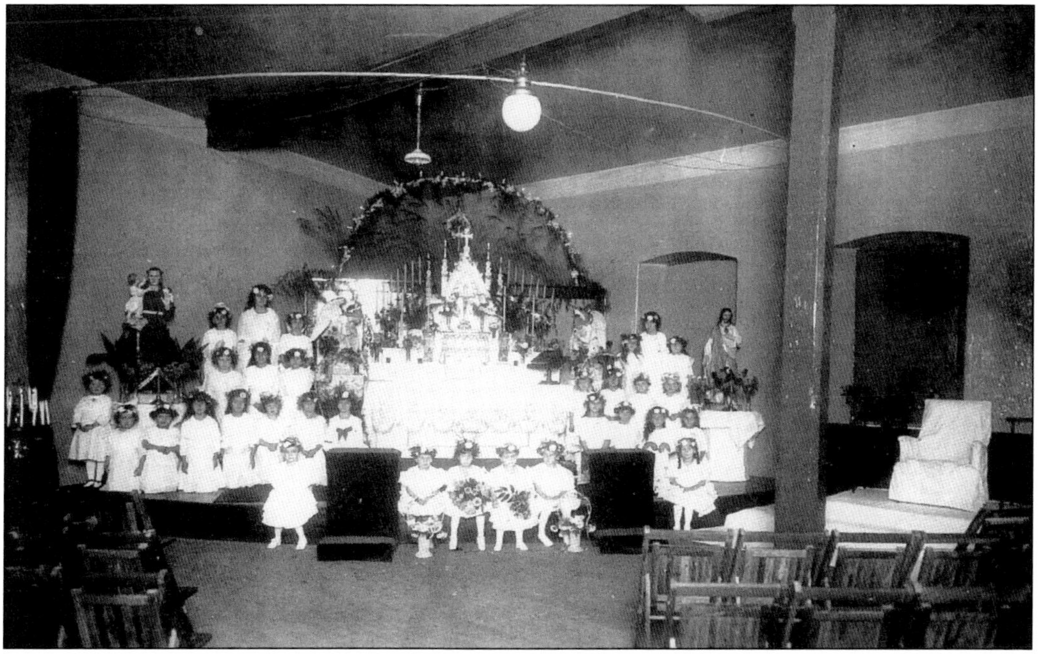

MAIN ALTAR OF THE ORIGINAL SAN ANTONIO CHURCH, C. 1923. Once the building for the welfare center was secured, the parishioners began a series of collections to purchase articles needed for the interior of the church. Shown in this photograph are the children who participated in the first May crowning at the church. (Courtesy of John Fariello.)

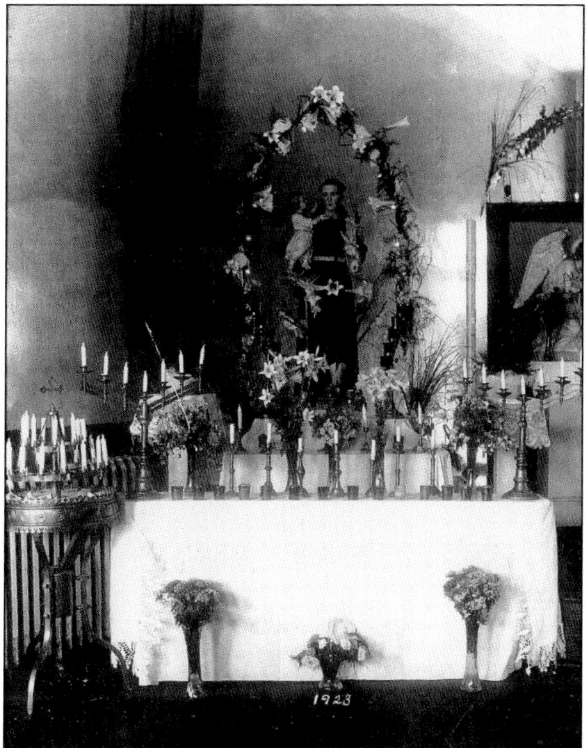

SIDE ALTAR OF ST. ANTHONY OF PADUA, 1923. St. Anthony was born in Lisbon, Portugal, in 1195 and died in Padua, Italy, on June 13, 1231. He was a Franciscan preacher and teacher and is often prayed to for recovery of lost things and against shipwreck. He is often represented with the infant Jesus, who appeared to him, and the lily, which symbolizes purity, innocence, and integrity. The Feast of St. Anthony is June 13. (Courtesy of John Fariello.)

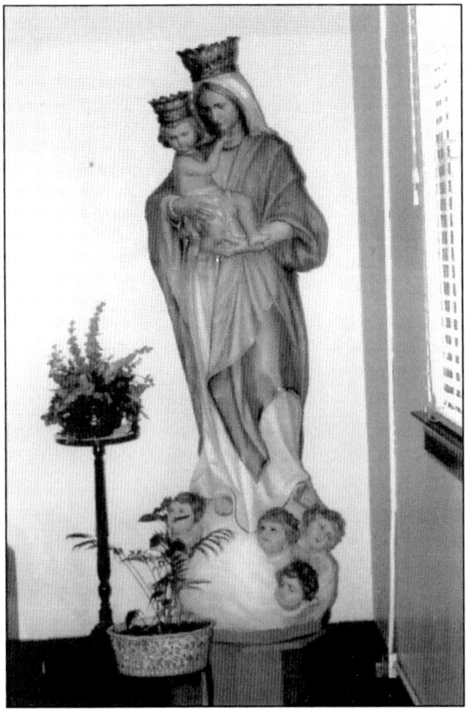

La Madonna Di Constantinopoli Statue. Although a recent photograph, this statue of the Madonna of Constantinopoli was inspired by a statue from the town of Felitto, in the province of Salerno, region of Campania, Italy. Religious processions take place to this day in Italy on the second Sunday of September in honor of the Madonna's feast day. The San Antonio congregation purchased this statue from Felitto. (Courtesy of Phil Sabatelli.)

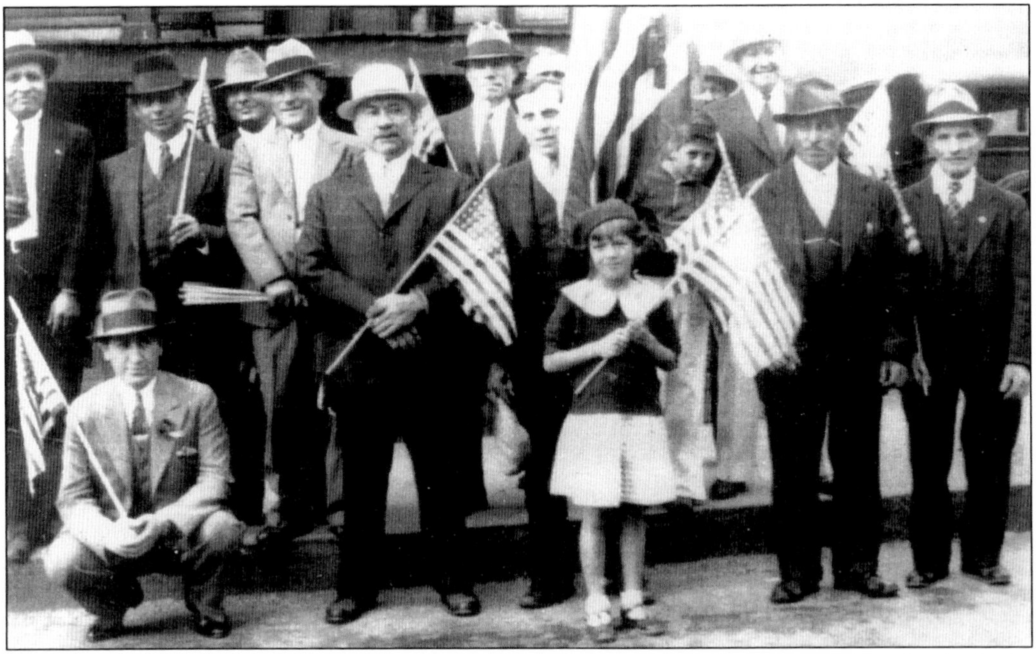

Holy Name Parade, c. 1933. The Holy Name Society is a confraternity within the Catholic Church whose primary mission is to promote love and reverence for the holy name of Jesus. Its origin began with the Council of Lyons in 1274, and it was placed under the leadership of blessed John Garbella of Vercelli, Italy. Society members demonstrate faith in the Catholic Church, loyalty to their country, and respect for all lawful authority. They also perform good works within their community. (Courtesy of Richard "Mussie" Minella.)

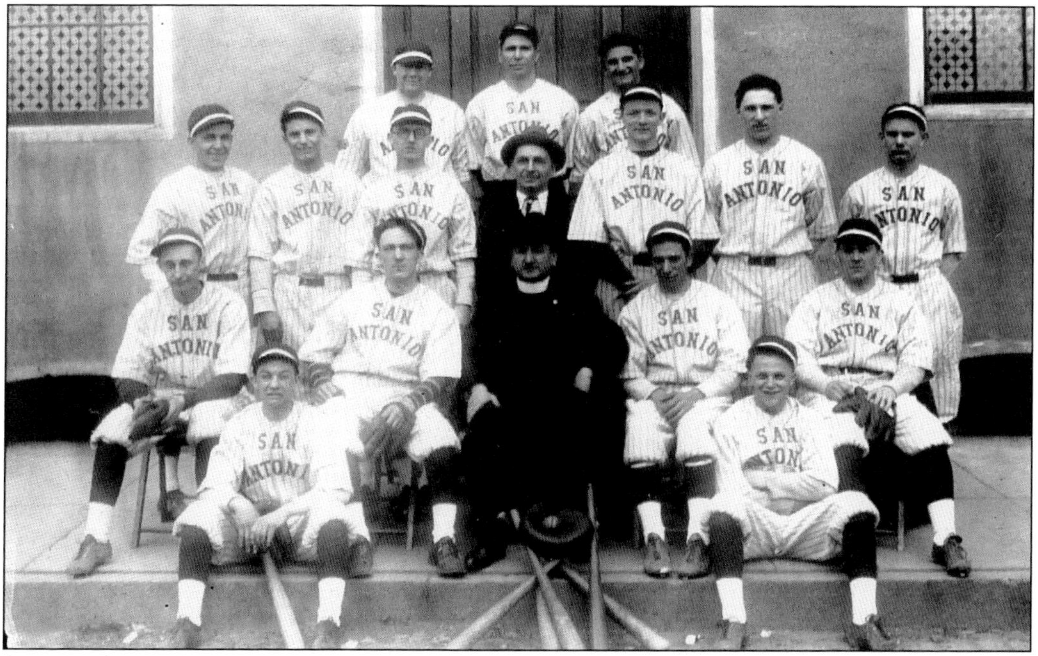

SAN ANTONIO BASEBALL TEAM, 1927. Fr. Vincent Graglia became the pastor of San Antonio during the summer of 1926. He also became the coach of the parish baseball team. He was later transferred to Dayton, and in October 1928, Archbishop John T. McNicholas placed San Antonio under the care of the Franciscan Order. (Courtesy of Richard "Mussie" Minella.)

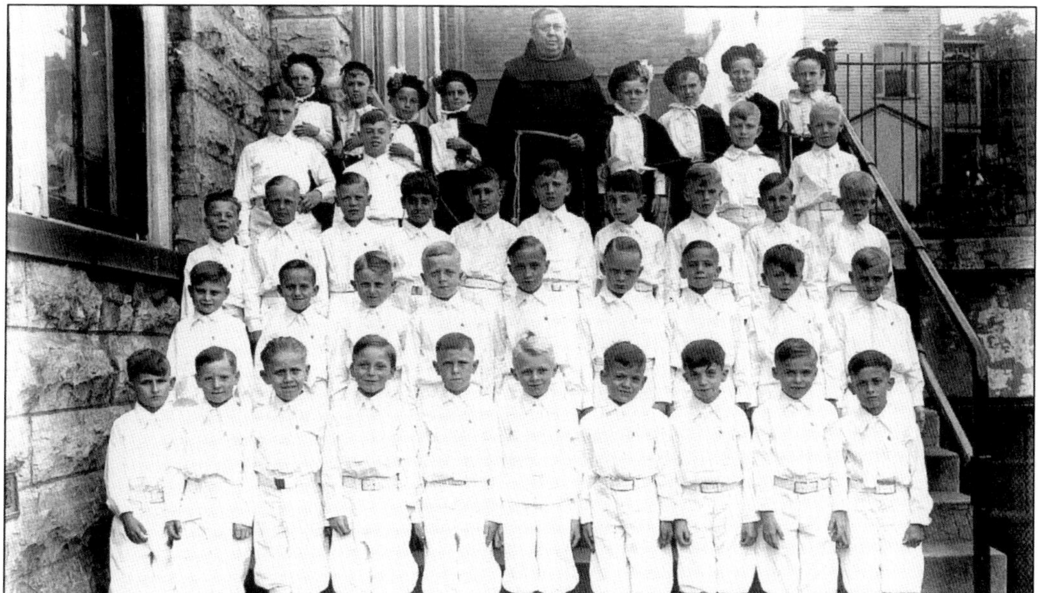

FIRST HOLY COMMUNION CLASS, C. 1931. This first communion class of St. Bonaventure Catholic Church was officiated by Father Odrich of the Franciscan Order. The sacrament of the Eucharist, Holy Communion, is one of the most important sacraments of the Catholic Church. Prior to receiving the "body and blood" of Christ, the children must first be baptized and have made their first confession. (Courtesy of Richard "Mussie" Minella.)

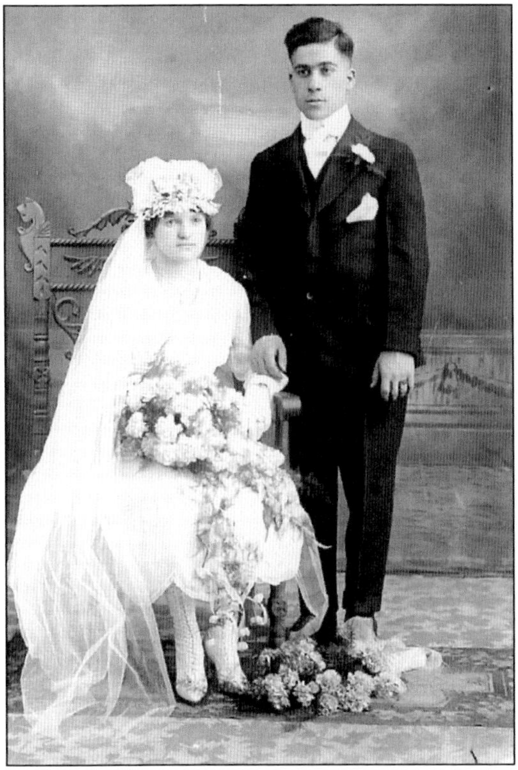

MARY SALERNO AND FILIPPO (PHILLIP) ANTONIO SABATELLI, APRIL 27, 1919. The Mary Salerno and Phillip Antonio Sabatelli wedding took place in Old Forge, Pennsylvania. Their families originated from Felitto, Salerno, Campania, Italy. Mary was born in America, and Phillip arrived in America in 1913. After working the coal mines of Old Forge, Pennsylvania, they settled in Cincinnati, where he first worked as a water boy for a construction company. (Courtesy of Phil Sabatelli.)

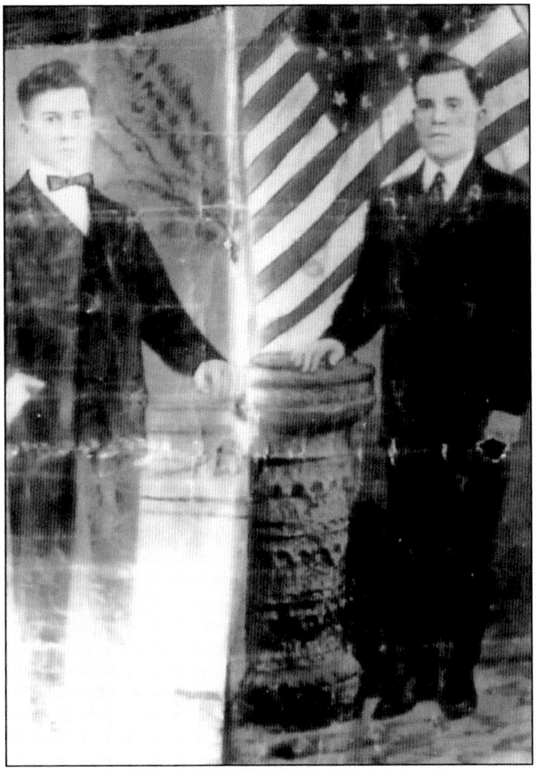

THE SABATELLI BROTHERS, C. 1914. Filippo (Phillip) Sabatelli (left) and his brother Giuseppe (Joseph) sent this canvas photograph to their parents, Pietro Giorgio and Raffaella Prinzo Sabatelli, in Felitto, Italy. The Sabatelli family in Italy still has the canvas and proudly shows it to visiting family members. (Courtesy of Phil Sabatelli.)

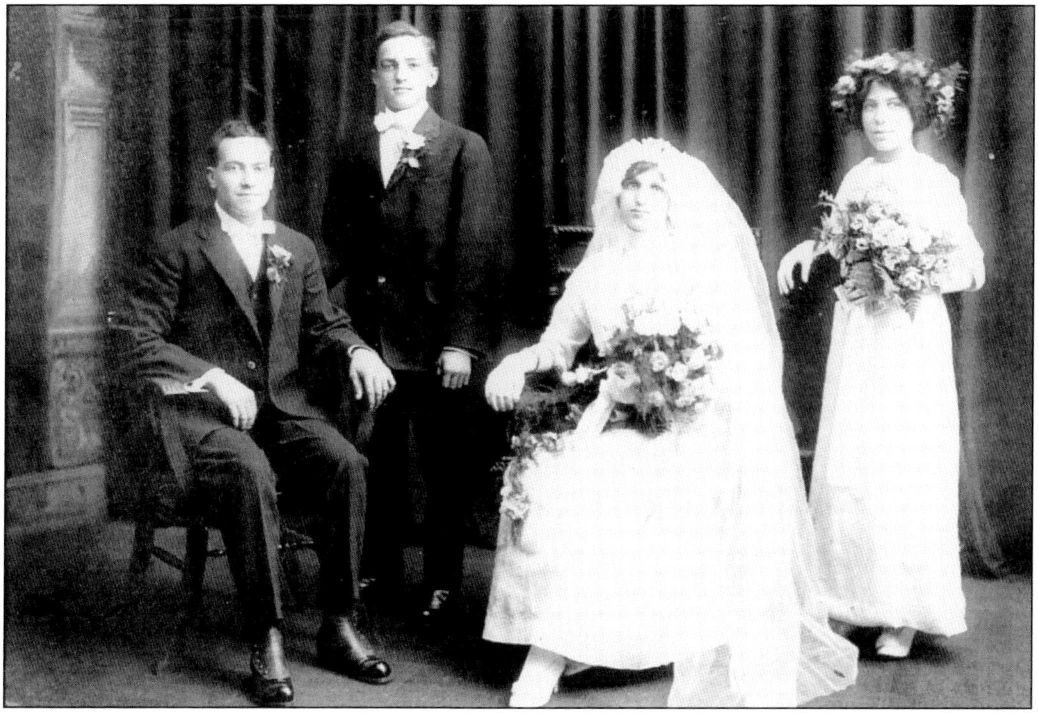

SILVANO AND DENA MINELLA WEDDING, SEPTEMBER 14, 1913. Silvano Minella emigrated at the age of 15 from Felitto, Italy, on June 11, 1903, aboard the *Roma*. His marriage to Bernardina (Dena) Panaro began with a carriage ride to Sacred Heart Italian Church. The bridal party is, from left to right, Silvano (seated), Carmen Guerrera, the bride Dena, and Vergie Prinzo. (Courtesy of Richard "Mussie" Minella.)

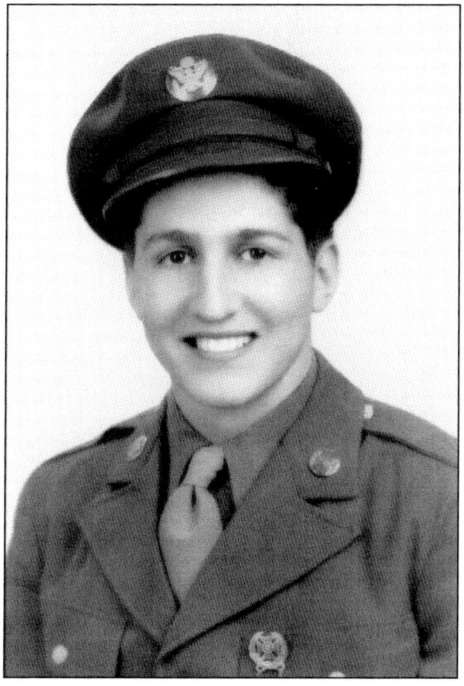

RICHARD MUSSOLINI MINELLA, 1944. Richard Mussolini "Mussie" Minella, at age 18, was drafted by the army to serve his country in World War II. He served six months in the Philippines as a forward observer in the artillery detachment. He fought in the Battle of Leyte Gulf, one of the largest naval battles in American history, and in Luzon. Minella was discharged in 1946. He remains active at San Antonio Church and with the Cincinnati Italian societies. (Courtesy of Richard "Mussie" Minella.)

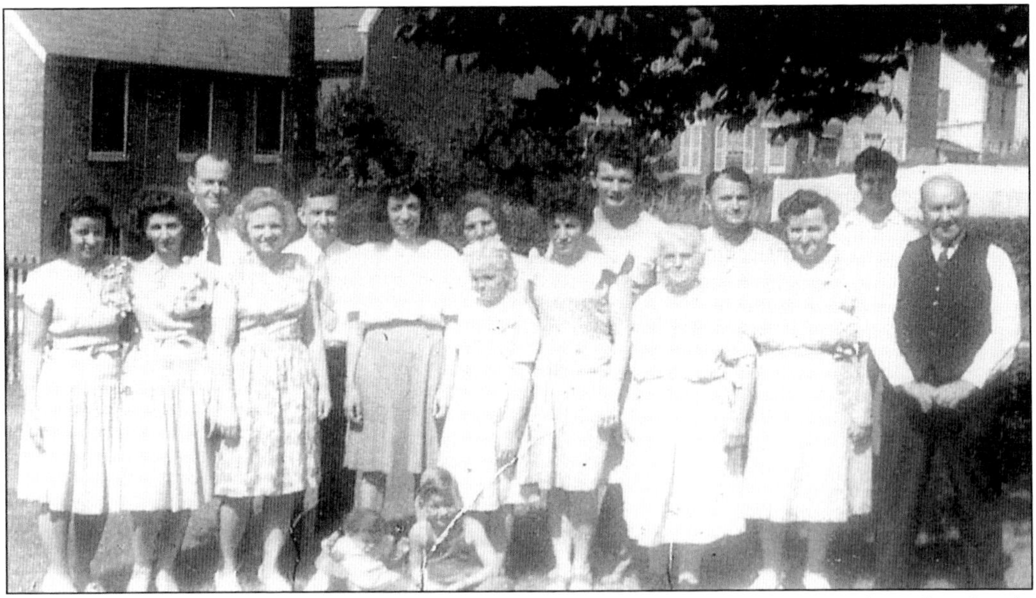

ANTHONY SCHIESZ AND MARY MINELLA WEDDING, JULY 4, 1947. Pictured in this family photograph are, from left to right, (first row) baby Judy Dattilo and Ron Wegmann; (second row) Betty Schiesz, the bride Mary Minella, Madelyn Schiesz, Rosie Cupito Young, Clara Jean Schiesz, Matilda Minella, Mary Josephine Panaro, Clara Schiesz, and Silvano Minella; (third row) the groom Anthony Schiesz, Lawrence Schiesz, Dena Minella, Elmer Wegmann, Victor Minella, and Richard "Mussie" Minella. (Courtesy of the Schiesz family.)

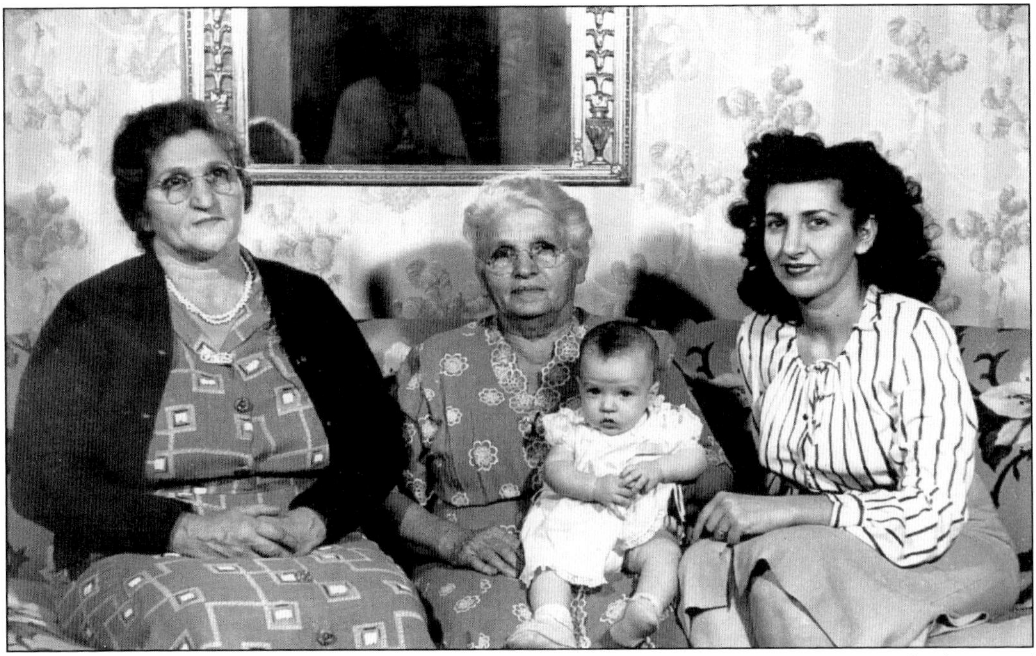

FOUR GENERATIONS. This photograph was taken at 1990 Queen City Avenue at the home of Josephine Palmire Panaro (center). At her left is her daughter Dena Panaro Minella, and at the far right is Dena's daughter Mary Minella Schiesz and baby Mary Jo Schiesz, daughter of Mary. (Courtesy of the Schiesz family.)

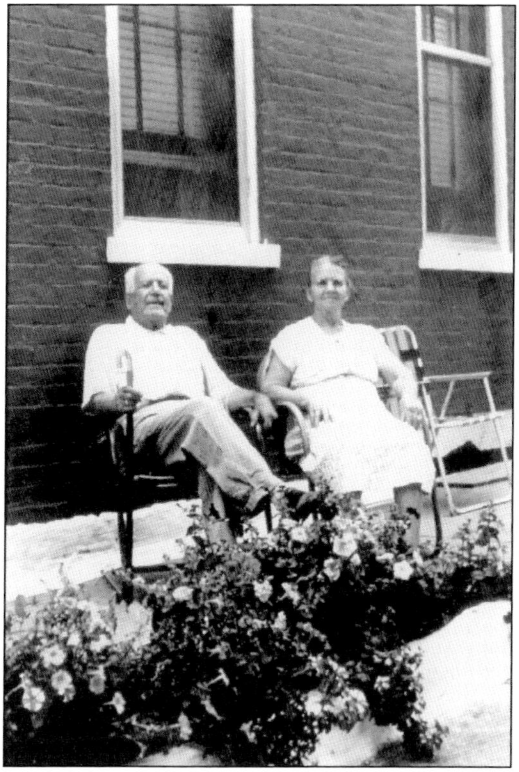

RAFFAELE AND PHILOMENA MINELLA. This photograph was taken in the side yard of the Minella home located at 1986 Queen City Avenue. Raffaele Minella first worked in the coal mines of Scranton, Pennsylvania, and then as a laborer for the Lunkenheimer Company in Cincinnati. He left there in 1912 for better employment at General Hospital, where he earned a salary of $16 per week. Philomena Minella took care of their eight children, Victor, Anna, Samuel, Matilda, Antoinette, Theresa, Rose, and Katherine. (Courtesy of Victor Minella.)

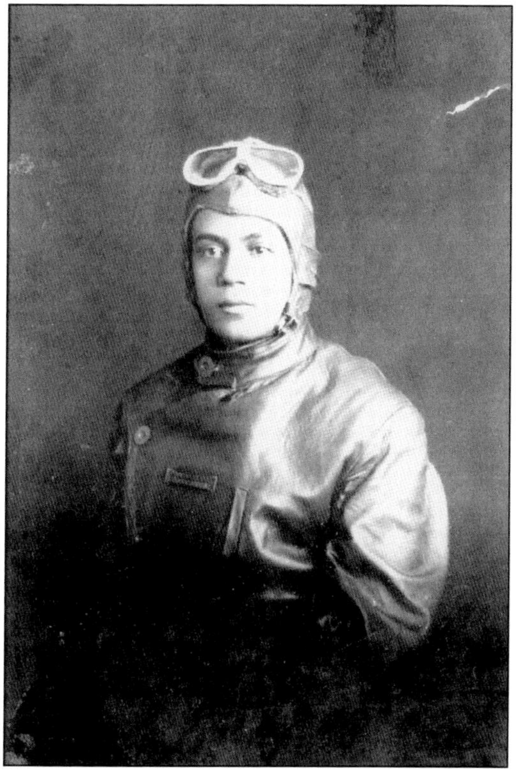

VICTOR MINELLA MOTORCYCLE OUTFIT. Victor Minella was born in Felitto, Italy, and immigrated to America with his parents, Raffaele and Philomena Minella, in 1901. He enlisted in the regular army on January 10, 1918, to fight in World War I and left from the armory located in Fort Thomas, Kentucky. His final assignment was with the American Expeditionary Forces from October 21, 1918, through June 28, 1919. He was honorably discharged on July 12, 1919, at Camp Sherman. (Courtesy of Victor Minella.)

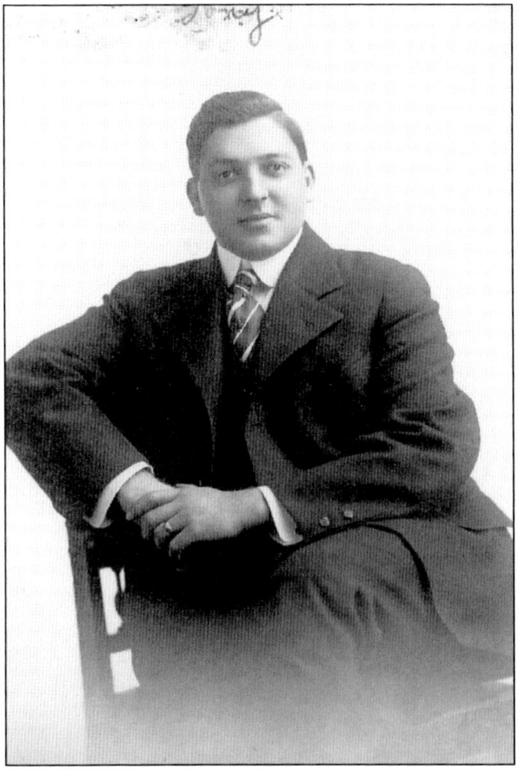

TONY PALMIRE. San Antonio men established the St. Anthony's Men's Society on August 12, 1922. As part of the society, Tony Palmire became the chairman of the San Antonio Church festival. The first festival was held in June 1923. (Courtesy of Richard "Mussie" Minella.)

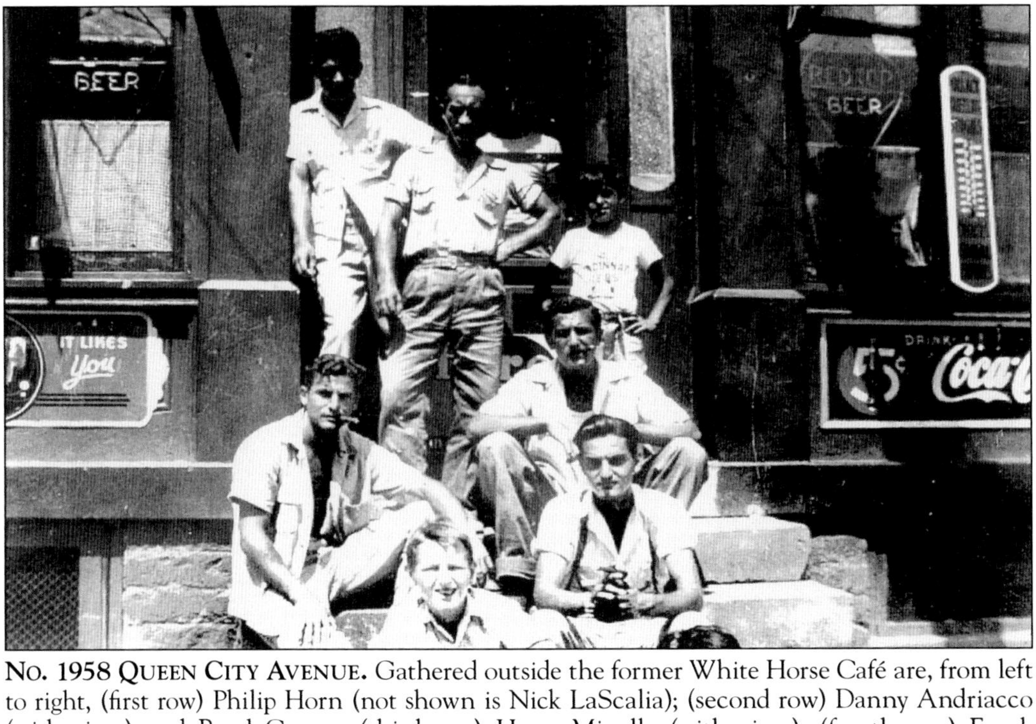

NO. 1958 QUEEN CITY AVENUE. Gathered outside the former White Horse Café are, from left to right, (first row) Philip Horn (not shown is Nick LaScalia); (second row) Danny Andriacco (with cigar) and Reed Carota; (third row) Herm Minella (with cigar); (fourth row) Frank Gramaglia, Nick Augustine, and Jimmy Fariello. (Courtesy of Richard "Mussie" Minella.)

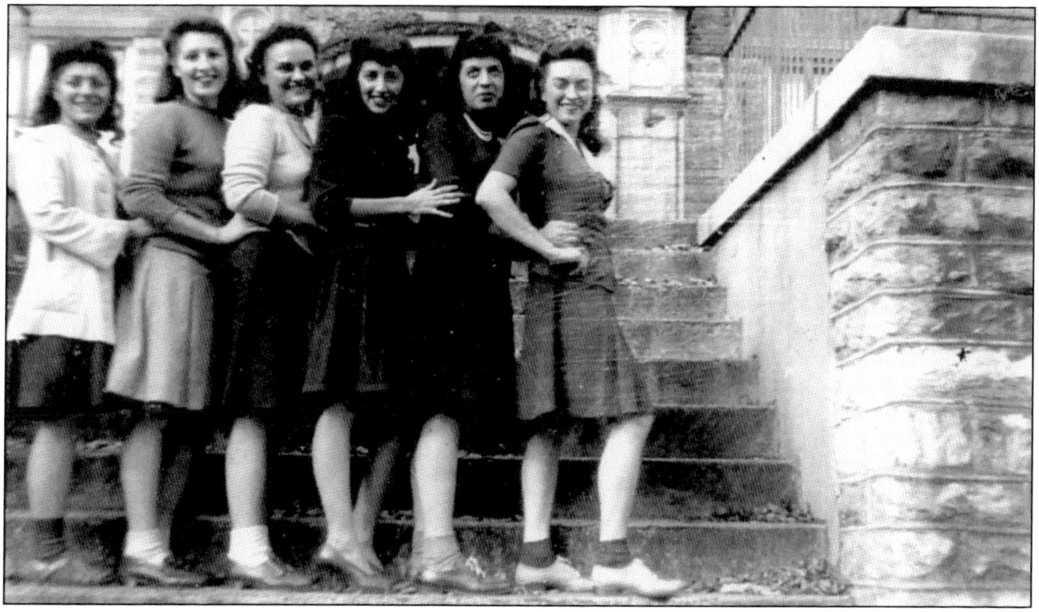

ST. BONAVENTURE ELEMENTARY SCHOOL, 1937. Former students of St. Bonaventure Elementary School pose for this photograph. From left to right, they are Mary Roberto, Loretta Horn, Eleanor Englameyer, Mary Minella, Rosie Cupito, and Ethel Englameyer. The girls were neighborhood friends who had attended the school that was associated with St. Bonaventure Catholic Church. The parish later merged with St. Leo in South Fairmount in 2003. (Courtesy of the Schiesz family.)

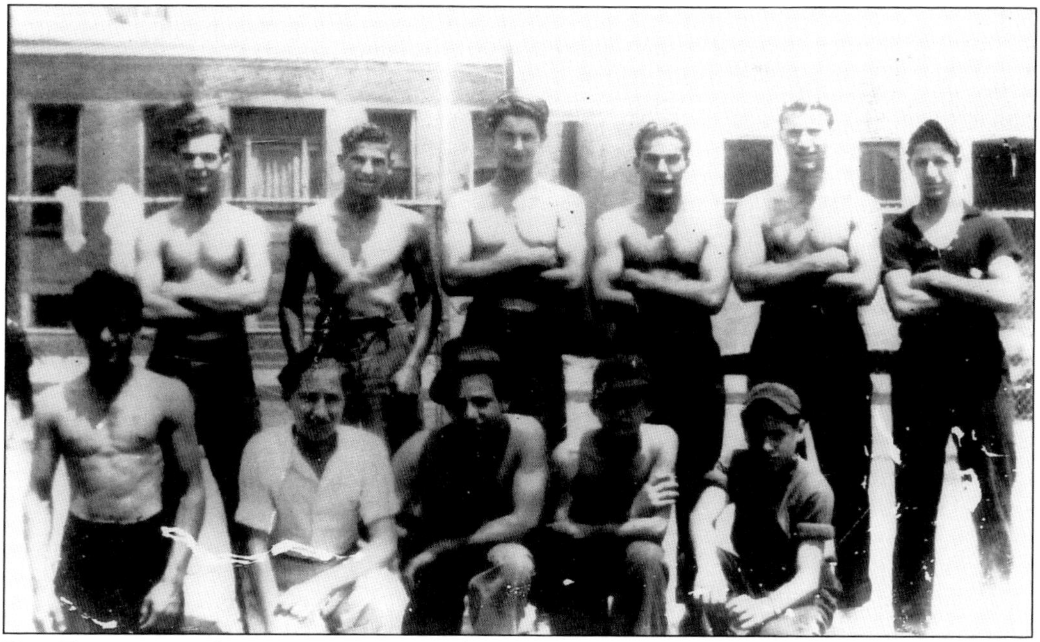

THE FAIRMOUNT GUYS, 1930S. Pictured are, from left to right, (first row) Tony Bor, Tony Esposito, Tony Gargano, Danny Delseno, and Jack Sarvie; (second row) Frank Bellissimo, Dan Andriacco, John "Gick" Dalessandro, Herb Garato, Joe Andriacco, and Danny Stevens. (Courtesy of Tim and Ann Dalessandro.)

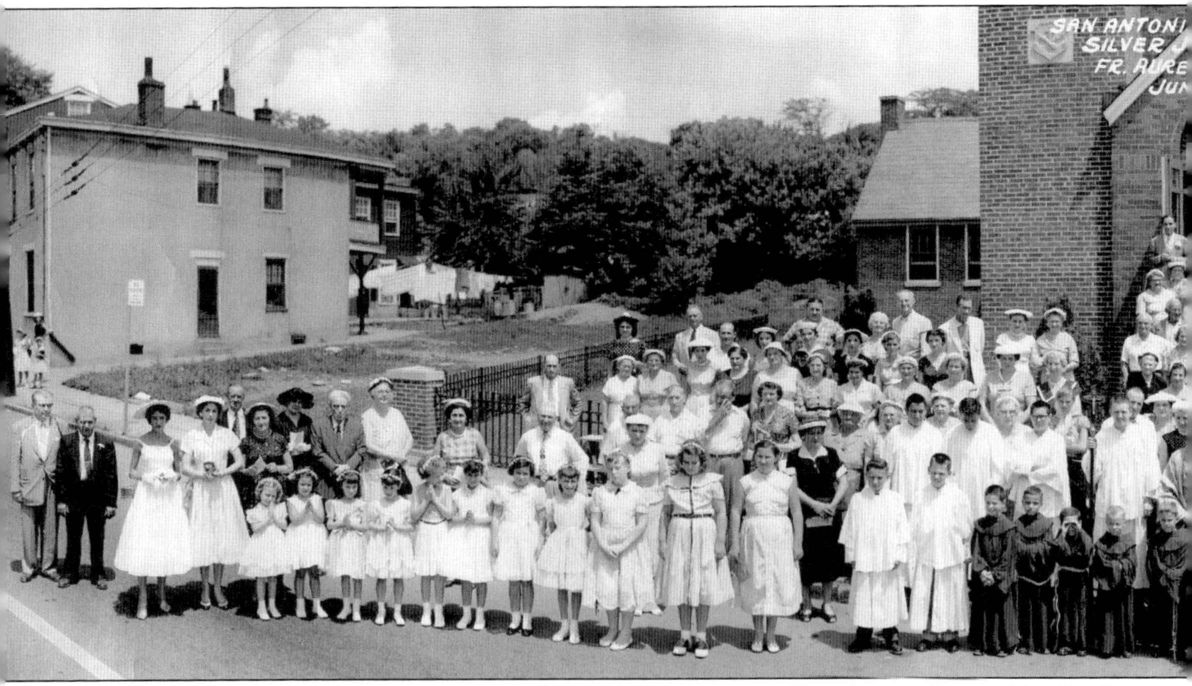

THE NEW SAN ANTONIO CHURCH. The new San Antonio Church was designed by Brother Bertrand Bailey, O.P., and was dedicated with a solemn High Mass on December 1, 1940, celebrated by pastor Fr. Ferdinand Nirmaier, the Most Reverend George J. Rehring, and the Very Reverend Adalburt Rolfes. A new bell tower was erected during the Marian year 1954. Bishop

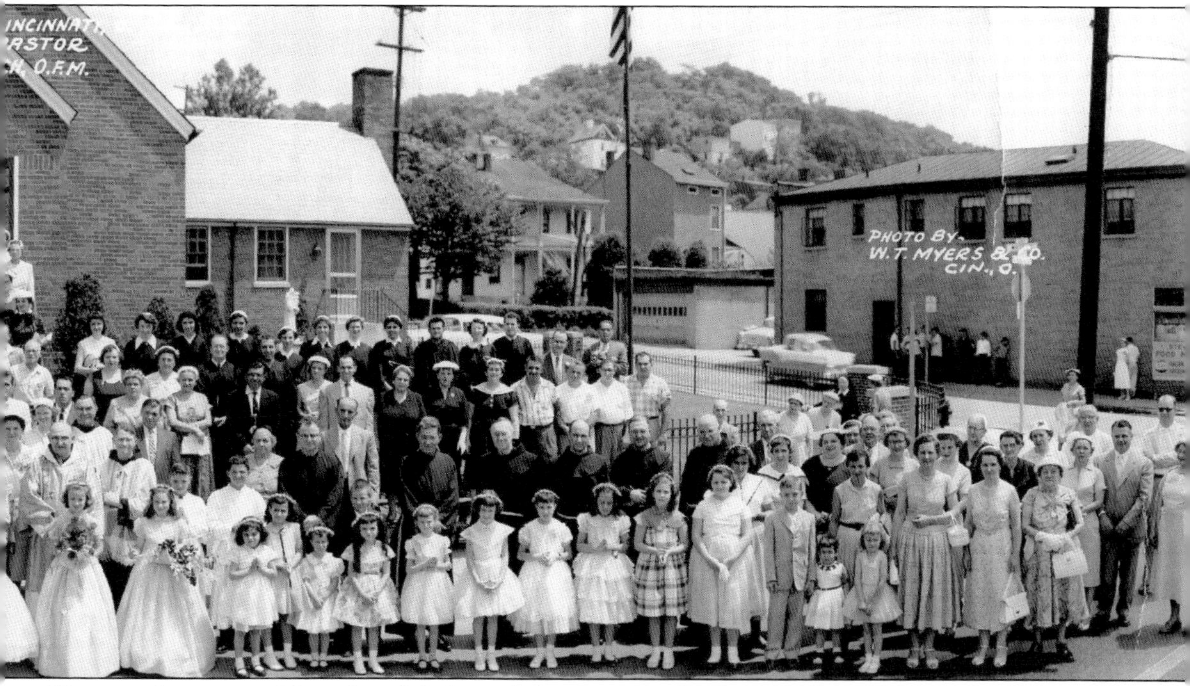

Clarence Issenmann blessed and dedicated the tower to the Immaculate Conception. Shown here is the congregation gathered out front on the occasion of the silver jubilee of Fr. Aurelian R. Munch, O.F.M, in 1957. Sunday mass and social gatherings continue to this day as San Antonio Church operates as a chapel under the St. Leo parish. (Courtesy of Margaret Fariello.)

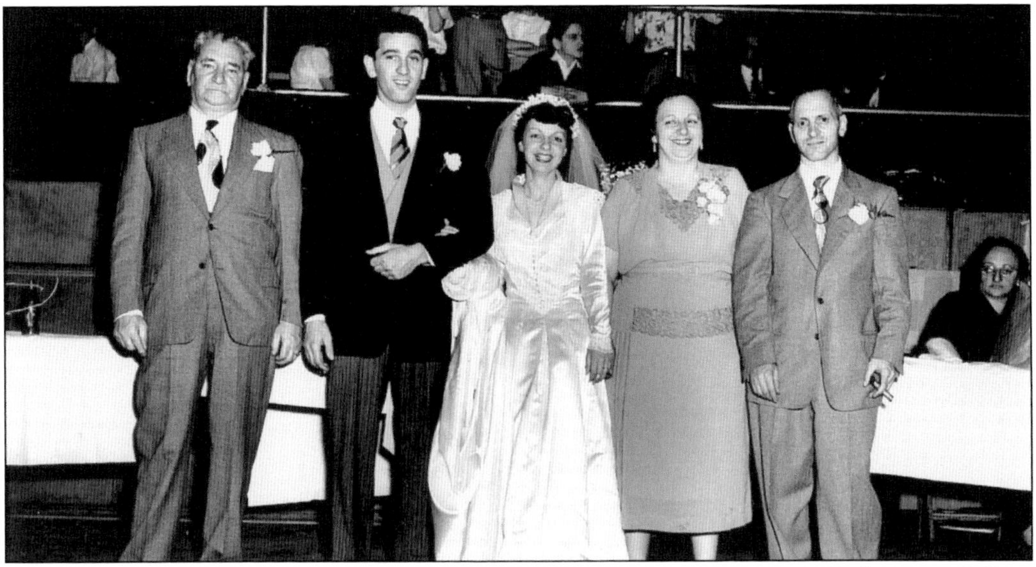

LOUIS ROBERTO AND FERN ROMELLI WEDDING, APRIL 4, 1951. Louis Roberto and Fern Romelli were married at San Antonio Church and raised a family of five children, LuAnn, Tony, Tina, Vincent, and Gina, on Bieglar Street in South Fairmount. Here they are shown with their parents; pictured are Pasquale Roberto (left), Louis, Fern, Caroline Romelli, and Joseph Romelli (right). Louis founded Pasquale's Pizza in 1954 with locations in Newport and Cincinnati. Today one can find Pasquale's Pizza parlors from New York to California. (Courtesy of Fern Roberto.)

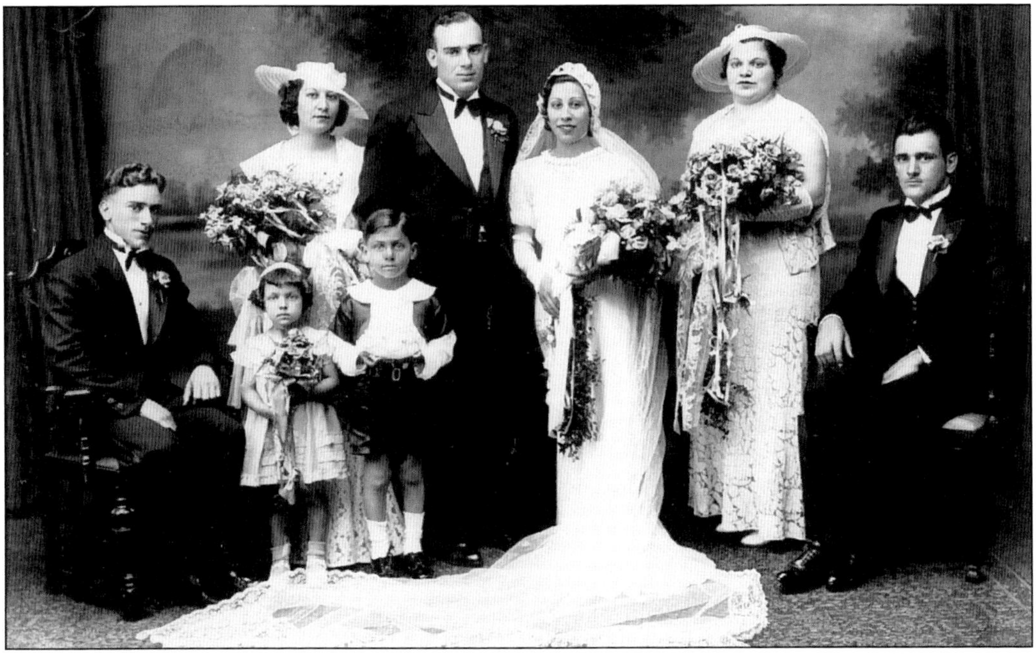

WEDDING OF CARMINE BONAVENTURA AND CARMELA SMERALDO. Carmine Bonaventura and Carmela Smeraldo were married on May 23, 1936, at San Antonio Church. Bridal party members are, from left to right, Joe Bonaventura (seated), Fern Romelli (flower girl), Jim Scrimizzi (ring bearer), and Frank Acito (seated far right). Standing in the second row are Rose Smeraldo, Carmine and Carmela, and Ann Bonaventura. (Courtesy of Estelle and Fern Bonaventura.)

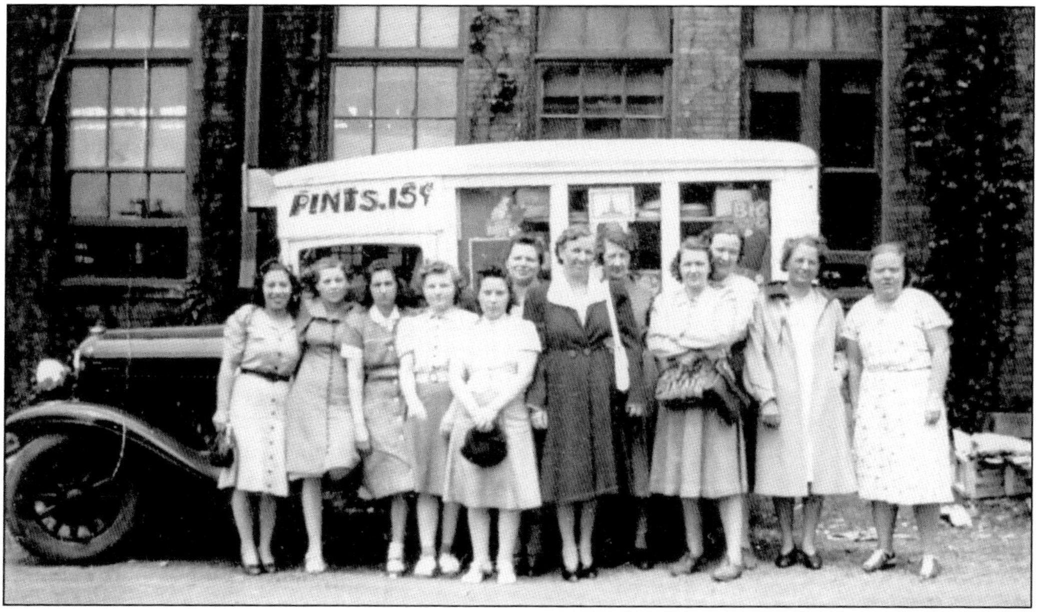

FASHION FROCKS WORKERS, 1938. Fashion Frocks, a leading manufacturer in women's ready-made apparel, employed Carmela Bonaventura and her fellow workers at their 3301 Colerain Avenue location. During World War II and the Korean War, the company produced parachutes, at its peak producing 20,000 weekly. The headquarters from 1935 to 1957 was placed on the National Register of Historic Places on October 27, 2005. (Courtesy of Estelle and Fern Bonaventura.)

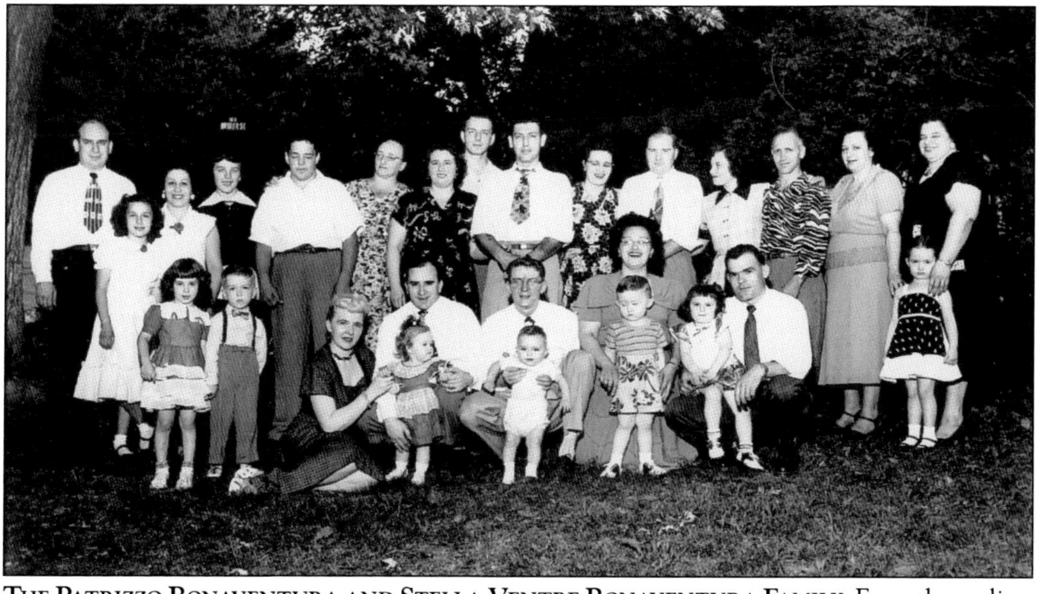

THE PATRIZZO BONAVENTURA AND STELLA VENTRE BONAVENTURA FAMILY. From the earliest years, the Bonaventura family enjoyed its Sunday gatherings on Biegler Street. The men played horseshoes and poker, all while puffing on their big black cigars. The women gathered in the kitchen stirring their rich savory pasta sauce while the children ran and played throughout the day. When it was dinnertime, everyone found a place to sit as they enjoyed their home-cooked Italian meal. (Courtesy of Estelle and Fern Bonaventura.)

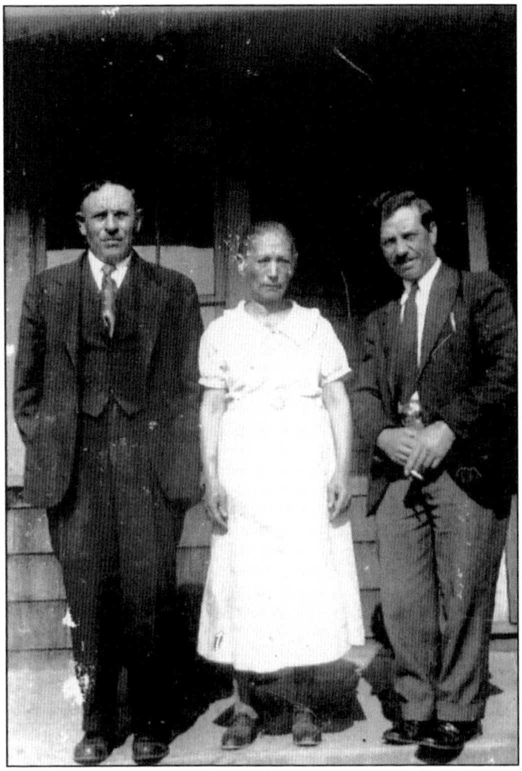

ROCCO SMERALDO AND FORTUNATA CUCIANATA SMERALDO. Rocco Smeraldo (left) was born in 1871 in the village of Varapodio, Reggio Calabria province, in the region of Calabria. At the age of 23, he married Fortunata Cucianata, age 20, and then immigrated to America in 1909. They first settled in West Virginia, then New York, and finally Ohio. Rocco was employed by the railroad his entire life. (Courtesy of Estelle and Fern Bonaventura.)

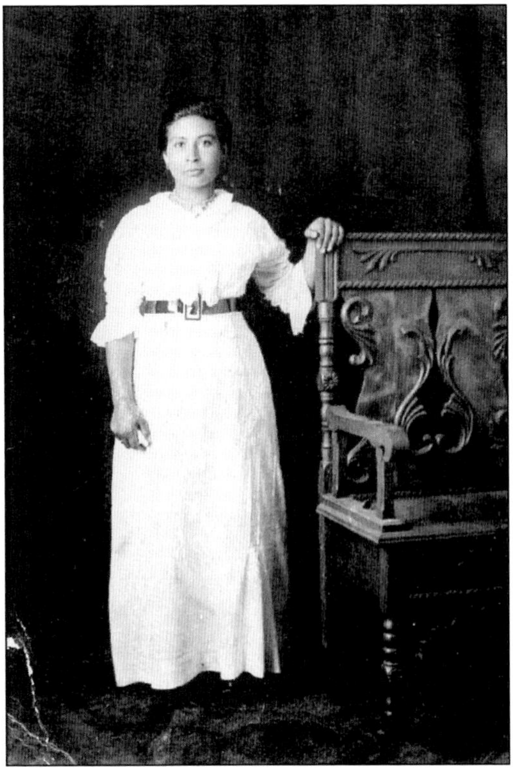

TERESA SMERALDO, 1915. Teresa Smeraldo was born in 1895 in Varapodio and arrived in America in 1914 for the prearranged marriage by her father, Rocco, to Sam Ricci. Many immigrants from Varapodio settled not only in the United States but also in Canada and Australia. The patron saint of Varapodio is Maria SS. del Carmine, Our Lady of Mount Carmel. (Courtesy of Estelle and Fern Bonaventura.)

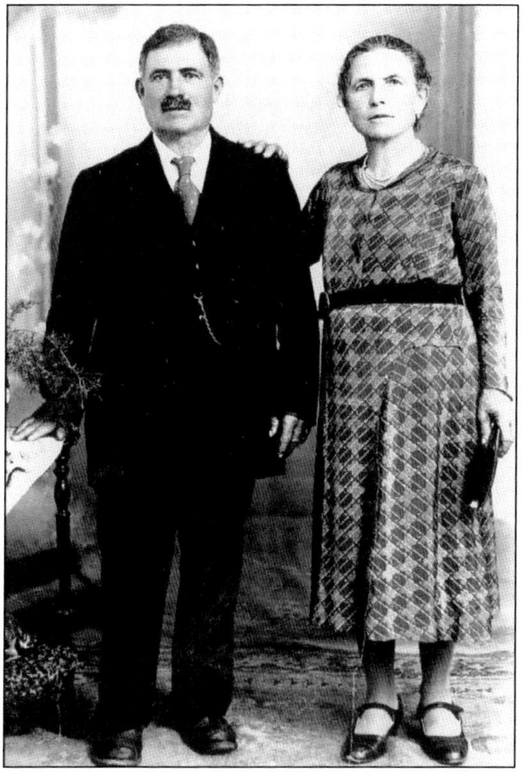

SABATO LINGARDO AND ROSA TROTTA LINGARDO, 1926. Sabato Lingardo, who was already a United States citizen, arrived at Ellis Island escorting his older son Antonio and daughter Rosaria on December 1, 1922, aboard the SS *Conte Rosso*. Sabato and Antonio stayed with relatives in Old Forge, Pennsylvania. Rosaria married Carmen Cerullo and moved to Cincinnati. (Courtesy of the Vito Lingardo family.)

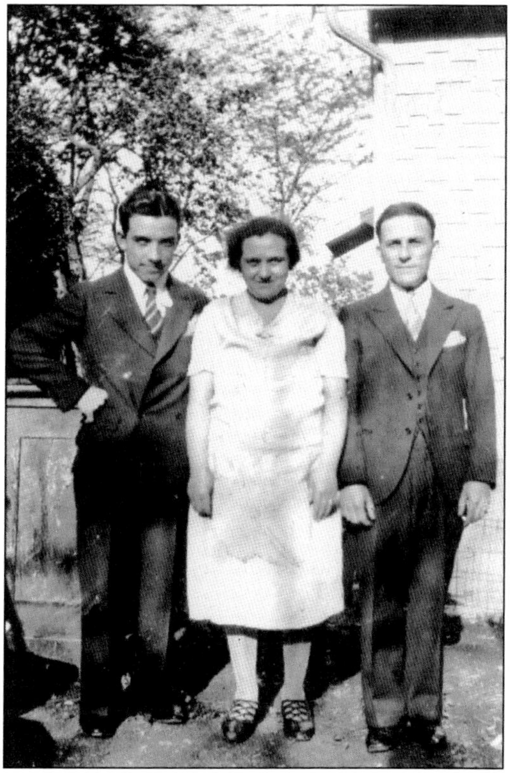

VITO, ROSARIA, AND ANTONIO LINGARDO. Vito Lingardo emigrated from Felitto, Salerno, Italy, in 1925 aboard the SS *Conte Verde*. Shortly thereafter, Sabato Lingardo returned to Italy, and Vito, along with brother Antonio, moved to Cincinnati and stayed with their sister Rosaria and her husband, Carmen Cerullo. (Courtesy of the Vito Lingardo family.)

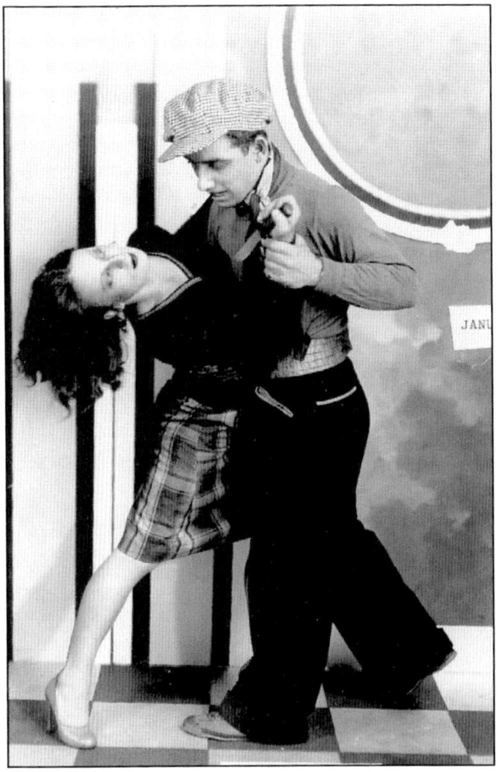

VITO LINGARDO AND VIRGINIA MEISSNER, C. 1931. Vito Lingardo enjoyed going to the Albee Theatre in downtown Cincinnati to watch the vaudeville acts. He took dancing with his friend Virginia Meissner at the Schuster-Martin School for Performing Arts. He even looked for a career in the silent movies by going to Hollywood in 1931 and joining the Screen Actors Guild (SAG). Unable to find steady acting work, he returned home in 1933. (Courtesy of the Vito Lingardo family.)

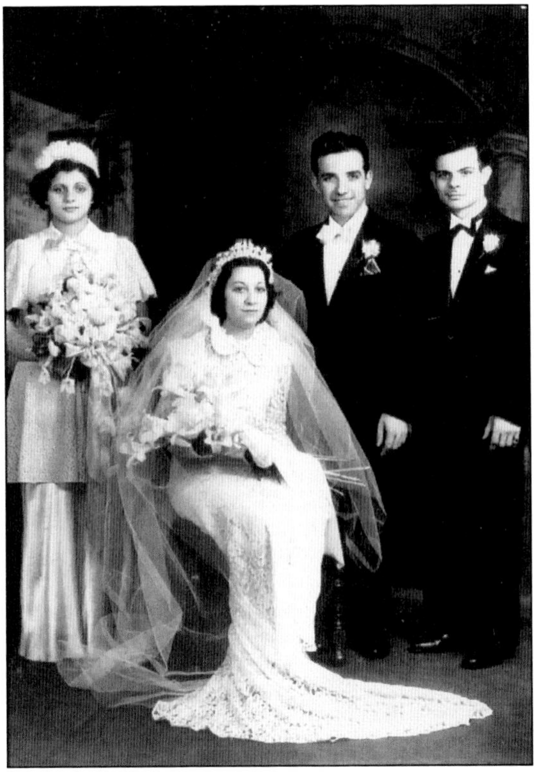

VITO LINGARDO AND ROSE SMERALDO LINGARDO. Vito and Rose Lingardo were married at St. Stephen Church in Hamilton, Ohio, on July 3, 1937. Felix Isgro witnessed the wedding along with Josephine Scrimizzi, whom he later married. The Lingardos raised four children on Harrison Avenue while living next to Vito's sister Rosaria. They later moved to South Fairmount. In 1977, Vito and Rose moved to Fallbrook, California, and built their retirement home. (Courtesy of the Vito Lingardo family.)

CINCINNATI STREET RAILWAY, C. 1939. Vito Lingardo attended class at Bloom Street School to learn the English language and finished his education at Hughes High School. In 1927, Lingardo found employment with the Cincinnati Railway Company. He was a car shifter and mechanic for the railroad. (Courtesy of the Vito Lingardo family.)

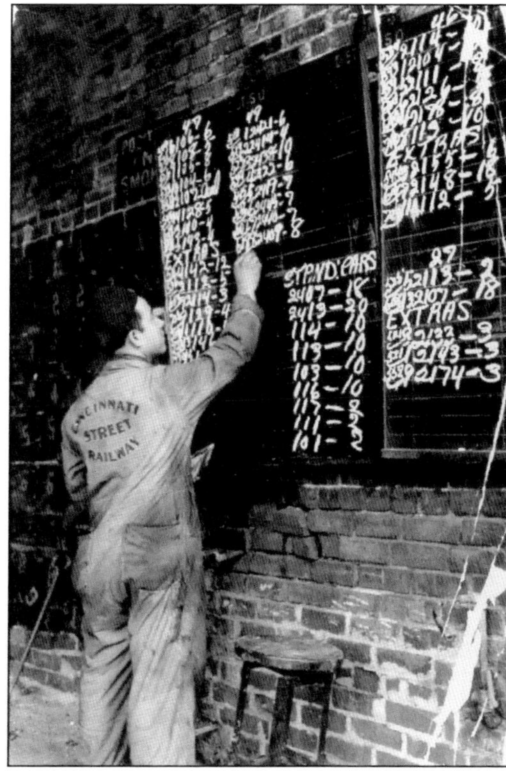

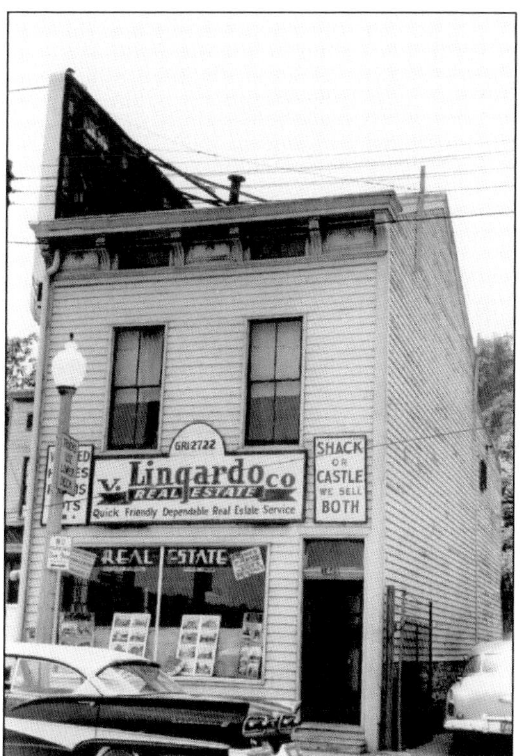

VITO LINGARDO REAL ESTATE, C. 1945. Vito Lingardo opened his first real estate office on Harrison Avenue near the Western Hills Viaduct. In 1961, he moved his location to Harrison Avenue in Cheviot. In 1978, while living in California, Lingardo, still having his SAG membership, began working as a bit player, doing commercials and movies. He was elected vice president of SAG for the San Diego Imperial Valley and Oceanside City. (Courtesy of the Vito Lingardo family.)

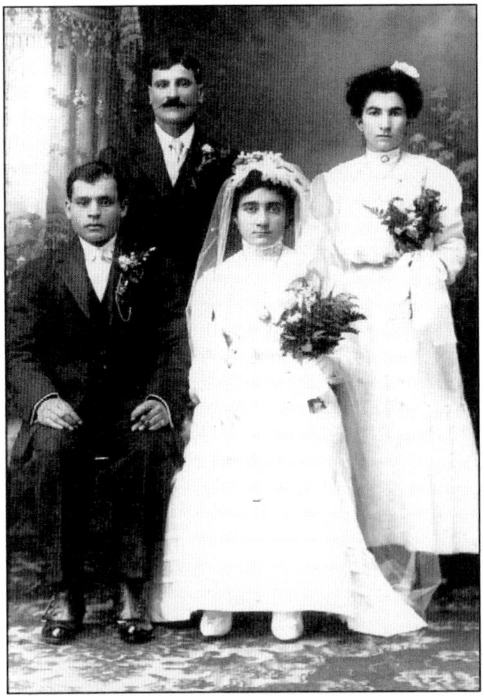

ANTONIO AUGUSTINE AND AGNES DIANGELO AUGUSTINE. Antonio and Agnes Augustine (D'Agostino in Italy) had a family of eight children before his untimely death in 1926. Raising a family on her own required Agnes to be resourceful by providing domestic services such as cooking, cleaning, and caring for infants and mothers as a midwife. The Augustine family resided at 1968 Queen City Avenue. (Courtesy of Jean Bromwell.)

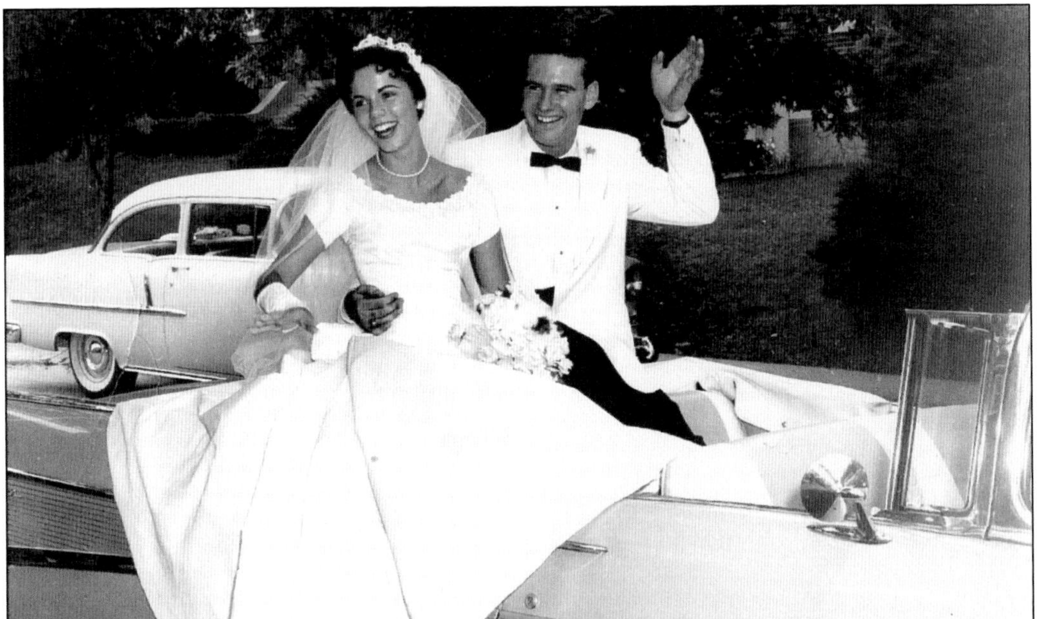

DAN AND CONNIE MCCLUSKEY. Connie Wakeman, the granddaughter of Antonio and Agnes Augustine, was married to Dan McCluskey at St. Clare Catholic Church in College Hill on August 3, 1957. The young couple borrowed Connie's uncle John Augustine's 1956 convertible to pose for this photograph. Connie's brother Vic Wakeman's Chevrolet is in the background. Together Dan and Connie built McCluskey Chevrolet and raised two children, Vicki, who married Mark Schmerge, and Keith, who married Kimberly Weeda. (Courtesy of Connie McCluskey.)

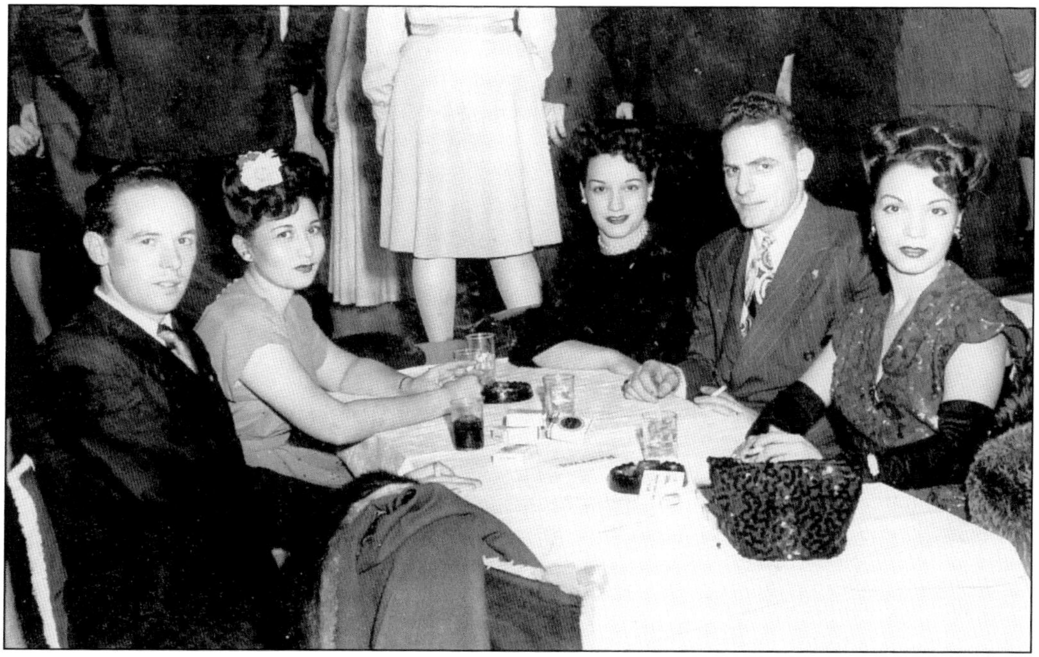

AUGUSTINE SISTERS. Three of the five daughters of Antonio and Agnes Augustine are shown in this photograph. Enjoying a night out are, from left to right, Jack Roda with his wife, Carmella, Jean and Andy Bromwell, and Ann Drahmann. Missing from the photograph are Mary Wakeman and Josephine LaCasella. (Courtesy of Jean Bromwell.)

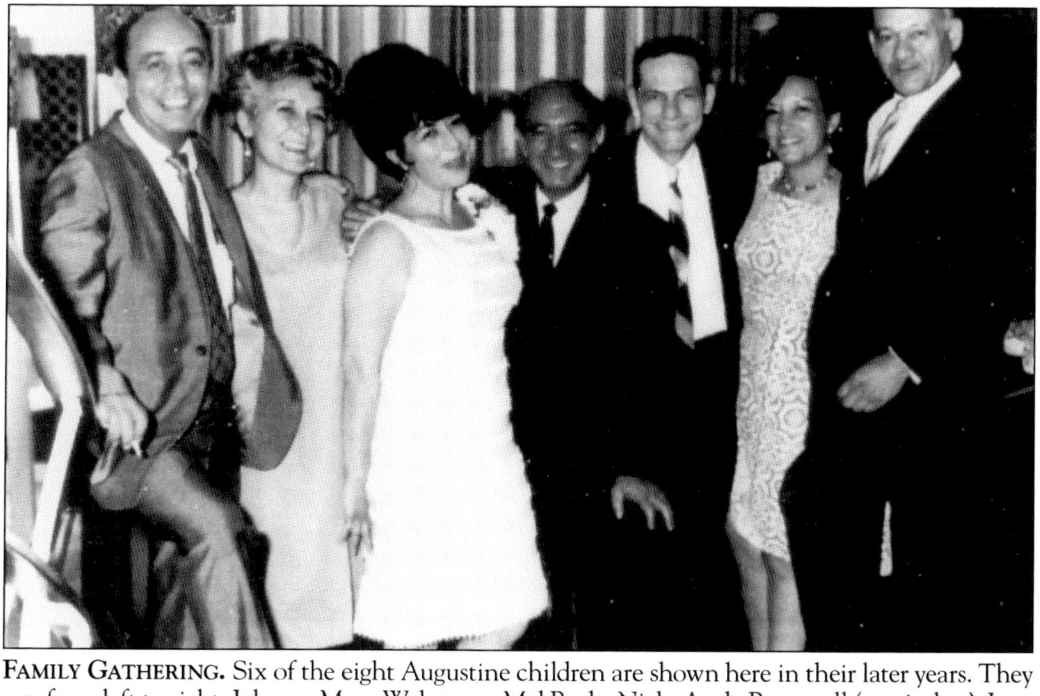

FAMILY GATHERING. Six of the eight Augustine children are shown here in their later years. They are, from left to right, Johnny, Mary Wakeman, Mel Roda, Nick, Andy Bromwell (son-in-law), Jean Bromwell, and Russell. After their father's death, the children would pick apples and pears to eat and blackberries to sell to help support the family. (Courtesy of Jean Bromwell.)

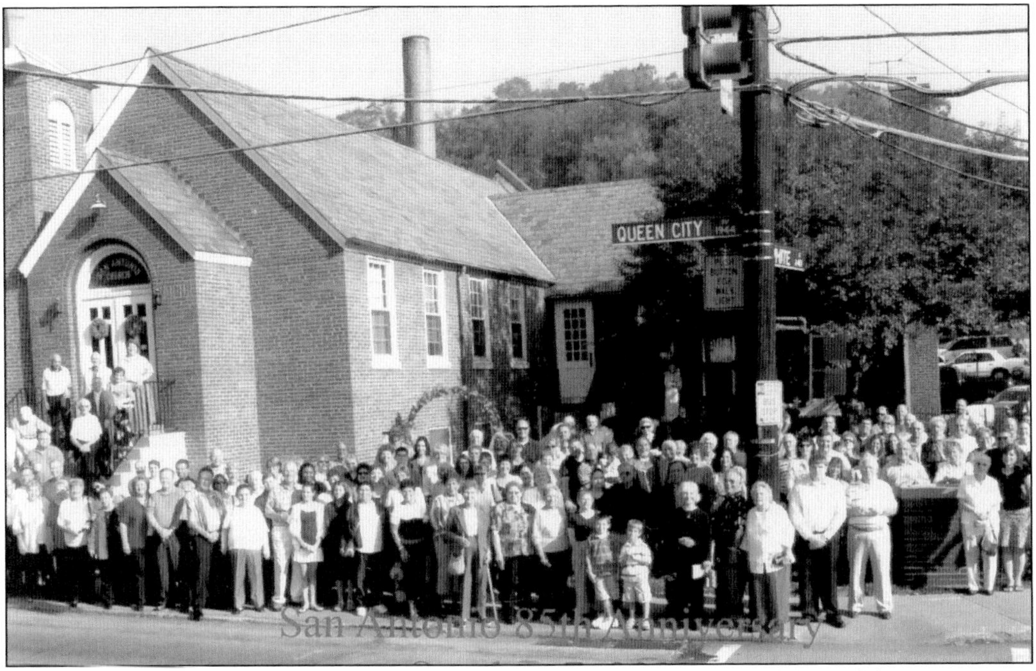

SAN ANTONIO 85TH ANNIVERSARY. On October 7, 2007, parishioners celebrated the anniversary of the formation of the San Antonio parish that began in 1922 with mass, a thanksgiving to the Sisters of Charity of Cincinnati, a dedication of a new brick walkway in the St. Anthony of Padua garden, and a social gathering. At the gathering, photographs of the early years were placed in the hall for all to review and remember. (Courtesy of TLC Pictures by Denise.)

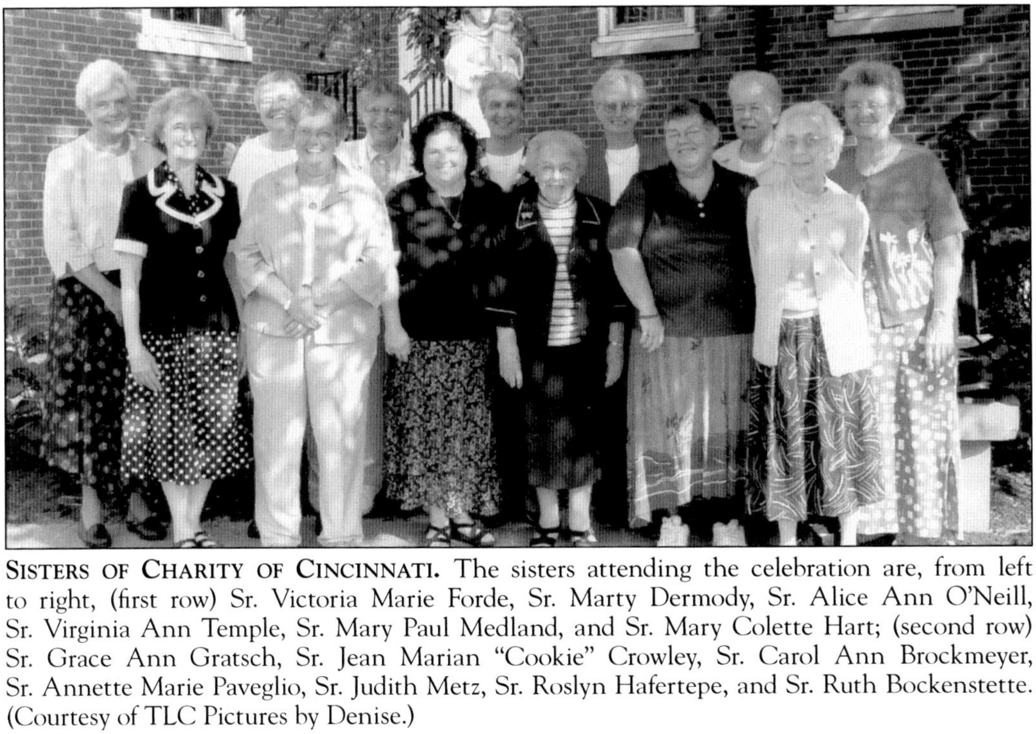

SISTERS OF CHARITY OF CINCINNATI. The sisters attending the celebration are, from left to right, (first row) Sr. Victoria Marie Forde, Sr. Marty Dermody, Sr. Alice Ann O'Neill, Sr. Virginia Ann Temple, Sr. Mary Paul Medland, and Sr. Mary Colette Hart; (second row) Sr. Grace Ann Gratsch, Sr. Jean Marian "Cookie" Crowley, Sr. Carol Ann Brockmeyer, Sr. Annette Marie Paveglio, Sr. Judith Metz, Sr. Roslyn Hafertepe, and Sr. Ruth Bockenstette. (Courtesy of TLC Pictures by Denise.)

Three

The Family Album

Humble beginnings, a sense of belonging, and eventual understanding of life in America helped make the Italians strong and dedicated to their new country without forgoing their Italian heritage. A focus on education and religion, along with a strong work ethic, made them good Americans.

By 1896, Cincinnati had over 8,000 Italians living in the area. Italian immigration into the area can be loosely classified as those who arrived in the 19th century, those who came before World War I, and those who came after World War II.

As with any family album, there is a mixture of photographs depicting family, religious events, entertainment, and fun. There is also a great sense of pride in the family business and in work in general that get captured in photographs. In 1900, over 85 percent of the early immigrants consisted of artisans such as tailors, shoemakers, blacksmiths, sculptors, musicians, and mosaic tile setters. Business owners, many of whom were first established in the area as street peddlers in one of the several public markets, such as Pearl Street, Wade Street, and Court Street Markets, established grocery stores and shops to sell their goods. Today Findlay Market is the lone original public market survivor with the rest given way to downtown development. Laborers completed the top-three employment categories with individuals working for the railroad, in factories, or as domestic servants. Professionals such as policemen, religious officials, and teachers and white-collar workers such as office personnel, salesmen, and bookkeepers accounted for the remaining 15 percent of employment.

Today, with the educational opportunities available to everyone, those of Italian descent have escalated up the ladder into more professional jobs. The way was paved by every generation before them that fostered a sense of pride in themselves and their new country. The Italian societies of Cincinnati offer college scholarships to those of Italian descent as a way to promote higher education. Family stories are shared in the following chapter to give all readers an appreciation for the times and trials faced by the young and not so young families living in the various communities of Greater Cincinnati.

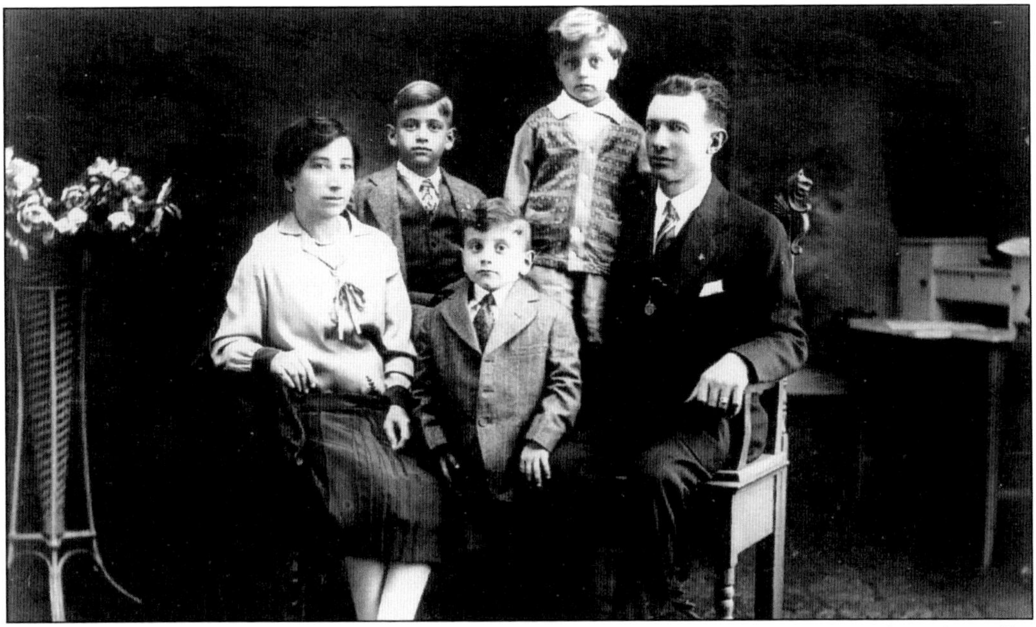

JOSEPH AUCIELLO FAMILY. Pictured are, from left to right, (first row) Beatrice Saulino Auciello, Dante Auciello, and Joseph Auciello; (second row) Alfred and Frank Auciello. Joseph immigrated to America from Pescolanciano, Italy, in 1898 to find work. He returned to Italy in 1914 and served four years in the Italian army. He married Beatrice in 1918, and while pregnant with Alfred, she journeyed from Civitanova, Italy, to America in 1920. (Courtesy of Alfred Auciello.)

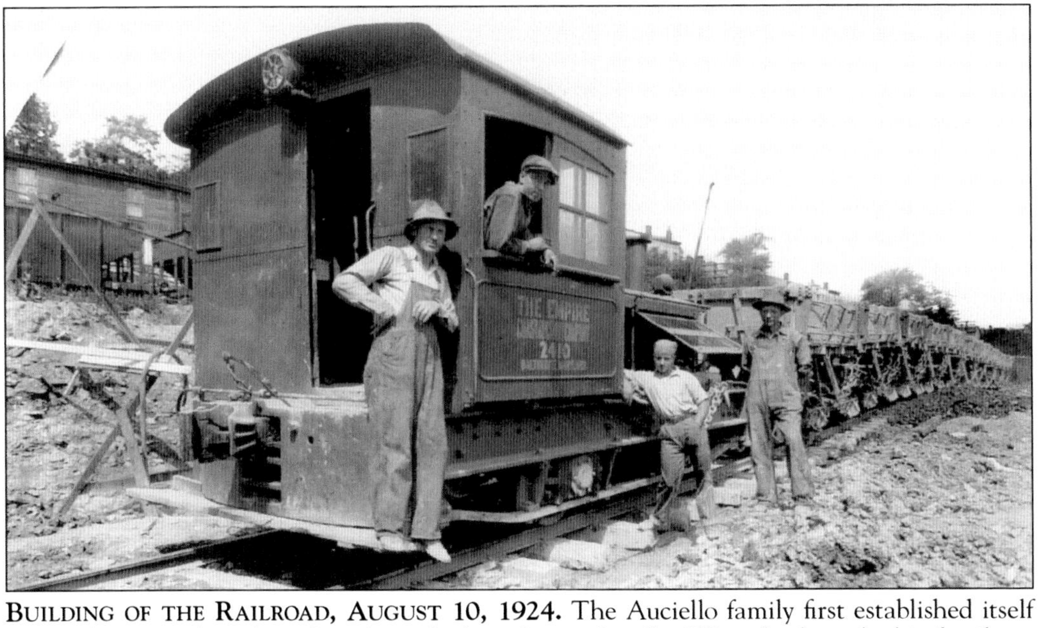

BUILDING OF THE RAILROAD, AUGUST 10, 1924. The Auciello family first established itself in Lynch, Kentucky, where Joseph worked in the steel mills. When he brought his family to Cincinnati, he worked as a laborer for the railroad. Joseph (far right) is working at the site of the Hopple Street viaduct. While in Cincinnati, the family lived in Cumminsville, then Coryville. Joseph later returned to Lynch with his family and opened a jewelry store. (Courtesy of Alfred Auciello.)

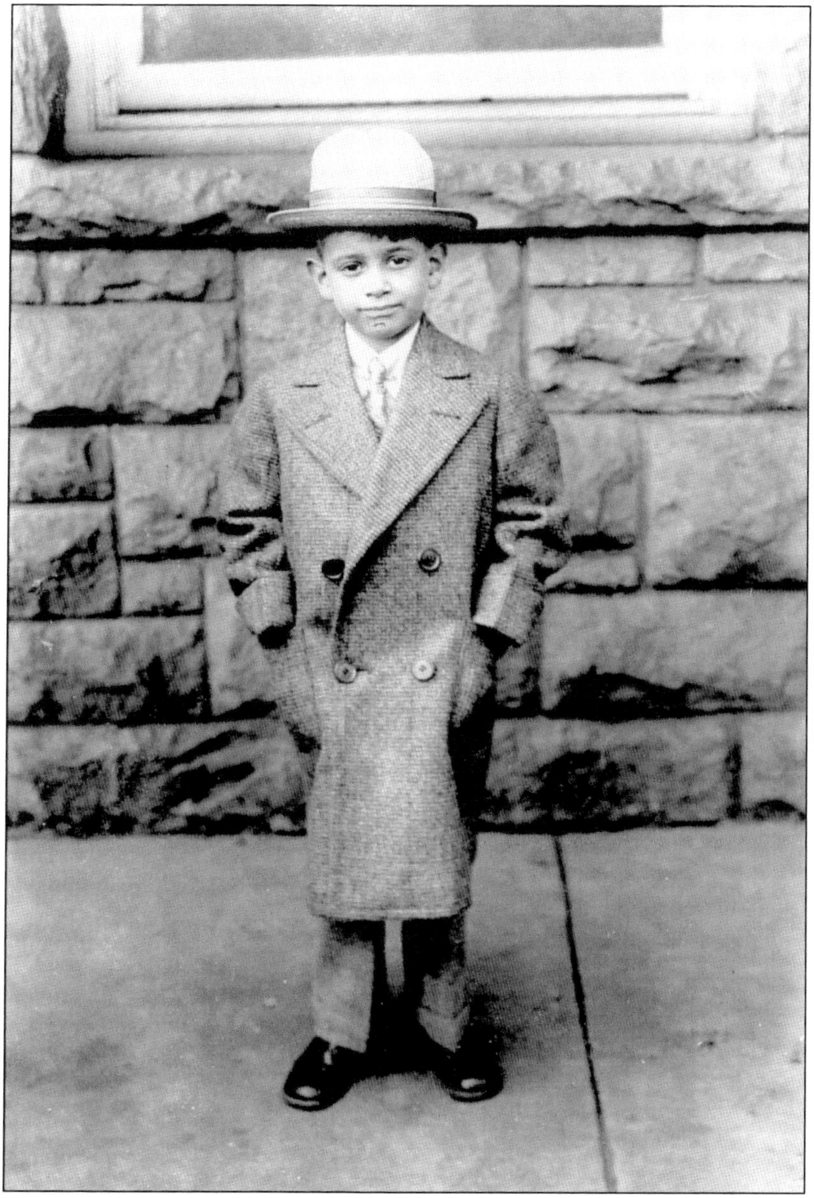

ALFRED AUCIELLO. Alfred Auciello, the eldest son of Joseph and Beatrice, was born on November 19, 1920, in Lynch shortly after his mother arrived in America. Here he is shown all dressed up in a coat made for him by his uncle Angelo Meccia. Alfred attended Lexington Latin School in Kentucky for three years, then moved back to Cincinnati in 1937 and graduated from Hughes High School in 1938. He then went into the seminary for four and a half years. About a year after he left the seminary, Alfred reconnected with Elena Siciliano in Cincinnati, and they were married in 1944. Alfred and Elena grew up together in Lynch, and their families knew each other well. Elena was born to Italian immigrants Angelo Siciliano and Concetta Ciulla Siciliano from Ena, Sicily. Elena worked as an Avon lady for 40 years, while Alfred worked for a heating and air company, eventually starting his own business. Alfred and Elena had eight children, Alfred Jr., Beatrice, Thomas, Vincent, Theresa, Joseph, Anthony, and Pamela. They lived in Cincinnati (Price Hill, then Delhi). (Courtesy of Alfred Auciello.)

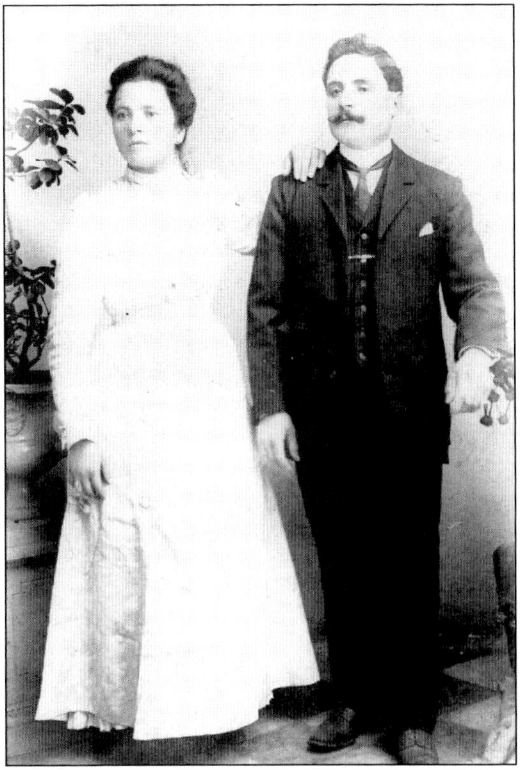

Elisena and Antonio Iacobucci. Elisena and Antonio Iacobucci came to America shortly after being married on December 7, 1907, in Chiauci, Campobasso (now Isernia), Molise, Italy. They first stopped off in Philadelphia, then went on to Cincinnati where the DiPilla family welcomed them. They raised four sons in the Cincinnati area, Vince, Louie, Joseph, and Frank. (Courtesy of Frank A. Iacobucci.)

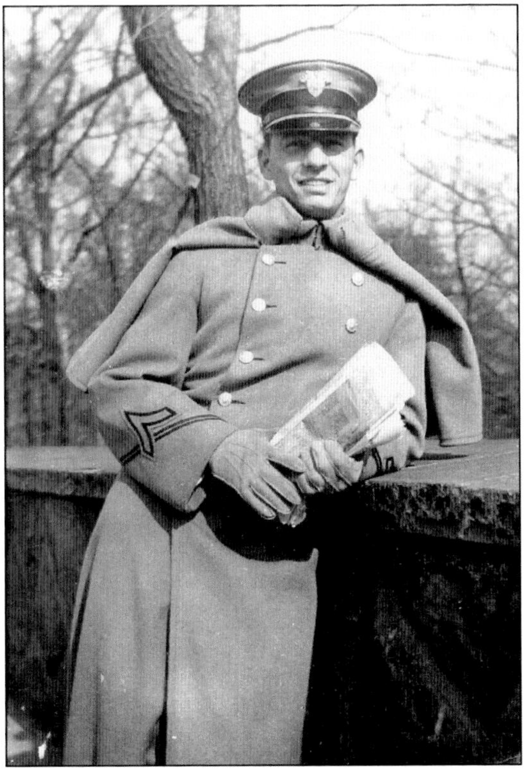

Capt. Joseph V. Iacobucci, c. 1938. Joseph V. Iacobucci graduated from West Point 23rd in his class of 448 in June 1940. He was a member of the Signal Corps and left for Manila, Philippines, in the autumn of 1941. After the fall of Corregidor on May 6, 1942, Iacobucci was taken to the Cabanatuan Prison Camp located in Fukuoka, Japan. (Courtesy of Frank A. Iacobucci.)

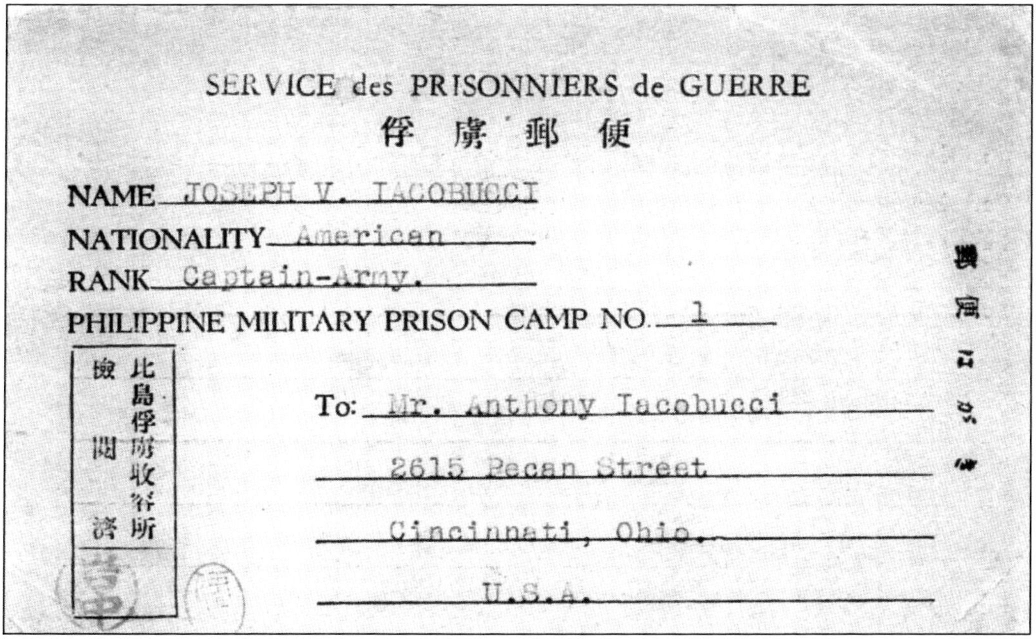
SERVICE des PRISONNIERS de GUERRE

俘虜郵便

NAME JOSEPH V. IACOBUCCI

NATIONALITY American

RANK Captain-Army.

PHILIPPINE MILITARY PRISON CAMP NO. 1

比島俘虜收容所
檢閲濟

To: Mr. Anthony Iacobucci
2615 Pecan Street
Cincinnati, Ohio.
U.S.A.

POSTCARD HOME. The family received this postcard after Capt. Joseph V. Iacobucci's death on March 14, 1945, at the age of 28 while a prisoner at Fukuoka Sub Camp 1, Kyushu, Japan. Remarkably he survived the arduous seven-week journey via the "Hell Ships" *Oryoku Maru*, which sunk in Subic Bay in December 1944, the *Enoura Maru*, which was sunk in the harbor of Taipei, Formosa, in January 1945, and the *Brazil Maru*, which ultimately transported the surviving prisoners of war to Moji, Japan. Iacobucci died as a prisoner of war due to starvation, dysentery, and exposure. (Courtesy of Frank A. Iacobucci.)

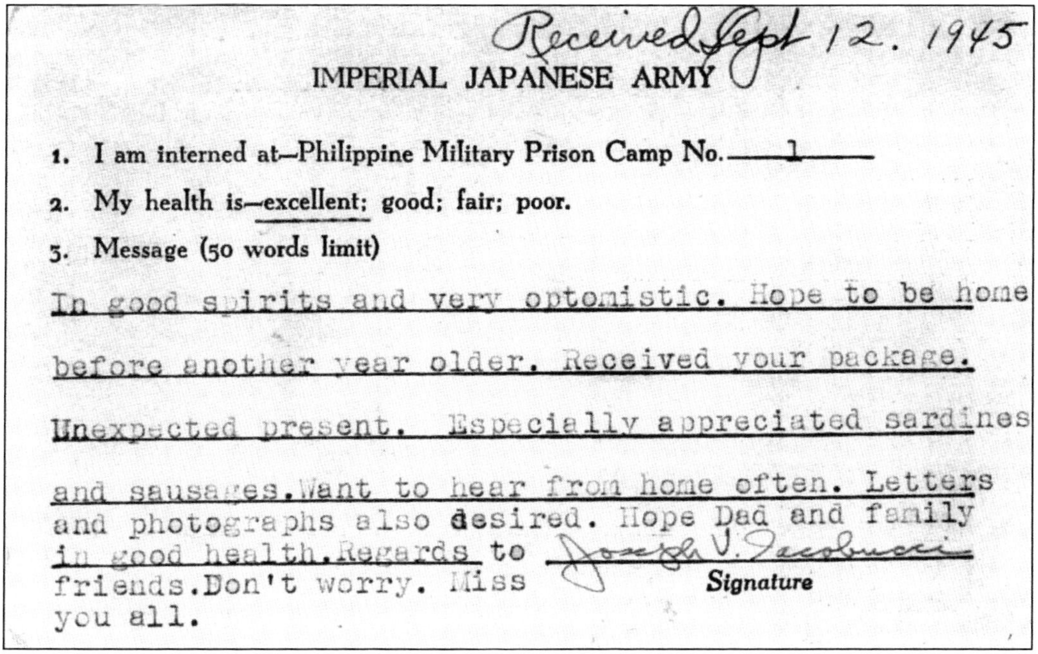
Received Sept 12. 1945

IMPERIAL JAPANESE ARMY

1. I am interned at—Philippine Military Prison Camp No. 1
2. My health is—excellent; good; fair; poor.
3. Message (50 words limit)

In good spirits and very optomistic. Hope to be home before another year older. Received your package. Unexpected present. Especially appreciated sardines and sausages. Want to hear from home often. Letters and photographs also desired. Hope Dad and family in good health. Regards to friends. Don't worry. Miss you all.

Joseph V. Iacobucci
Signature

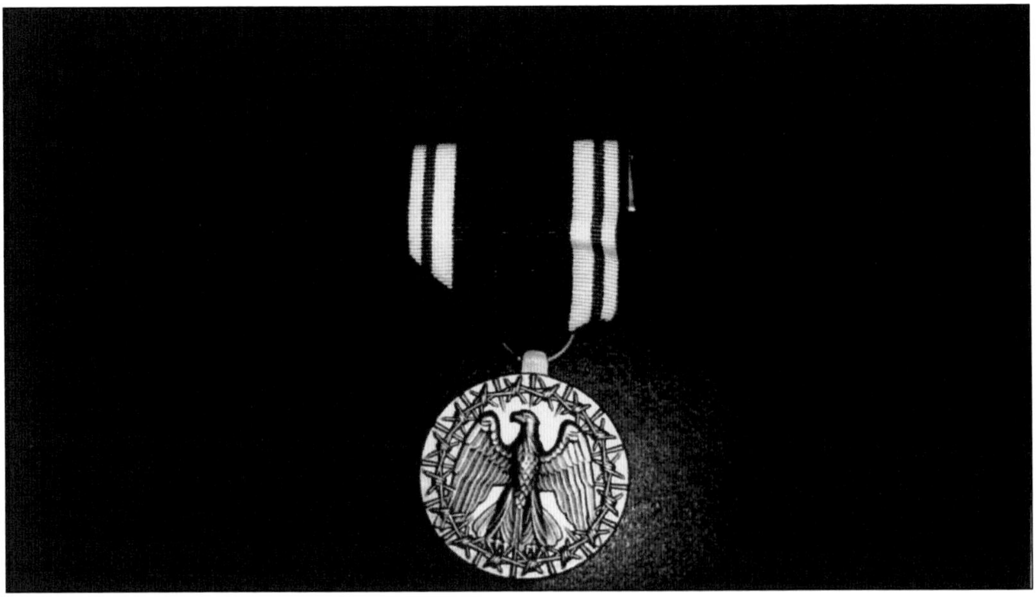

PRISONER OF WAR MEDAL. The family of Joseph V. Iacobucci, a captain in the U.S. Army, was awarded the Prisoner of War Medal for Iacobucci's honorable service while a prisoner of war. On the front of the medal is an eagle, symbol of the United States and the American spirit. Barbed wire and bayonet points surround it as a symbol of hope that upholds the spirit of the prisoner of war. After the surrender of Japan in 1945, Japanese general Masaharu Homma was convicted of war crimes, including the atrocities of the death march out of Bataan and atrocities at Camps O'Donnell and Cabanatuan. General Homma was executed on April 3, 1946. Shown below, Frank A. Iacobucci, also a West Point graduate, visits the mass grave of his brother and his comrades interred at Jefferson Barracks National Cemetery in St. Louis. (Courtesy of Frank A. Iacobucci.)

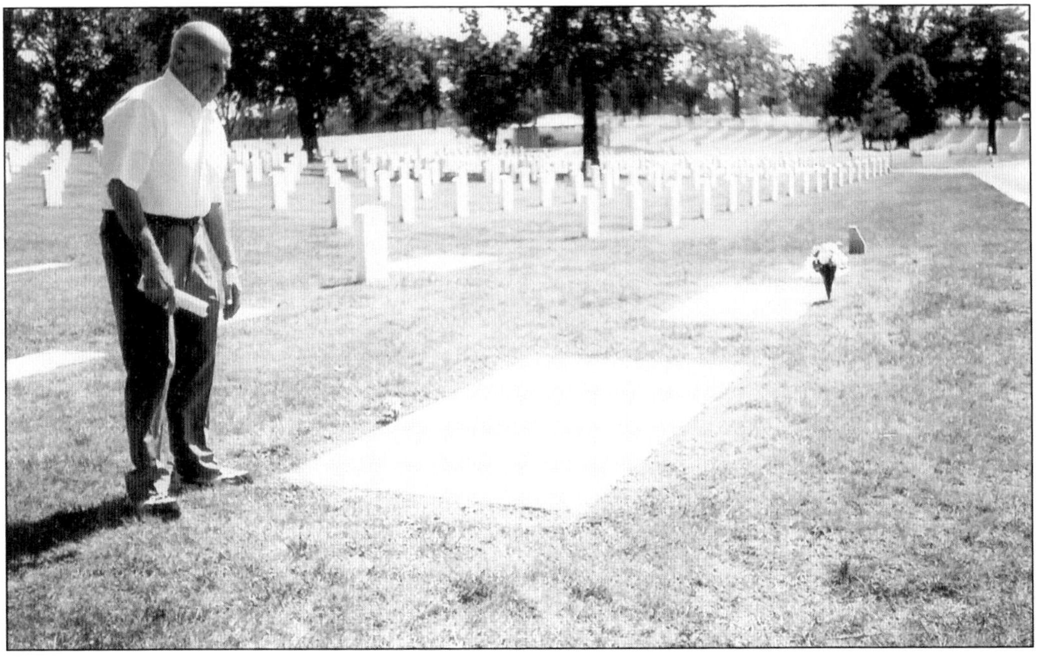

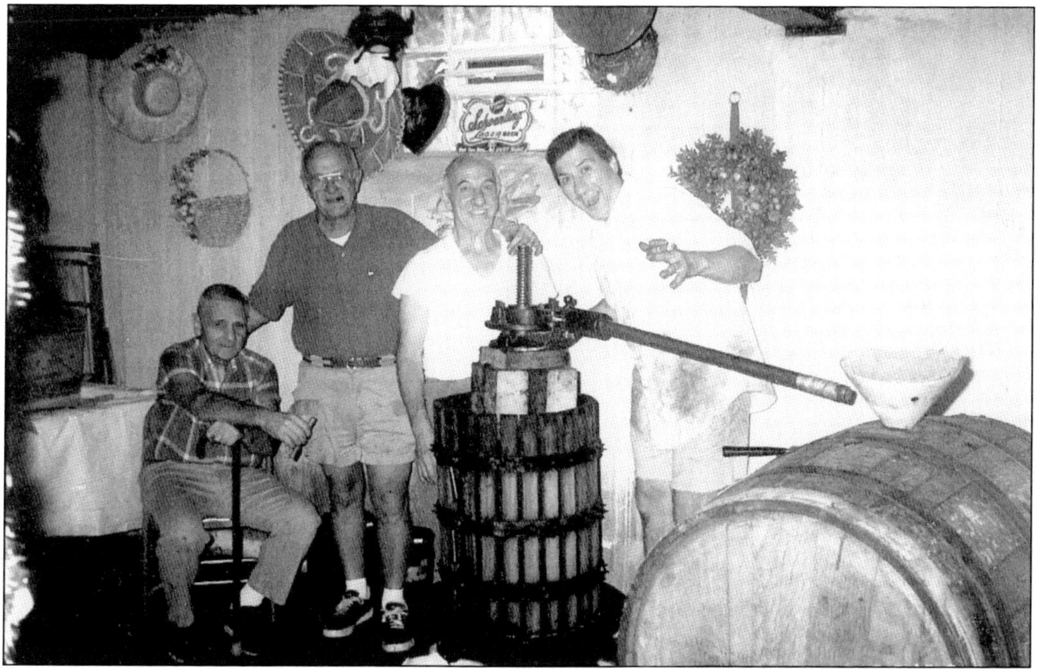

HOMEMADE WINE. Wine making is an Italian family tradition. Shown with the wine-making equipment are, from left to right, Tony Iacobucci, Bill Bradley, Frank A. Iacobucci, and Jim "Giacomo" Pferrman. On the Feast of St. Martin, which is celebrated on November 11, the wine is tasted as it is bottled. It is also customary to dip aniseed-flavored biscotti, made in the saint's honor, into sweet wine. (Courtesy of Frank A. Iacobucci.)

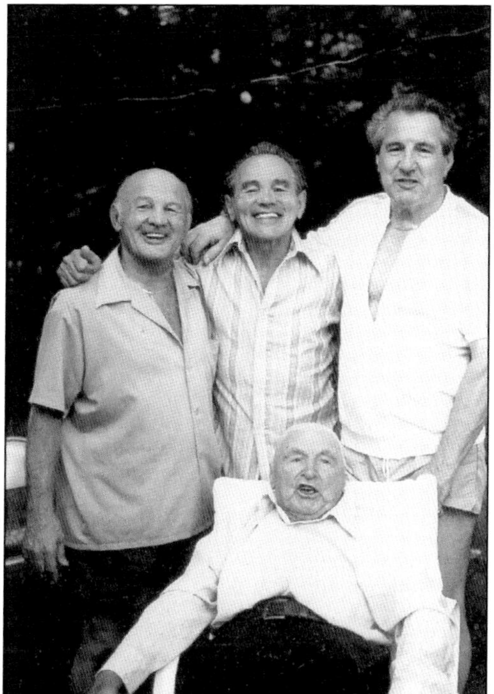

CARMINE IACOBUCCI AND SONS. Seated is Carmine Iacobucci at the age of 93 with his sons, shown from left to right, Pat, Carmine, and Tony. Carmine came to America at the age of 17 and returned to Chiauci, Italy, to escort his wife M. Concetta to America on March 2, 1924, aboard the ship *Colombo*. Carmine operated a grocery store in Findlay Market. (Courtesy of Pat Iacobucci.)

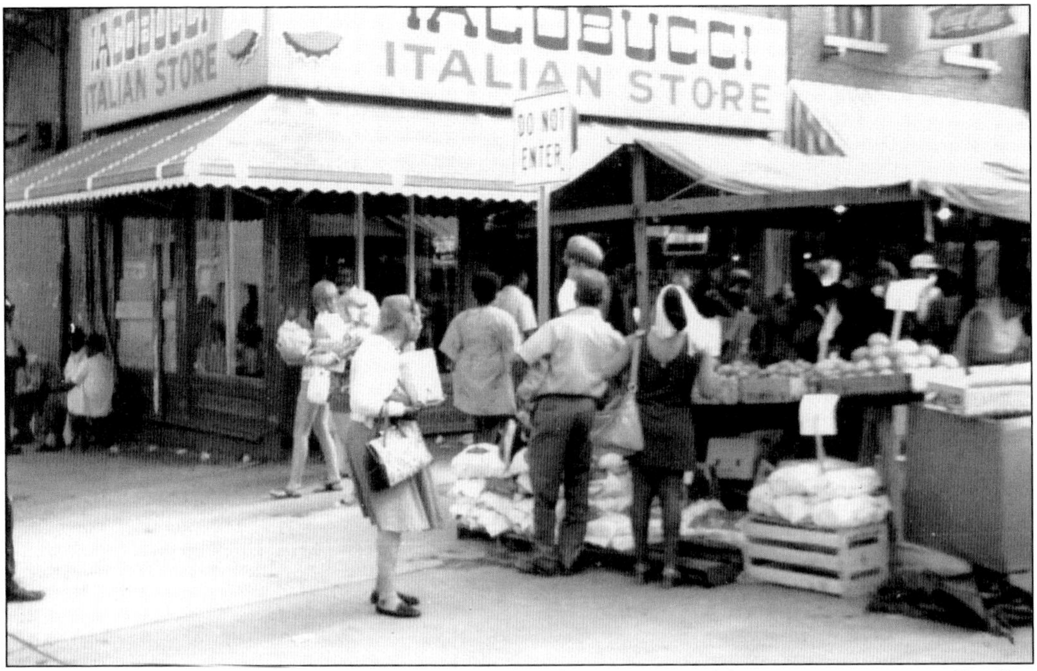

IACOBUCCI ITALIAN STORE, 1972. Carmine Iacobucci operated his grocery store in Findlay Market for 60 years, ending his stay with his retirement in 1982. The store offered Italian luncheon meats, cheeses, and pastas, along with fresh fruits and vegetables. Shown below in front of the meat slicer is his niece Santa Iacobucci, who immigrated to America in 1962, and standing behind the counter are, from left to right, Santa's sister Incoronada Iacobucci and Diva Bimenna Gruber. Findlay Market is located at 1801 Race Street and was listed on the National Register of Historic Places in 1972. (Courtesy of Santa Iacobucci.)

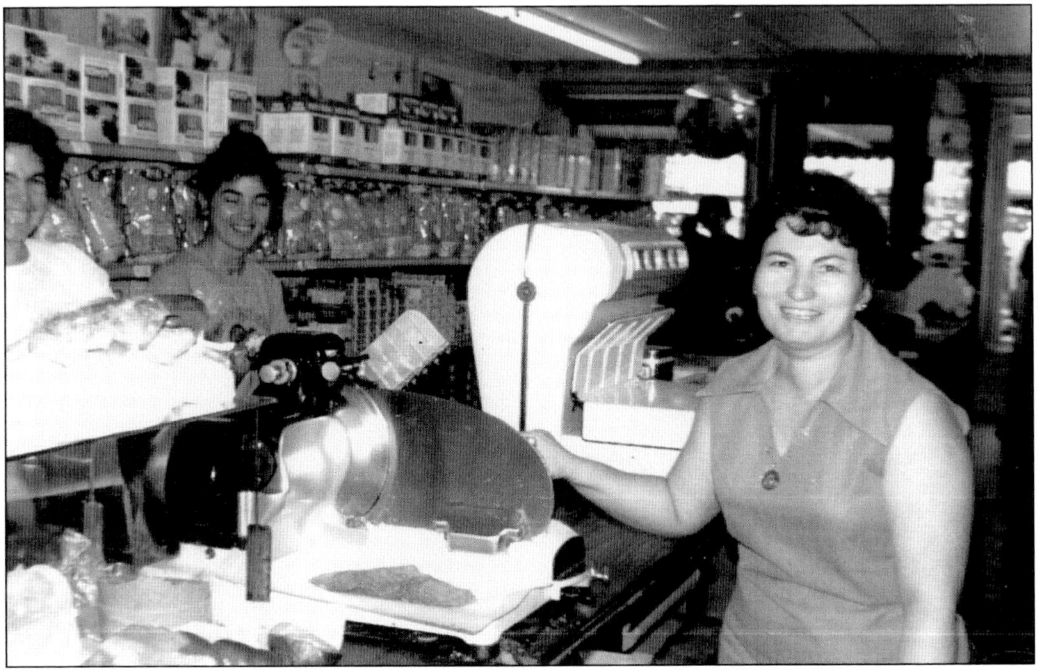

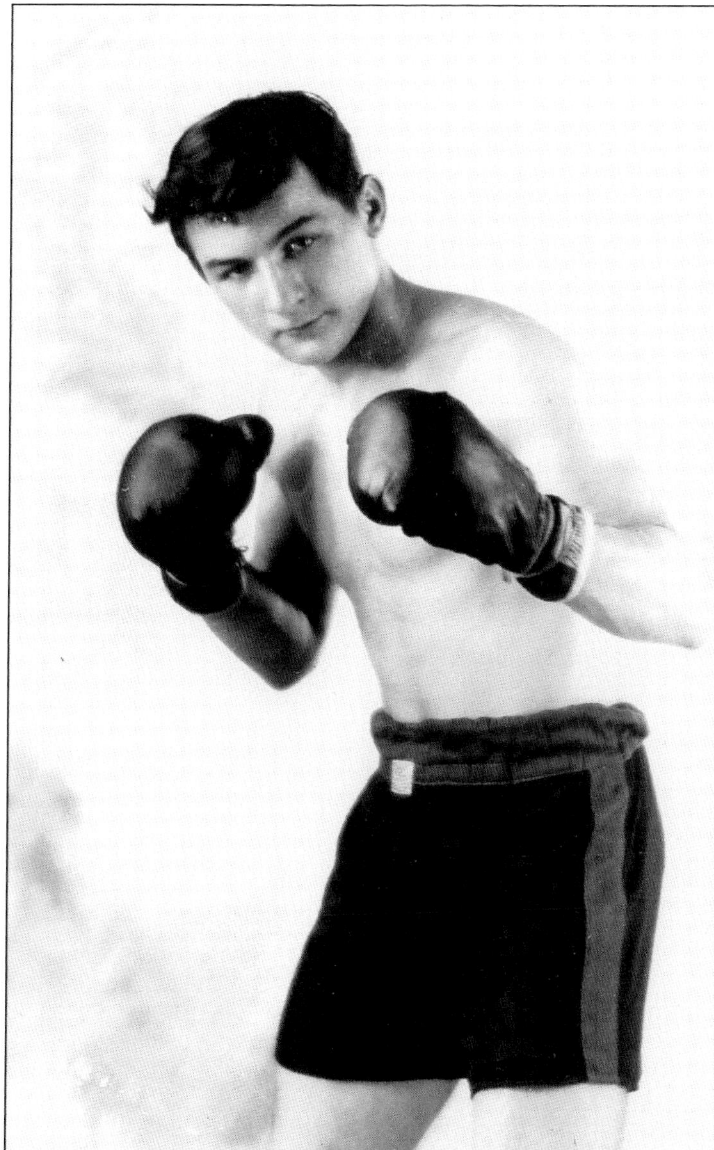

PAT IACOBUCCI. Pat Iacobucci began amateur boxing while attending Roger Bacon High School and earned the title of bantamweight champion in 1943 and featherweight champion in 1944. Iacobucci began his professional career at age 16; during his eight-year career, he fought 81 bouts and won 56, lost 17, had 8 draws, and had 16 knockouts. His significant accomplishments included winning 22 consecutive bouts from 1945 to 1947, boxing the semifinal in two world title bouts (Tony Zale–Rocky Graziano at Chicago Stadium and Sugar Ray Robinson–Rocky Graziano at Madison Square Garden), and having the distinction of fighting two 10-round bouts without a clinch. The first such bout came in his first feature 10-rounder against Benny May of New York on October 21, 1946, at Cincinnati Music Hall. The second such bout came against Eddie Lacy on April 20, 1950, in Minneapolis. After his fighting days, Iacobucci remained involved in amateur and professional boxing as a trainer, second, referee, and judge for over 40 years. He was inducted into the Hamilton County Hall of Fame in 1980 and Roger Bacon Hall of Fame in 1983. (Courtesy of Pat Iacobucci.)

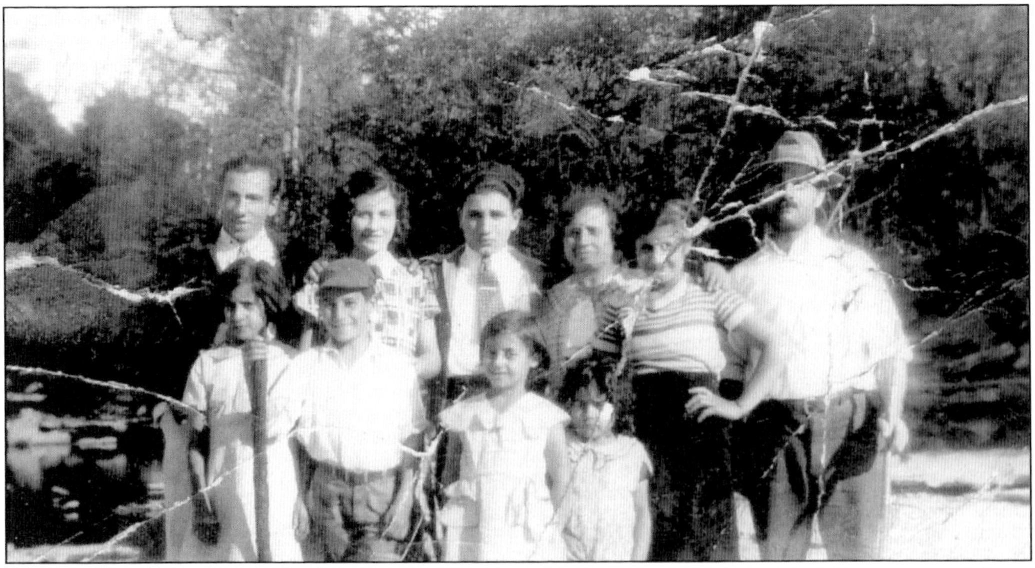

VIRGINIA VESPASIAN FUNARO CHILELLI. Virginia Vespasian Funaro Chilelli emigrated from Naples, Italy, and married immigrant Nicola Funaro in Youngstown. After Funaro was killed in a steel mill accident, Virginia married James Chilelli, who emigrated from Calabria, Italy. Family members shown are, from left to right, (first row) Rose Chilelli Antony, Ralph Chilelli, Marie Chilelli Cahill, and Carmela Chilelli Schabell; (second row) August Funaro, Anna Funaro Carlisle, Pete Funaro, Virginia Vespasian Funaro Chilelli, Julia Chilelli Shields, and James Chilelli, husband of Virginia. (Courtesy of Ralph Chilelli.)

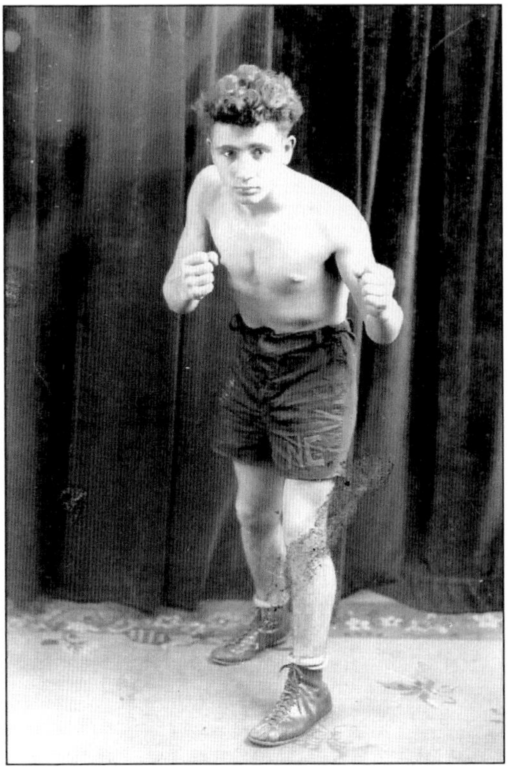

PETE FUNARO. Pete Funaro began amateur boxing at the age of 15 or 16. In 1931, he became the featherweight champion of Greater Cincinnati and Northern Kentucky. After that, he worked for Palazzolo's factory making pasta. Funaro married Pauline Nicholas in 1941. He was drafted to serve in the United States Army during World War II and was stationed at Fort Biehl, California, as a cook. (Courtesy of Ralph Chilelli.)

RALPH CHILELLI. Shown here is Ralph Chilelli with his nephew Jimmy Shields, niece Lelia Shields Kroger, and nephew Wayne Carlisle. The Funaro/Chilelli family moved from a farm in Batavia, Ohio, to Thirteenth Street in Newport. The Funaros, Chilellis, Carlisles, and Shieldses had various moving, trucking, construction, demolition, and excavating companies. These companies worked on many projects that helped shape the region, including the building of floodwalls and steel mills. (Courtesy of Ralph Chilelli.)

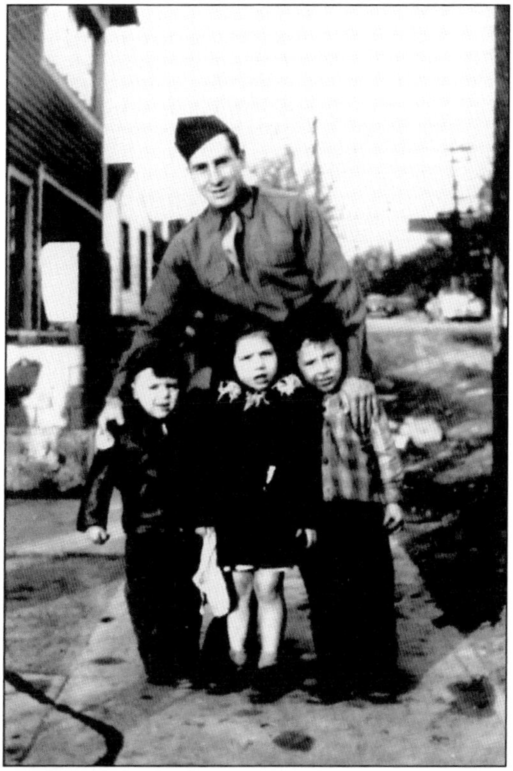

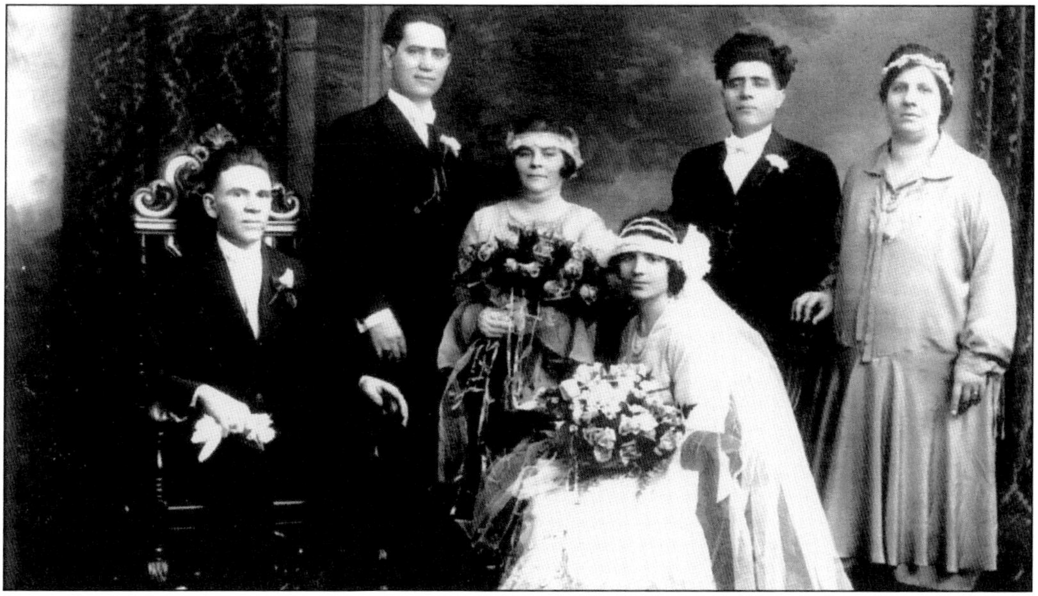

PANGALLO WEDDING. Joseph Pangallo emigrated from Roccaforte del Greco in Reggio, Calabria, Italy, and married Mary Incordona in 1911 in Chicago. Joseph and Mary raised eight children, Dominick, Fortunato "Anthony," Eleanor, Mario, Frank, Florence, Josephine, and Marino. Both Joseph and Anthony were professional bondsmen, and Frank was deputy clerk of common pleas court. Joseph purchased the home located at 4758 Glenway Avenue in Price Hill in 1910, and it remained Pangallo-owned until 2002. (Courtesy of Karen Pangallo Schellinger.)

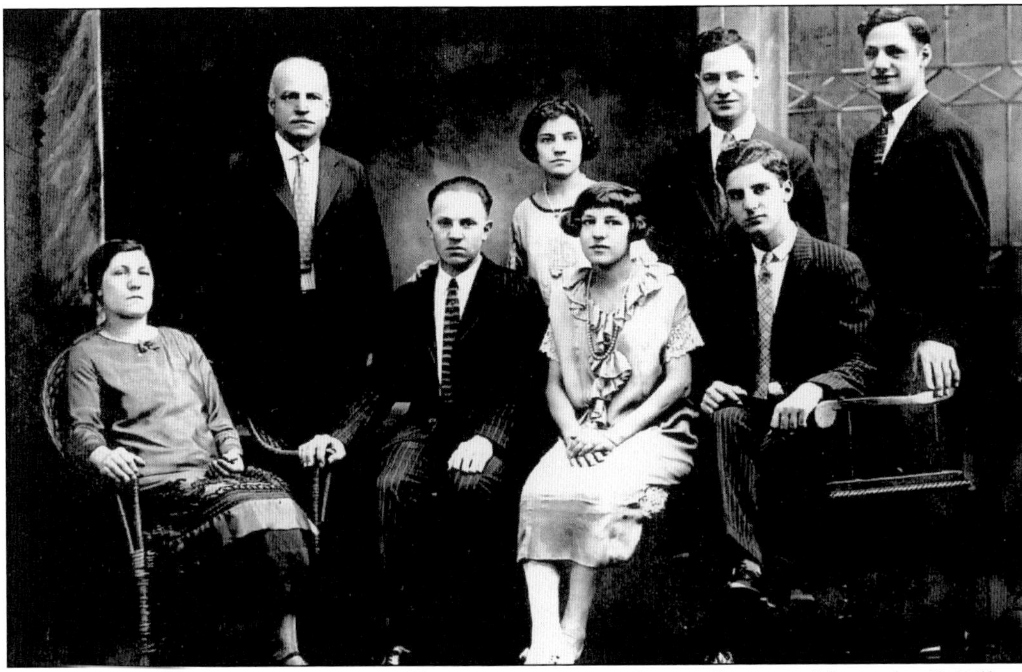

ALEXANDER DIPILLA AND MARIA TERESA PADULA DIPILLA FAMILY. Alexander DiPilla, a tailor, and Maria Teresa Padula DiPilla originated from the town of Chiauci and arrived at Ellis Island on December 18, 1901, aboard the ship *Hohenzollern*. Their sons operated DiPilla Custom Tailors Shop in Cincinnati. Family members are, from left to right, (first row) Maria Teresa, Albert, Louise, and Guido; (second row) Alexander, Amelia, Gino, and Joe. (Courtesy of the Ciafardini family.)

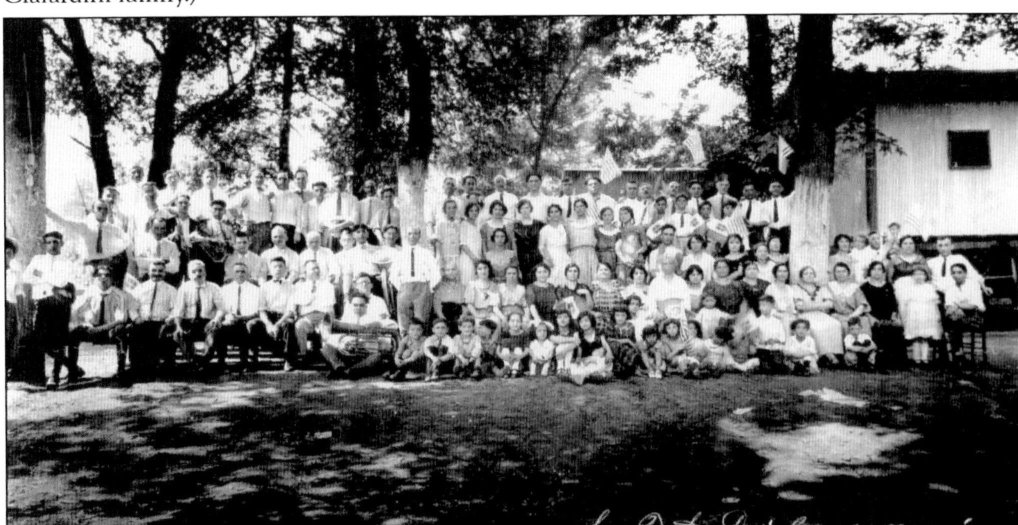

CHIAUCI, ITALY, FAMILY PICNIC, 1923. The Ionna and DeBaggis families emigrated from the town of Chiauci, in the province of Campobasso, Molise region of Italy. The DiTomaso family came from a nearby town down the mountain from Chiauci, which is located near the Trigno River, surrounded by beautiful forests and the Foce waterfall. The picnic was a way to celebrate their Italian heritage with others from their region. (Courtesy of Mike DiTomaso.)

NICOLA SCOCCO. Nicola Scocco was born in Casalvecchio di Puglia, Italy, on December 11, 1883. He left for America through Naples aboard the *Napolitan Prince* on May 10, 1906, arriving at Ellis Island on June 2, 1906. He petitioned for naturalization on January 6, 1936, and took his oath of allegiance to become a United States citizen on June 28, 1937. (Courtesy of Phyllis Scott Johnson.)

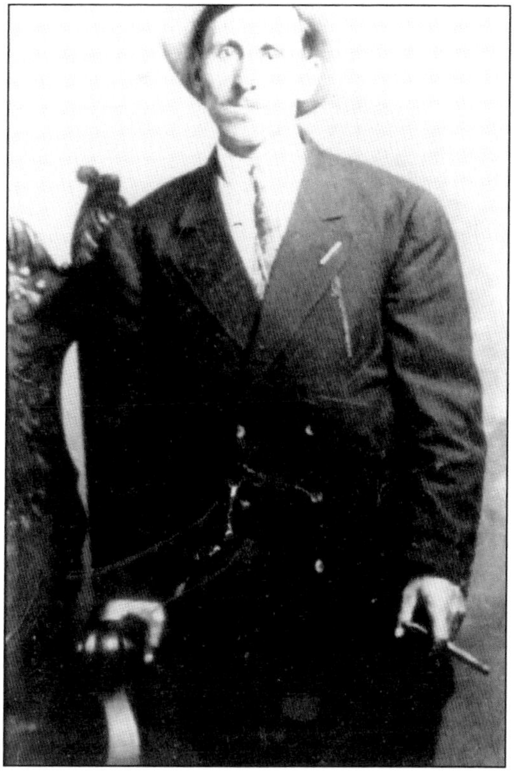

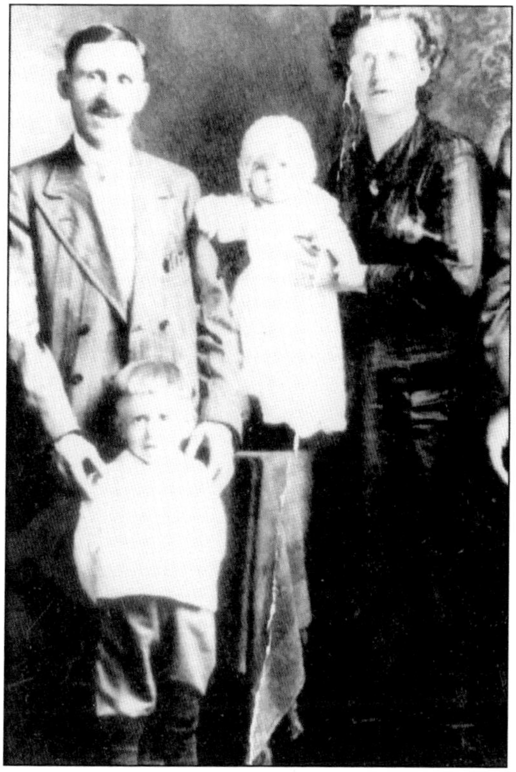

SCOTT (SCOCCO) FAMILY, C. 1918. Nicola Scocco married Mary Frances McGlasson on July 30, 1912. The family began using the surname of Scott and resided at 110 Second Street in Addyston. The Scotts raised 13 children. Shown here are the oldest children, Michael, born on May 1, 1915, and Loretta, born in 1918. (Courtesy of Phyllis Scott Johnson.)

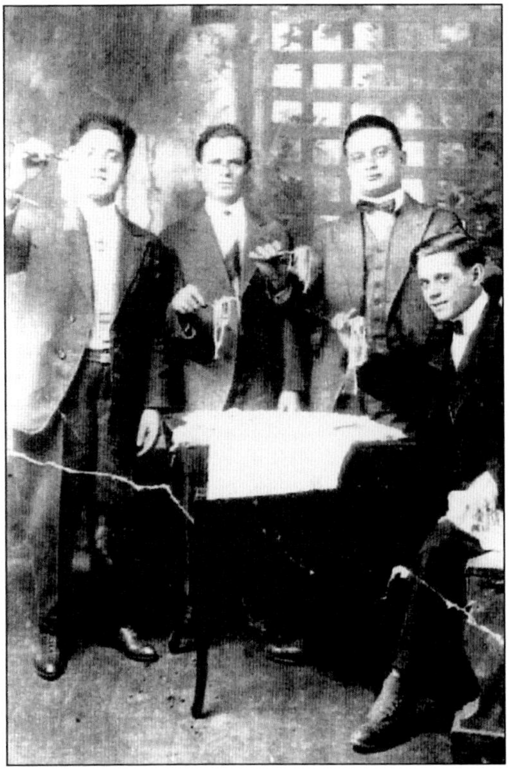

Potito Diego Francesco DiMuzio and Friends. Potito "Pete" DiMuzio was born on April 22, 1896, in Ascoli Satriano, Italy. He was one of 10 children born to Guiseppe DiMuzio and Guiseppina Ammanese DiMuzio. He emigrated from Italy on November 13, 1912, at 16 years of age aboard the *America*. While traveling as a steerage passenger on the ship, he ate from a block of cheese given to him by his mother. (Courtesy of Tony DiMuzio.)

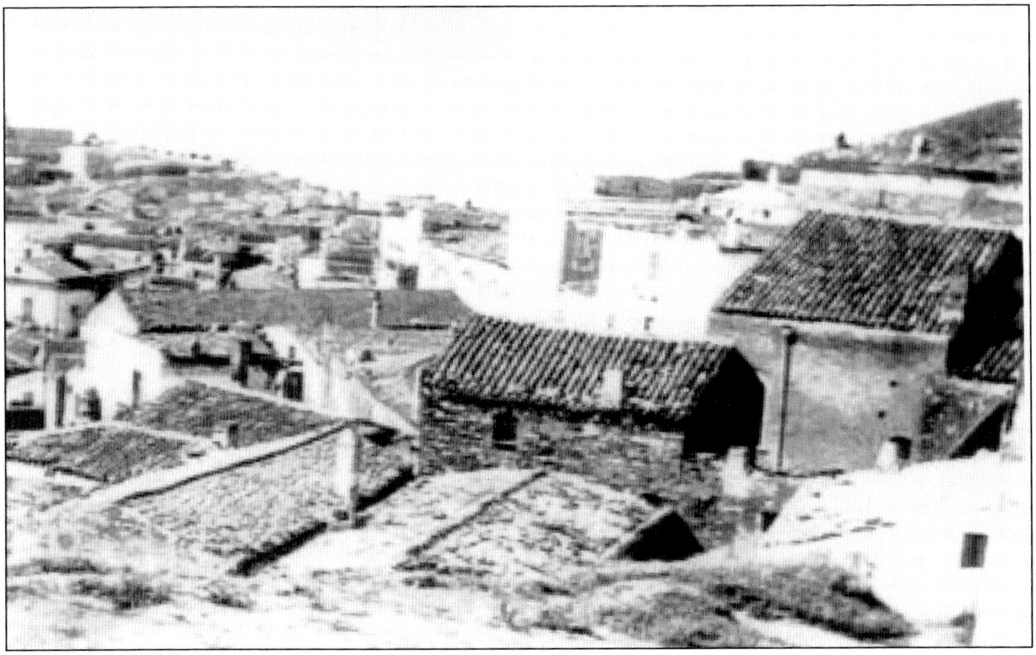

Town of Ascoli Satriano, Italy, c. 1910. Pete DiMuzio learned the trade of stonemasonry from his father and shoemaking from his uncles who lived in the town. He joined his brother Vincenzo and older sister Michelina, who had already immigrated to America and were living in Cincinnati. (Courtesy of Tony DiMuzio.)

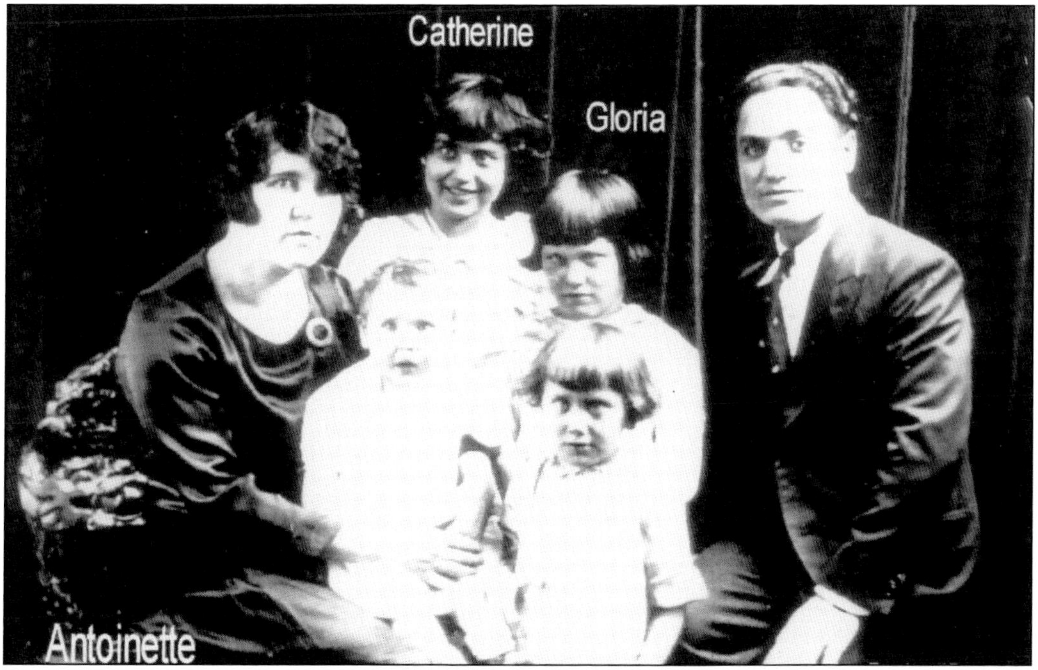

PETE DIMUZIO AND ANTOINETTE GEIMAN DIMUZIO FAMILY. Pete DiMuzio and Antoinette Geiman married in June 1919 at her parish of St. John's Catholic Church in Wilder, Kentucky. They lived the early years of their marriage in Cincinnati on Milton Street and later moved to Newport. They are shown here with four of their seven children, baby Josephine, Norma, Catherine, and Gloria. Born later were Johnny, Tony, and Julia. (Courtesy of Tony DiMuzio.)

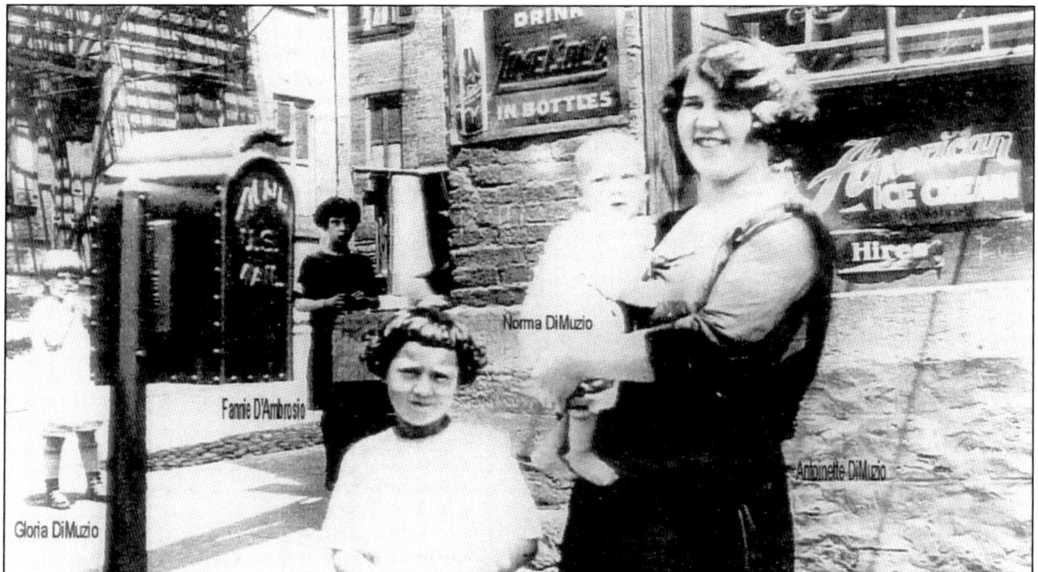

DIMUZIO ITALIAN GROCERY STORE, 1920S. Pete DiMuzio opened several grocery stores in Cincinnati and owned a pool hall near Sycamore and Mohawk Streets. He also held a variety of other jobs and secured additional money by renting out two rooms of their home at 439 Milton Street, which was the first home they owned. (Courtesy of Tony DiMuzio.)

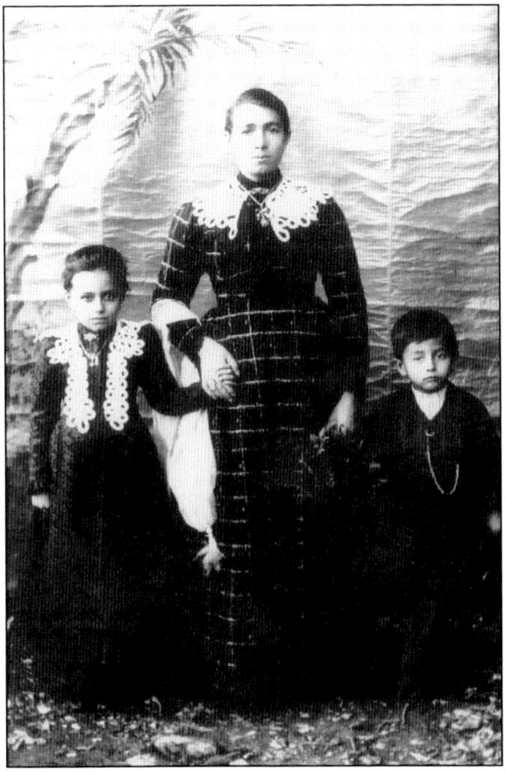

ROSA CARDARELLI. Rosa Cardarelli is shown here with her two children, Assunta and Dominic. As was often the case with family members, only part of the family would leave Italy for America. Dominic was the only member of this family to start a new life in America. He emigrated from Italy in December 1920. (Courtesy of Rosie Ferrara Steele.)

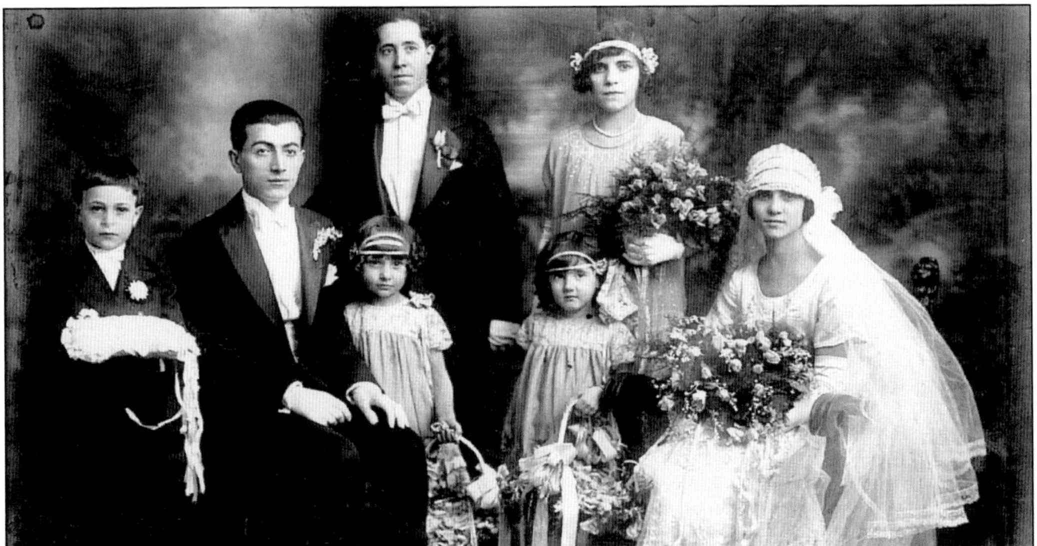

WEDDING OF DOMINIC CARDARELLI AND MARY FERRARA, NOVEMBER 20, 1926. Dominic Cardarelli and Mary Ferrara met while working at Silverstein Tailoring Company in Cincinnati. They married at St. Vincent de Paul Catholic Church in Clifton (Newport), Kentucky, and moved to Cincinnati. Members of the bridal party are, from left to right, Herman Ferrara (bride's brother), Dominic Cardarelli, Delores Ferrara (bride's sister), Louise Desalvo, and Mary Ferrara. Standing in the second row are witnesses Phillip Bruno and Rosa Ferrara. (Courtesy of Rosie Ferrara Steele.)

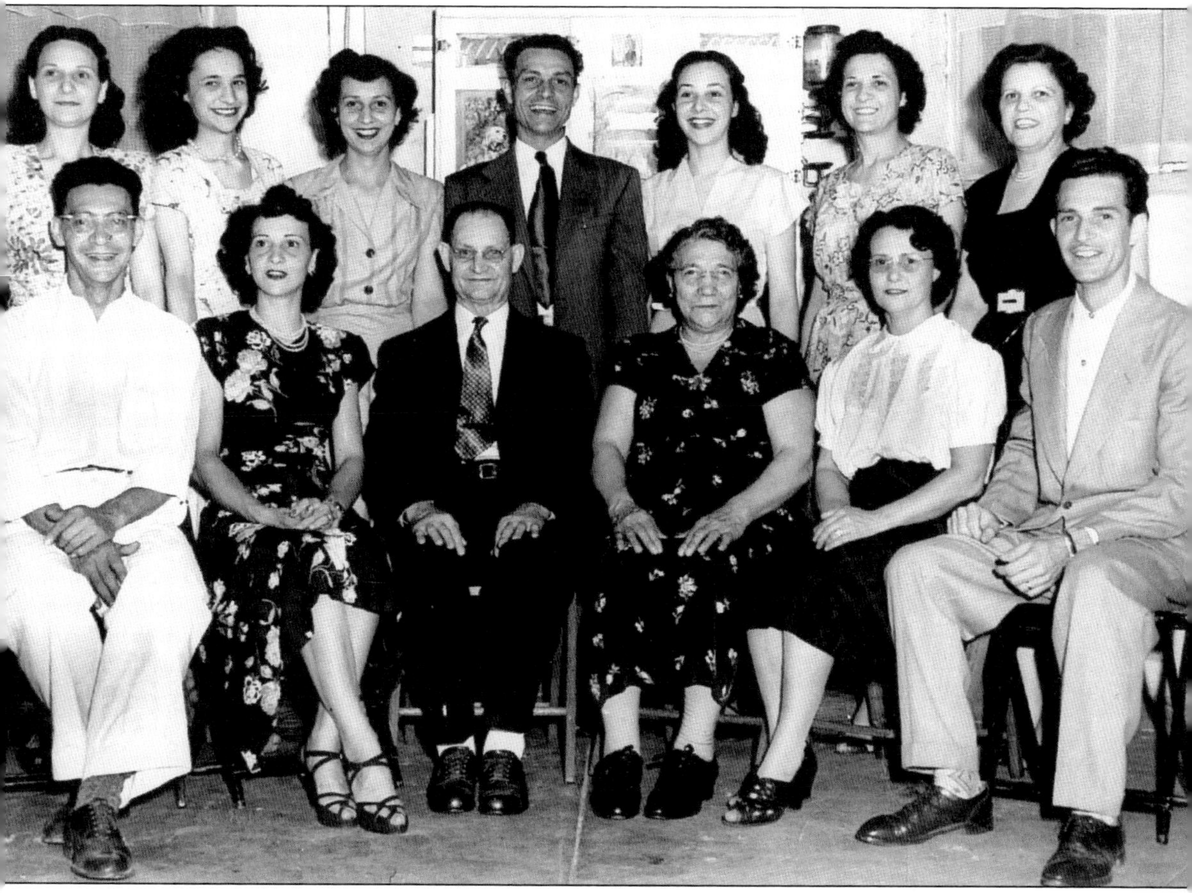

ROMOLO FERRARA AND FELICITA DIGIACOMO FERRARA FAMILY. Romolo Ferrara and Felicita Digiacomo were married in Italy on May 21, 1902. In the early years, Romolo made bricks and concrete blocks. He also built houses. He lost his first home on Biehl Street in Clifton (Newport) during the Great Depression. He eventually moved his family to Milton Avenue in Mount Auburn. Romolo found work as a tailor, retiring from that profession after 35 years. The Ferraras raised 12 children, including, from left to right, (first row) Alexander (Al), Philomena Ritter, Romolo, Felicita, Mary Cardarelli, and Herman; (second row) Delores McCarthy, Louise Yockey, Michalena Light, Paul, Phyllis Smithson Otis, Suzie Zinco, and Rosa Bruno. Missing from the photograph is Nicholas. (Courtesy of Rosie Ferrara Steele.)

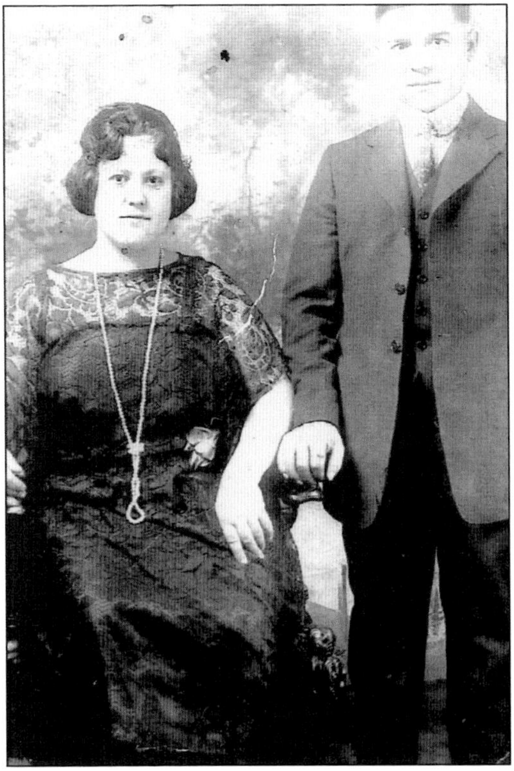

PASQUALE MORRELL AND LENA ANDICIA MORRELL. In Italy, Pasquale Morrell's surname was Mazzeo. He immigrated through Ellis Island around 1910 and went to Williamson, West Virginia, to work in the coal mines. While there, he stayed at a boardinghouse owned by Lena Andicia's mother. Pasquale and Lena married in West Virginia and later moved to 257 West McMicken Avenue in Cincinnati. Pasquale worked at Kroger's candy manufacturing plant. (Courtesy of Shirley Stevens.)

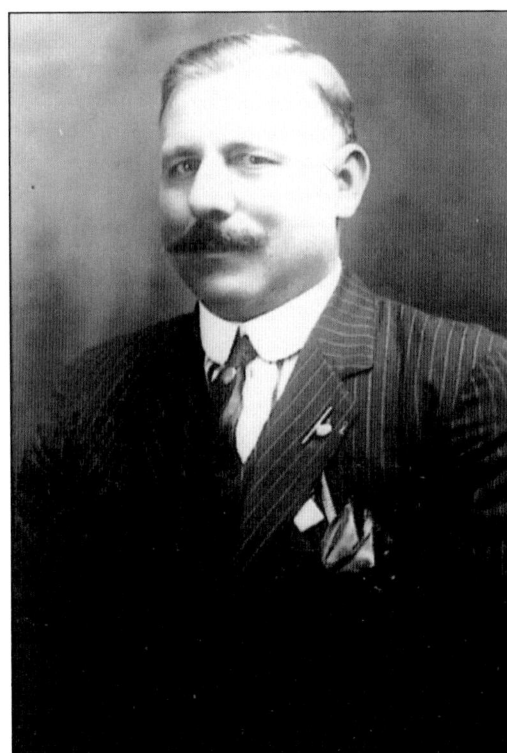

DOMENICK CARUSONE. Domenick Carusone arrived in Cincinnati when he was 11 years old. He operated a fruit stand in Findlay Market in downtown Cincinnati under the name D. Caruso and Sons for over 40 years. Domenick could also be seen on Queen City Avenue driving his truck and selling fruits and vegetables in the area. He married Antoinette Mussula, and they raised a family of five children. (Courtesy of Tim and Ann Dalessandro.)

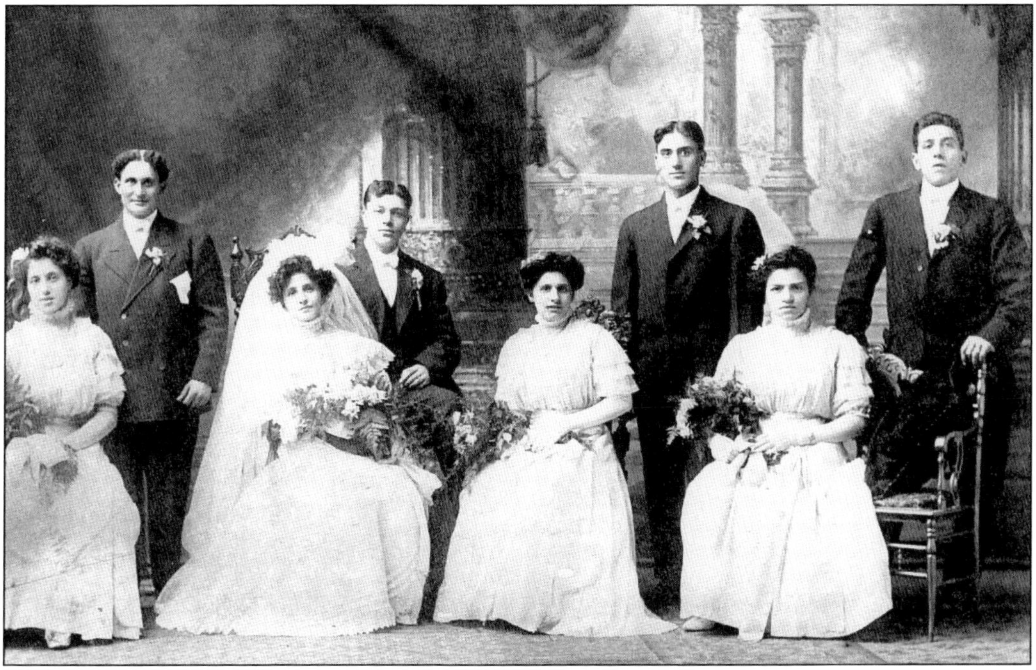

WEDDING OF AGOSTINO (GUS) COSTA AND ROSE DATILLO COSTA, OCTOBER 22, 1908. Agostino (Gus) Costa immigrated to America when he was nine months old. He and Rose Datillo were married in Cincinnati and resided at 525 Dandridge Street. Gus worked in the produce business in downtown Cincinnati. The family remained in Cincinnati until 1947 when they moved to Newport. (Courtesy of Joanna Teismann Barnett.)

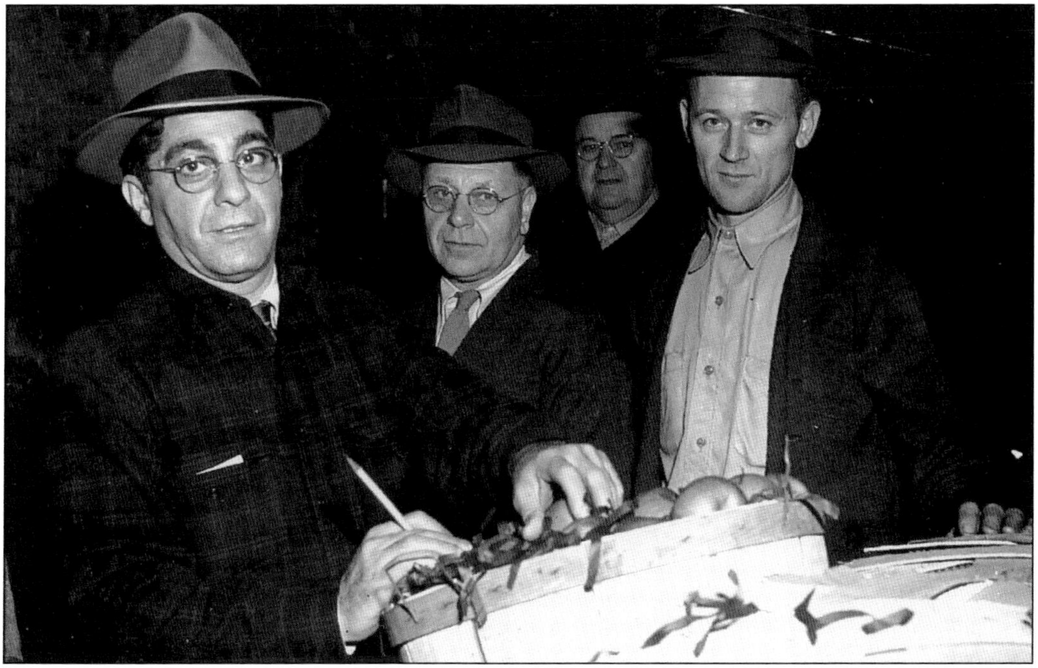

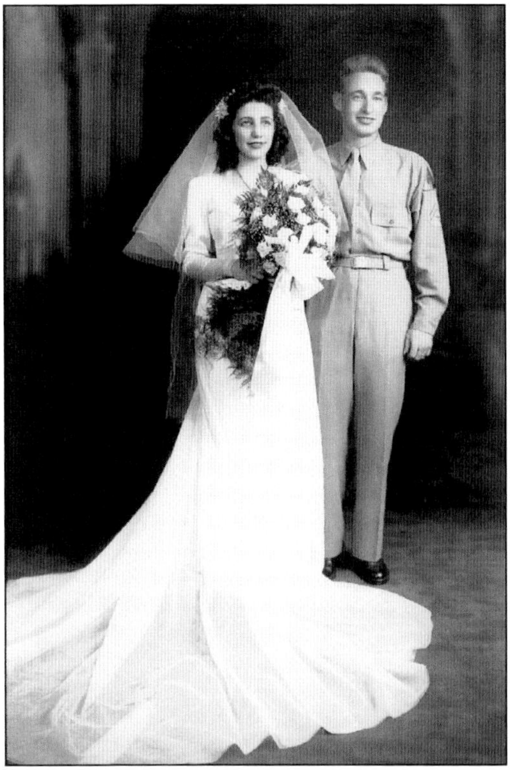

GENE TEISMANN AND ROSEMARIE COSTA TEISMANN, JUNE 27, 1945. The youngest child of Gus and Rose Costa, Rosemarie Costa married at St. Paul's Church in Cincinnati. Her husband, Gene Teismann, was a printer for the *Cincinnati Post* newspaper, and Rosemarie worked for Gibson Art Greeting Card Company. They raised three children, Peter, Geraldine, and Joanna. (Courtesy of Joanna Teismann Barnett.)

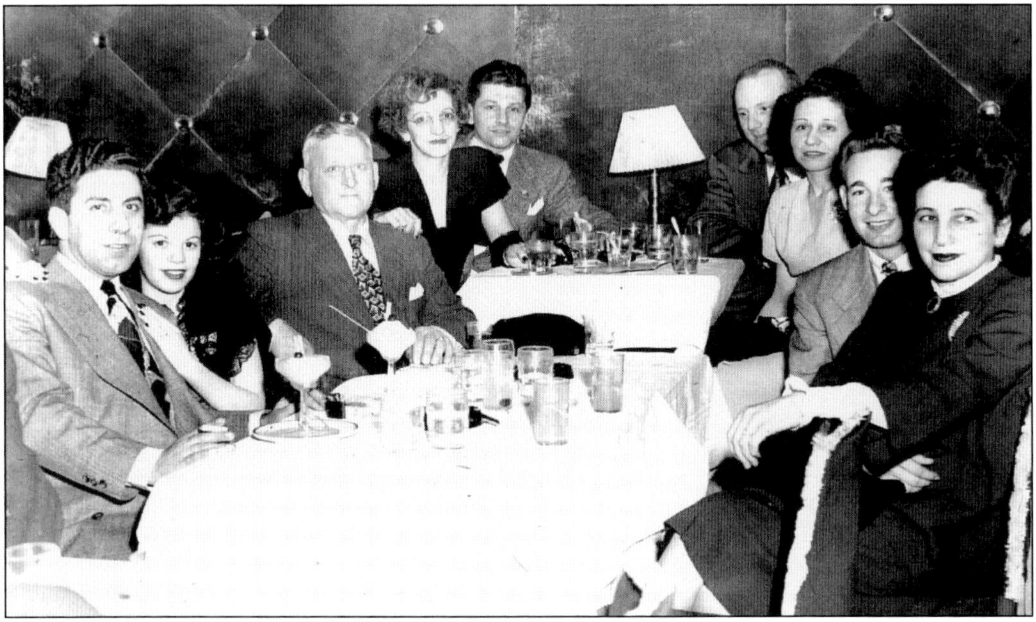

LOOKOUT HOUSE. Dining at the famous Lookout House restaurant located in Fort Wright, Kentucky, are, from left to right, three unidentified, Angela Rombach, and Jerry Costa (son of Gus and Rose); across from Jerry are Mel Schlueter, Frances Costa Schlueter (daughter of Gus and Rose), Gene Teismann, and Rose Costa Teismann (daughter of Gus and Rose). Josephine Costa Meno (daughter of Gus and Rose) is not shown. (Courtesy of Joanna Teismann Barnett.)

ALBERTINA THERESE MECONIO AND MORRIS KRAVITZ WEDDING, JUNE 4, 1938. Albertina Therese (Bertha) Meconio was born aboard the ship *Konig Albert* on May 28, 1909. She weighed one and a half pounds and slept in a shoebox aboard the ship. Her parents, Marco and Catherine Meconio, felt it fitting that she be named Albertina, after the ship's name. She was raised on Mulberry Street in Cincinnati and married at Sacred Heart Italian Church. (Courtesy of Rita Kravitz.)

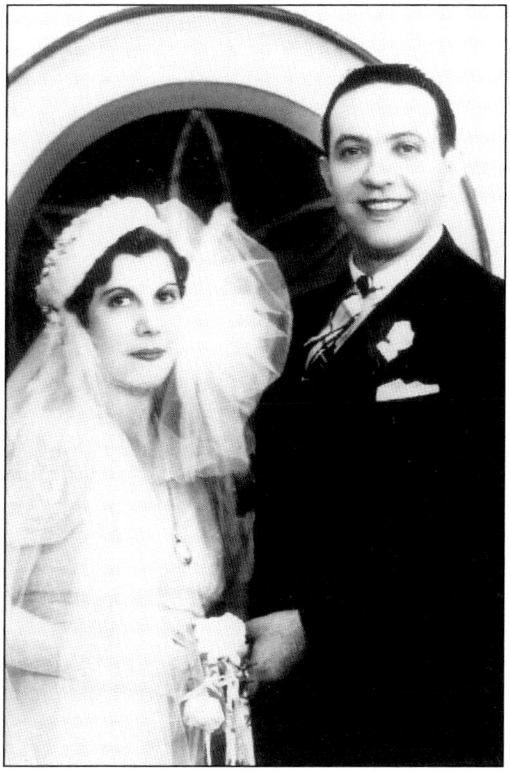

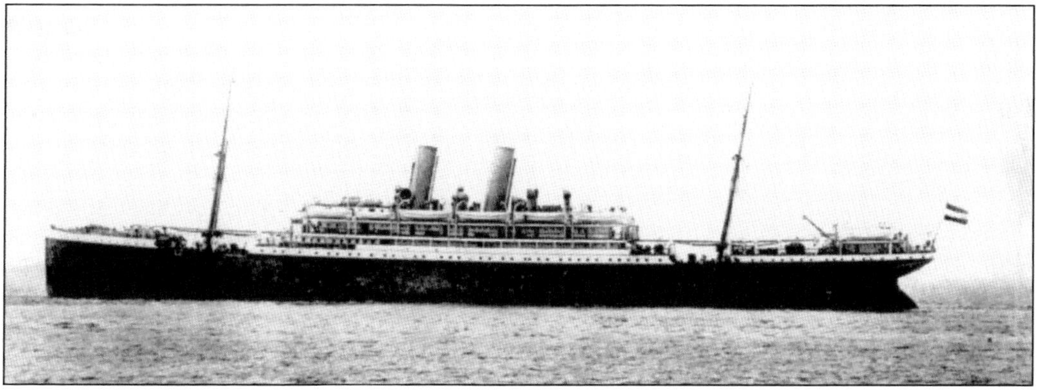

THE *KONIG ALBERT*, C. 1899. The *Konig Albert* was built by the A/G Vulcan Shipyard in Stettin, Germany, and offered Mediterranean–New York service after 1905. Its history involved being seized by the Italian government in 1914 and renamed the *Ferdinando Palasciano*, transferred to Navigazione Generale Italiana Line in 1920 and renamed *Italia* in 1923, and later being refitted as a transport for the Italian navy and scrapped in Italy in 1926. (Courtesy of the Statue of Liberty–Ellis Island Foundation.)

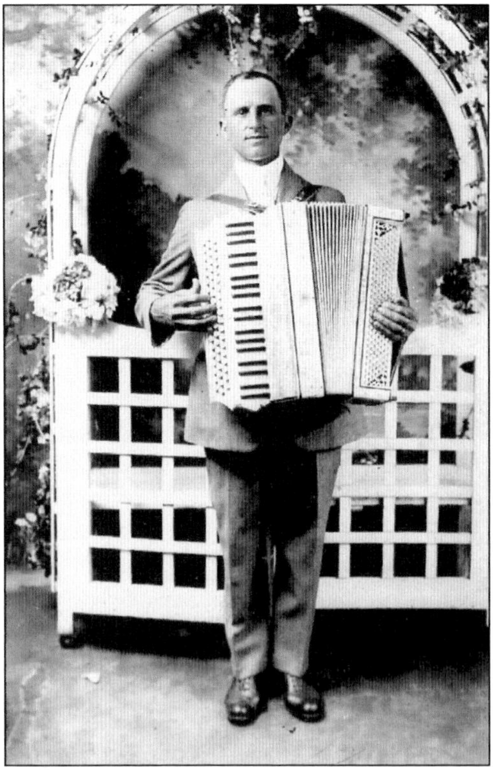

LUIGI NATALE WITH ACCORDION. Luigi Natale arrived at Ellis Island on February 19, 1903, aboard the *Sardegna* that sailed from Naples, Italy. He was 21 years old and single from the town of Atessa, Italy. His brother Pasquale was already living in Cincinnati, and Luigi joined him there. (Courtesy of Madelyn Lehr.)

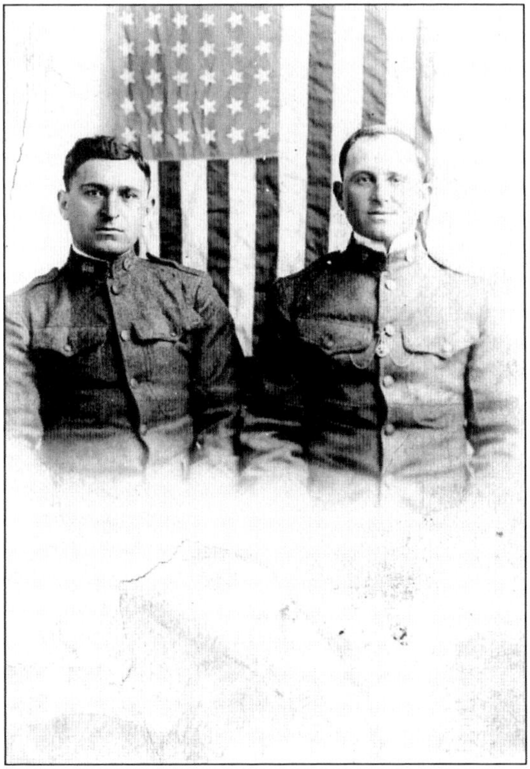

LUIGI NATALE, WORLD WAR I, DECEMBER 15, 1918. Luigi Natale (right), as well as many of the early immigrants, served in World War I. Charles Ginocchio, the Italian consul in Cincinnati, stated he had sent 250 Italians from the American Expeditionary Forces 1st Regiment to fight in the war and another 2,200 men to fight for Italy as of September 1917. The soldier at the left is unidentified. (Courtesy of Madelyn Lehr.)

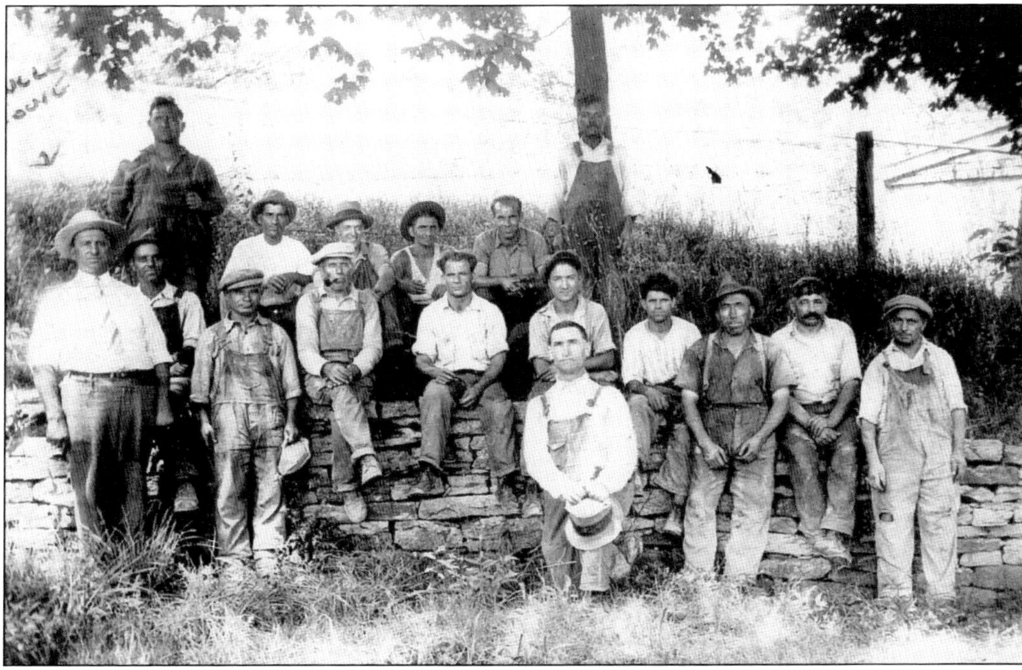

LUIGI NATALE WITH WORK CREWS. Although these photographs are undated, they certainly are reminiscent of the hard labor used to build various infrastructures within the city and its outlying area. Shown below, Luigi Natale, as a foreman for the gas company, and his crew are laying gas lines on Eastern Avenue in Cincinnati. (Courtesy of Madelyn Lehr.)

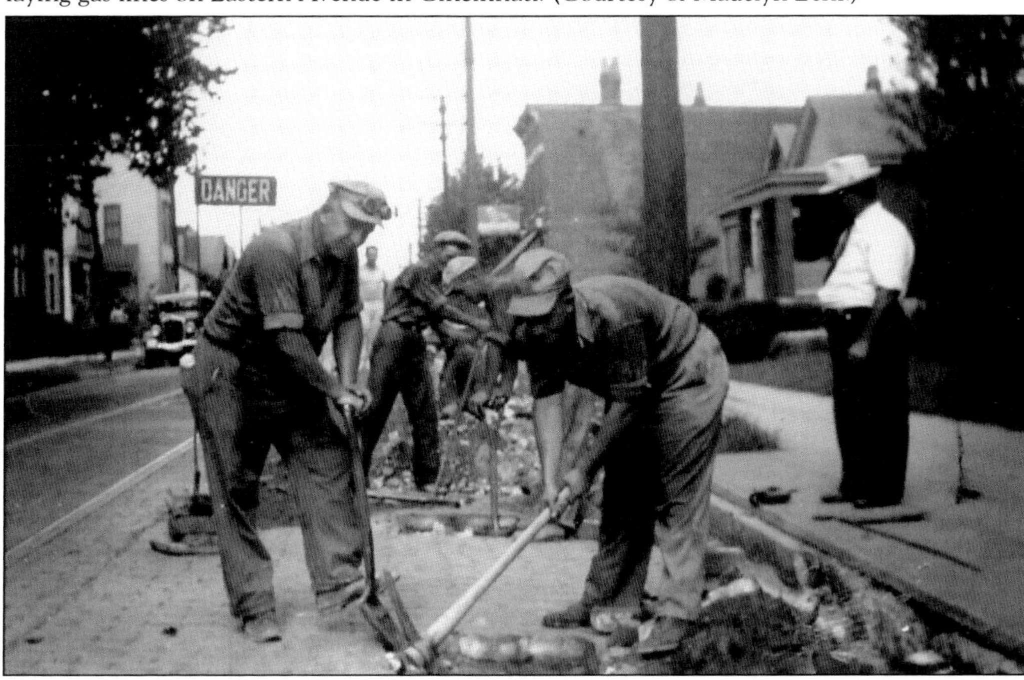

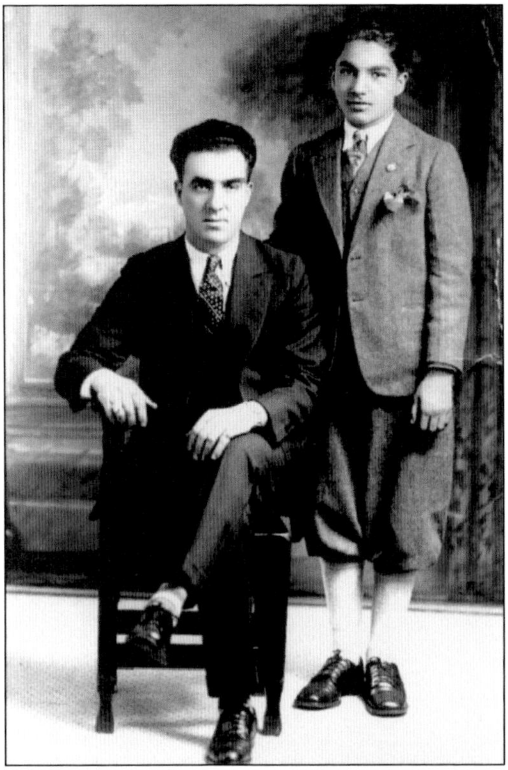

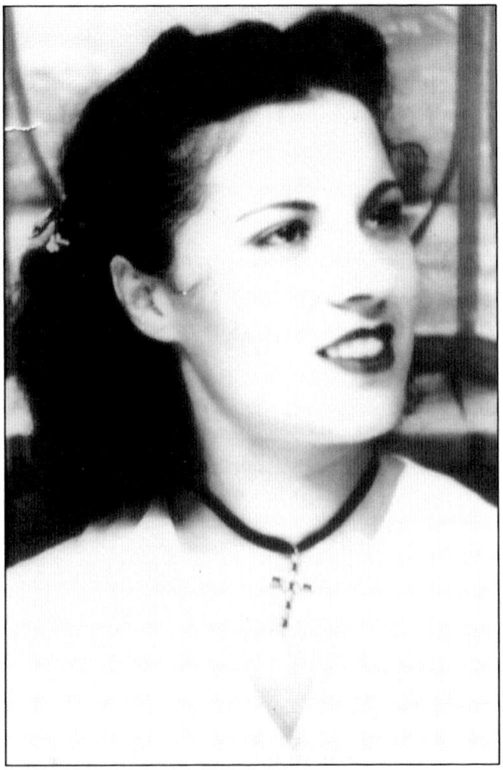

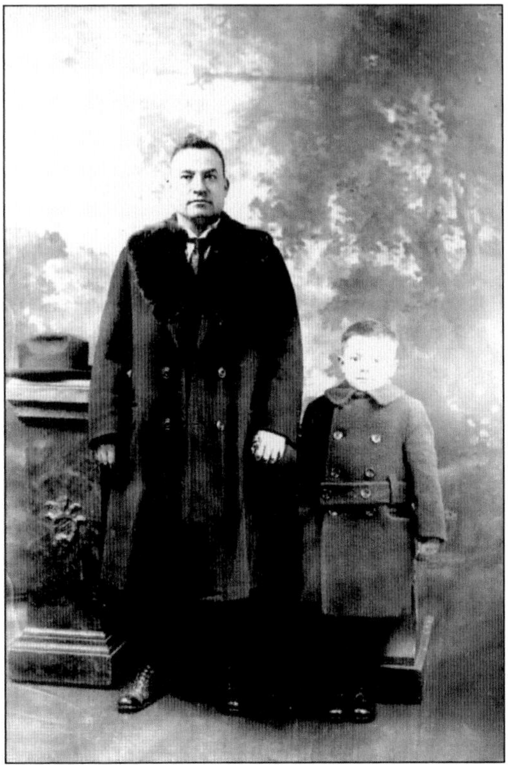

FRANCESCO (FRANK) AND JOHN MIGLIO. Francesco (Frank) Miglio (above left) immigrated at the age of 21 from Strongli, Catanzaro, Calabria, Italy, aboard the *Sant Anna*, arriving at Ellis Island on January 23, 1912. He first settled in Welch, West Virginia, before moving to Cincinnati. His son John, who was born in America, is standing next to him. Marie Miglio immigrated to America on September 17, 1928, at the age of 16 aboard the *Patria*. According to the ship manifest, she was going to visit her father, Francesco, at 1114 Clay Street in Cincinnati. Luigi Faillace (shown at left) arrived at Ellis Island on July 29, 1912, at the age of 18 from San Lorenzo, Calabria, Italy. Faillace was a tailor at Globe Tailoring Company and resided at 1575 Race Street in Cincinnati. His son Lou, standing next to him, would grow up to marry Marie Miglio (above). (Courtesy of Richard Faillace and Lou Faillace.)

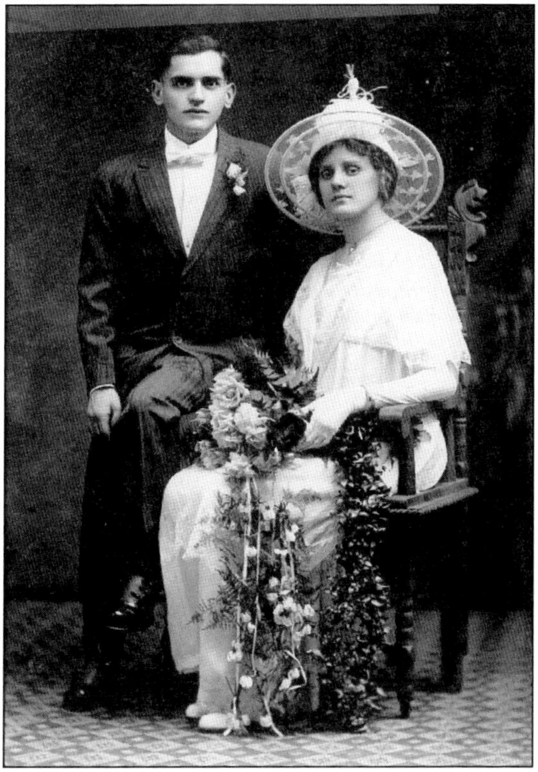

NICHOLAS AND HENRIETTA FARRO WEDDING, JUNE 10, 1915. Nicholas Farro was born in Newark, New Jersey, on October 15, 1892. His wife, Henrietta, was born in Ohio in 1895. They first resided at 1118 Broadway Street in Cincinnati and later moved to 524 Hodge Street in Norwood. Henrietta was a homemaker, and Nicholas was a machinist at American Tool Works. He later worked for R. K. LeBlond in Norwood. (Courtesy of Henry Forte.)

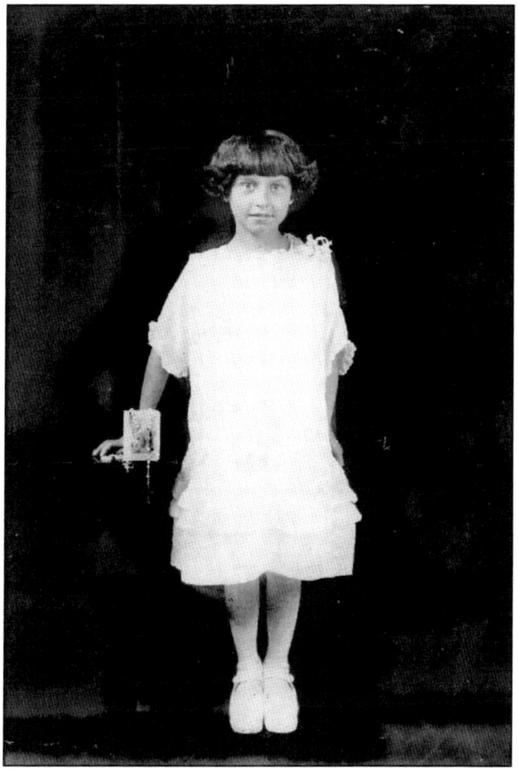

ANTOINETTE FARRO'S FIRST HOLY COMMUNION, MAY 17, 1924. Antoinette Farro's brother, Nicholas (above), raised her after the death of their mother in 1919. She attended St. Stephens Catholic Church on Eastern Avenue, where she made her first Holy Communion. After elementary school, she attended vocation school and later married Valentine Strub and raised three sons, Ralph, Nick, and Dan. (Courtesy of Henry Forte.)

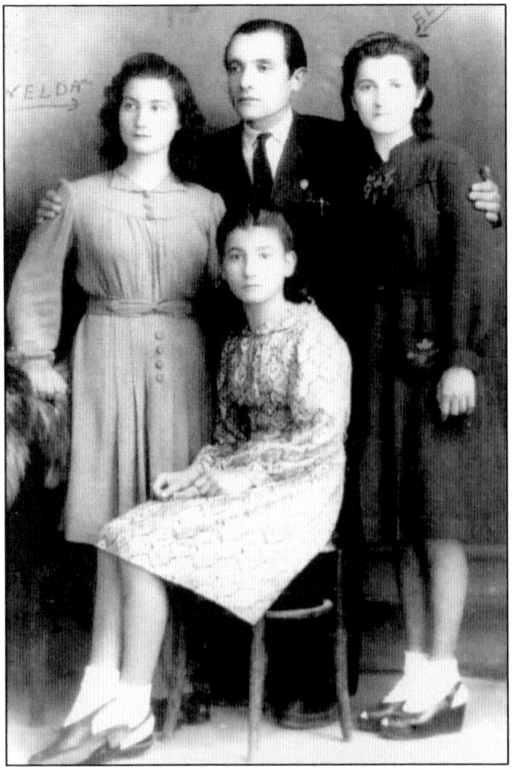

THE PASQUALE AND NELDA MEALE FAMILY. The Meale family emigrated from Fossalto, Campobasso, Molise, Italy, to Cincinnati in 1946. Pasquale Meale learned automotive mechanics in Rome and served in the Italian army during World War II, repairing tanks. Seated is Nelda Meale's sister Ida, and standing behind her from left to right are Nelda, Pasquale, and Elena, another sister of Nelda's. All three Meale women worked at Hyde Park Clothes in Newport as seamstresses. (Courtesy of Mario and Gina Onorini.)

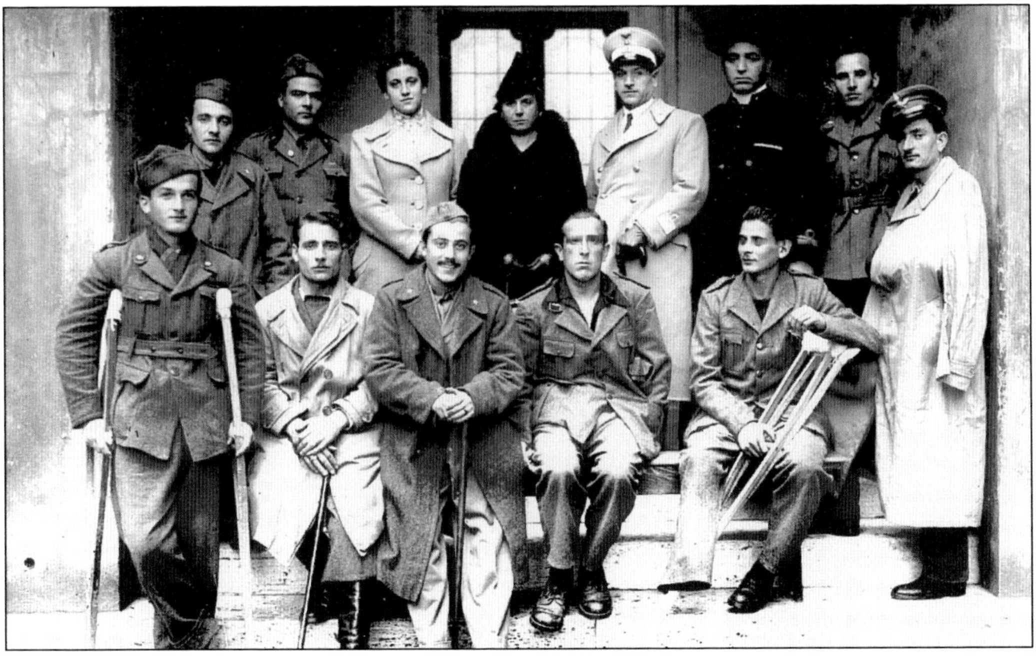

INJURED ITALIAN SOLDIERS, WORLD WAR II, 1942. All these wounded men were released from the Italian army in 1942. They served in the same platoon with Pasquale Meale, who was injured in the right leg by shrapnel. He is shown in the first row, left side, standing while using his crutches. (Courtesy of Mario and Gina Onorini.)

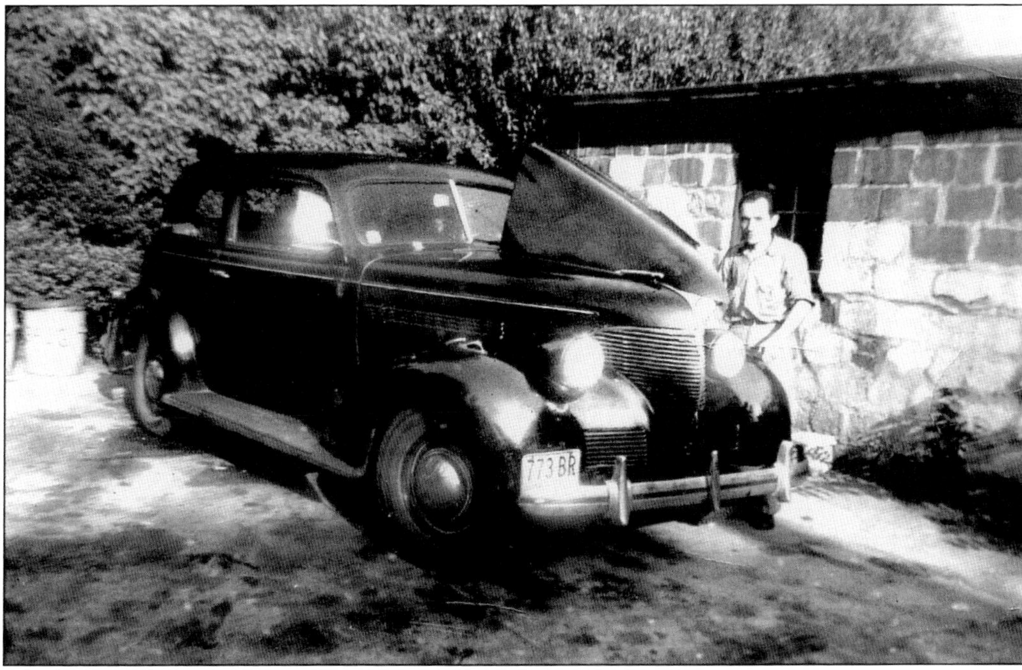

MEALE CAR REPAIR AND GAS STATION. In 1950, Pasquale Meale opened his own car repair shop and specialized in repairing foreign cars. His business was located at 1953 Burnett Avenue in Cincinnati. Shown below is Meale on the ladder fixing a sign at his gas station. Meale was always thankful that he learned his trade while serving in the Italian army during World War II. Because of his skill, he walked behind the troops, a position he felt saved his life on many occasions. (Courtesy of Mario and Gina Onorini.)

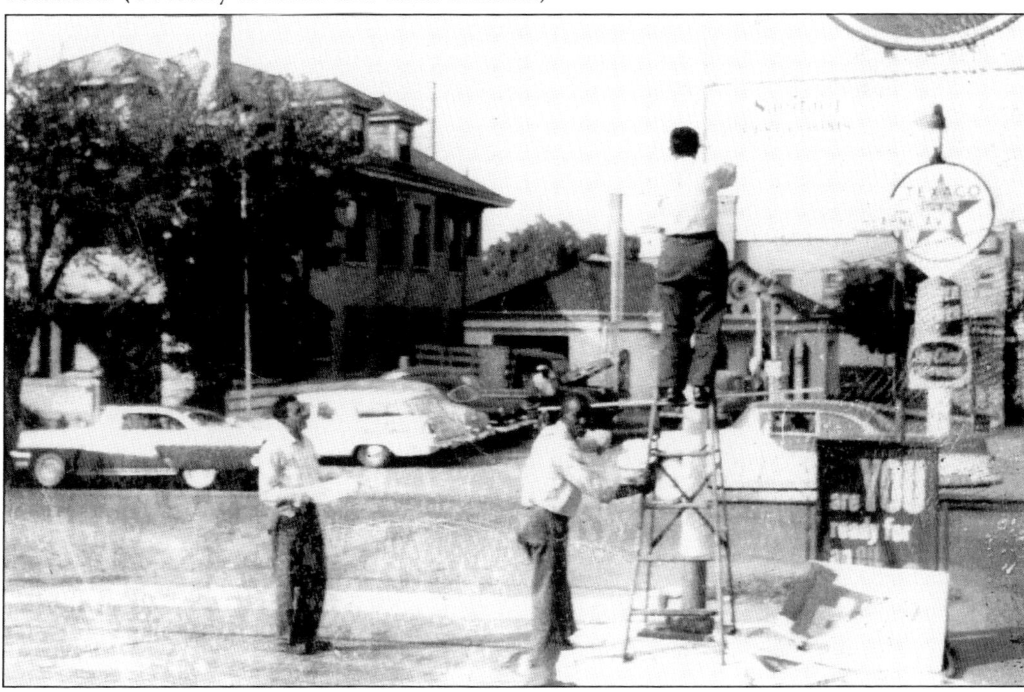

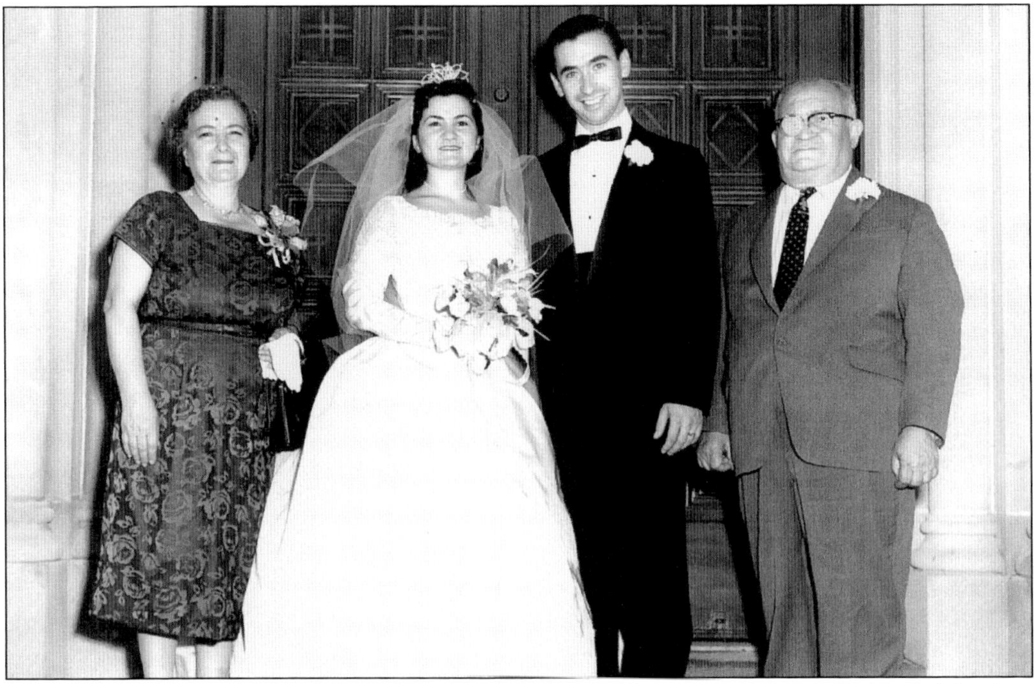

WEDDING OF NATALINA MEALE AND ADELO FOLCHI, SEPTEMBER 3, 1960. Both Natalina Meale and Adelo Folchi immigrated to America in the 1950s. Natalina is shown here with her parents, Guiseppe and Carmela Meale. Adelo started Folchi's Formalwear in 1975, located in Kenwood, and today his two sons Michael and Mark along with his daughter Marisa run the expanded business. Adelo, shown below at the far left with Michael standing next to him wearing his tuxedo, presented their formal wear during a fashion show at Tri-County Mall in 1982. (Courtesy of Mario and Gina Onorini.)

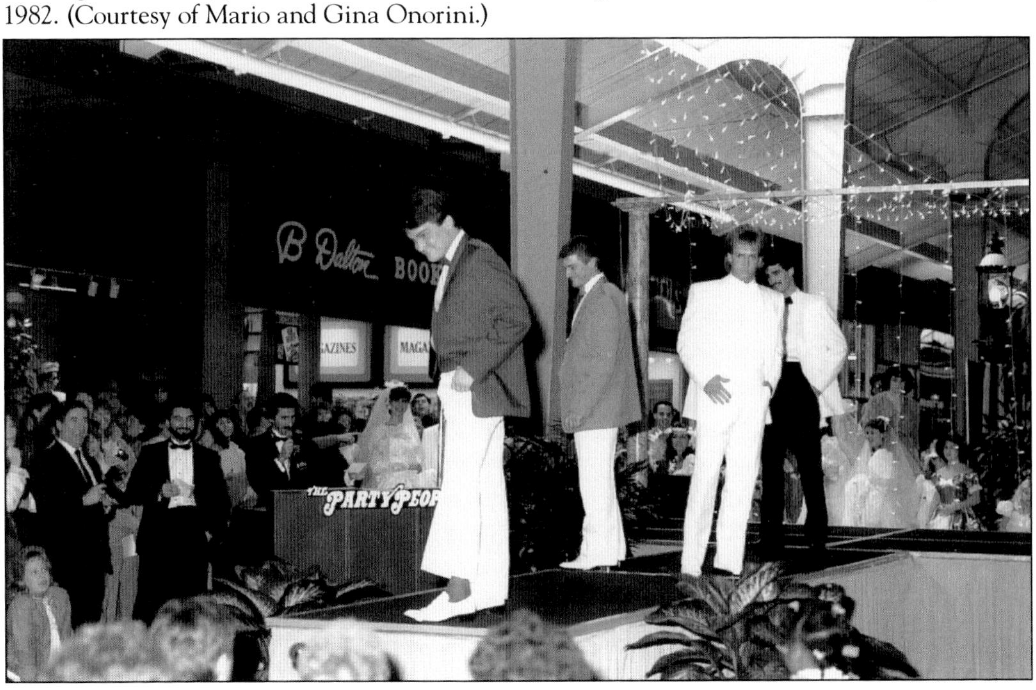

AGOSTINO CIANCIOLO AND DESCENDANTS. Agostino Cianciolo, seated at the far right, came to America and married Maria Palmisano on September 18, 1892, at Sacred Heart Italian Church. The two were natives of Sicily, where Agostino earned his living as a fisherman. In America, he began selling fruits throughout the city from his horse-drawn cart and then in the open-air markets. They raised nine children. Standing in the back row is their son Anthony, and his son, August (Gus), is standing next to Agostino. (Courtesy of Annie Cianciolo O'Donnell.)

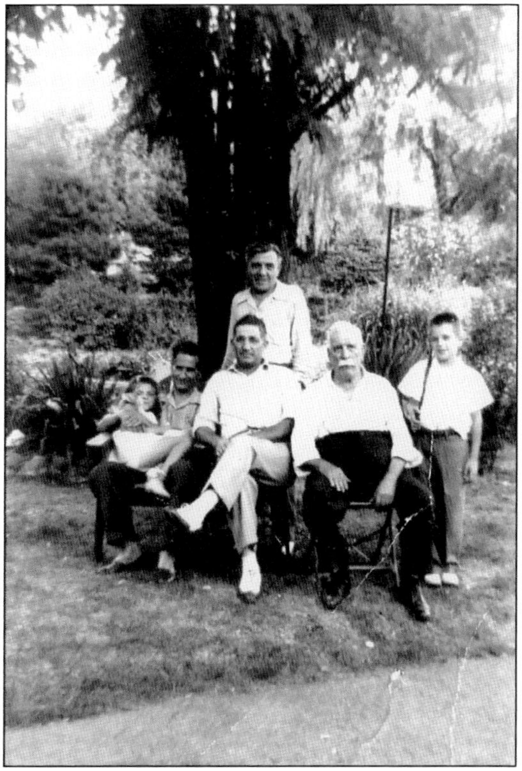

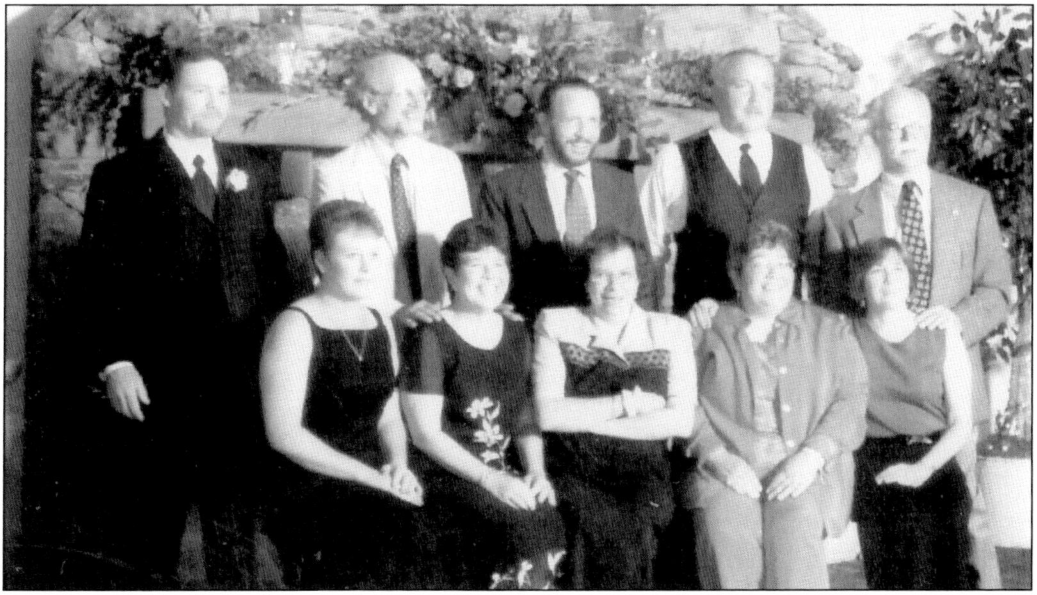

GUS AND PAT CIANCIOLO FAMILY. Pictured are members of Gus and Pat Cianciolo's family. From left to right are (first row) Eve Cianciolo (daughter-in law) and Gus and Pat's daughters Maggie Leugers, Ellen Cianciolo, Annie Cianciolo O'Donnell, and Patricia Cianciolo; (second row) William Cianciolo (son), Michael Leugers, Anthony (Tony) (son), Dennis O'Donnell, and Chuck Ganzert. Missing from the photograph are son Daniel and daughter Theresa. (Courtesy of Annie Cianciolo O'Donnell.)

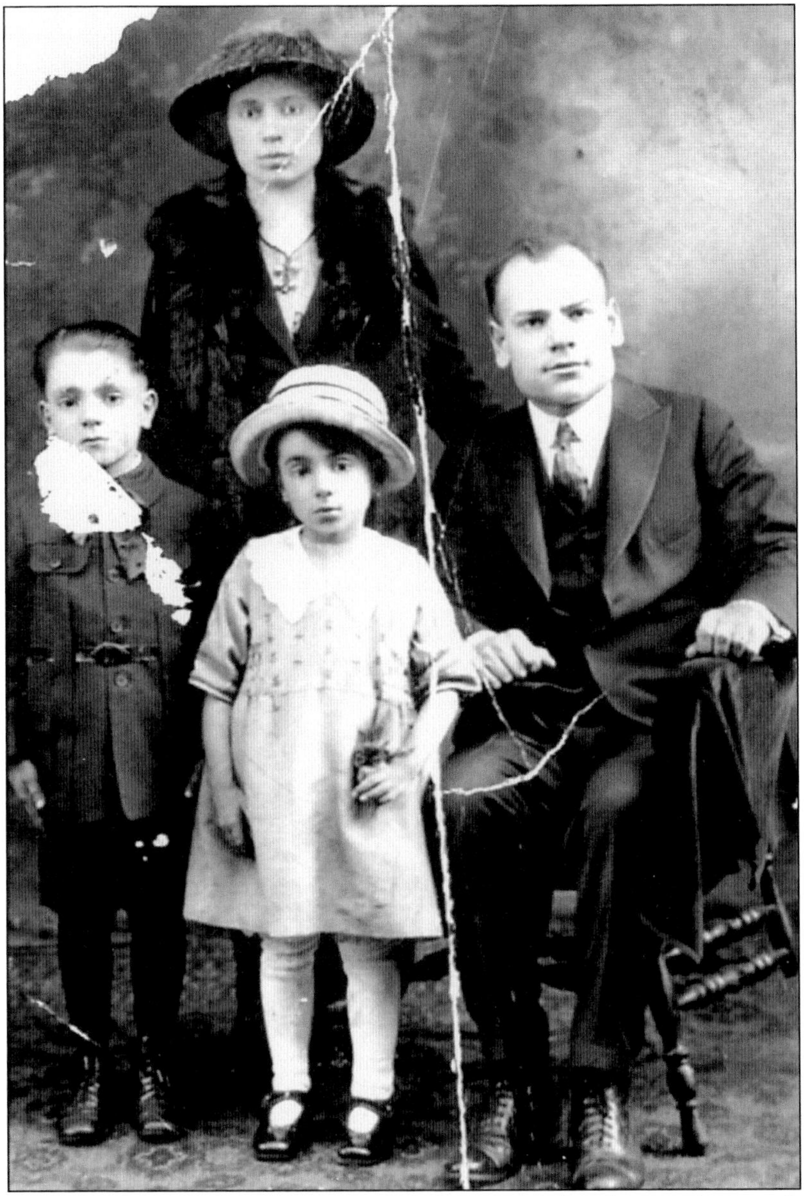

Carrelli Family. Dominic Carrelli and Elvira Gallo Carrelli, along with two of their three children, Angelo and Incranada "Mary," emigrated from Fossalto, Italy, in 1920. They also had a son Victor, born in America. Dominic was a tailor, and Elvira was a seamstress. The family resided in Norwood. Angelo became the first chairman of the United Auto Workers in Cincinnati and was founder of the Democratic Party in Blue Ash, and he also worked for the City of Cincinnati for 22 years. He and his wife, Sarah, raised six sons and five daughters. Incranada, being uncomfortable with her name, changed her name to Mary at the urging of her third-grade teacher. She married Francis "Jerry" Truax and raised one son and three daughters. Victor served in the army in the Philippines during World War II and received the Bronze Star. After the war, he was an FBI agent for 27 years. He also was appointed as a chief deputy sheriff under Sheriff Lincoln J. Stokes. He and his wife, Kay, raised one son and two daughters. (Courtesy of Mary Carrelli Truax.)

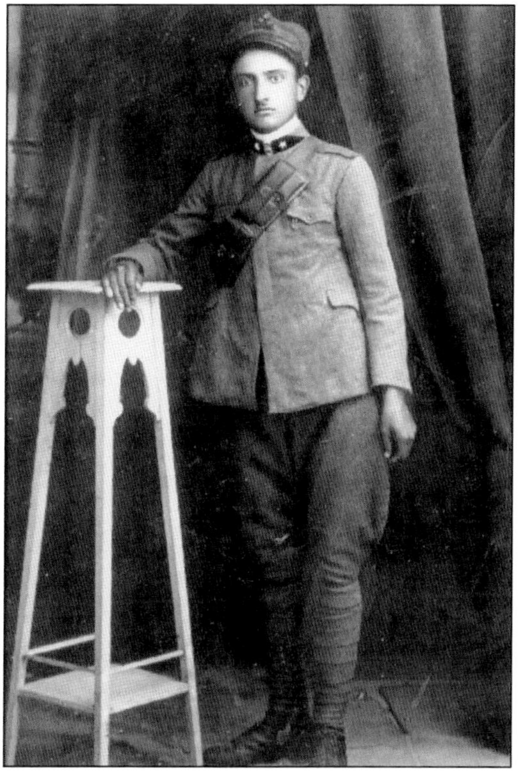

VITO CIUCCIO. Vito Ciuccio was born in Felitto, Italy, to Pasquale and Grazia Ciuccio and had two siblings, Rosaria and Guiseppe. Vito served in the Italian army during World War I and then came to America and worked the coal mines of Pittsburgh, Pennsylvania. Vito sent for his wife, Chiarina, and son Pasquale to join him in Cincinnati. Here he worked for Cincinnati Gas and Electric Company. (Courtesy of Lillian Ciuccio.)

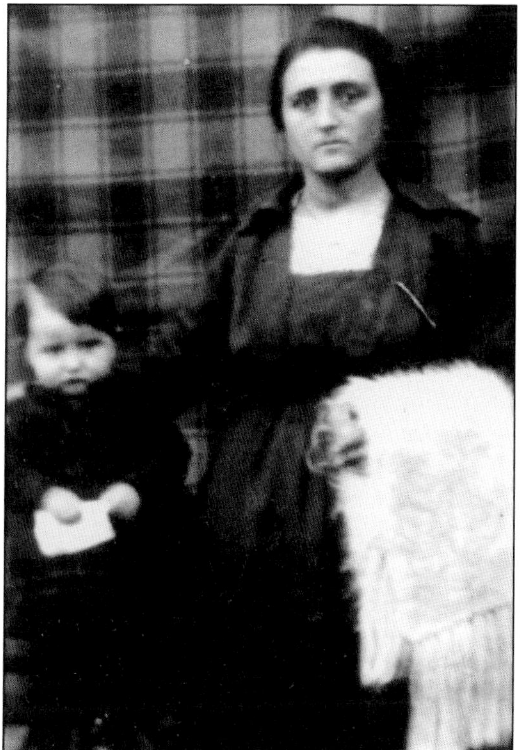

CHIARINA CIUCCIO WITH SON PASQUALE. Chiarina Ciuccio, the daughter of Pasquale Della Palma and Antonia Guazzo Della Palma, arrived at Ellis Island with her three-year-old son Pasquale (Pat), on July 30, 1928. The Della Palma family lived in the town of Compatroni di Castels, Lorenzo, Salerno. The trip to America was very difficult on Chiarina as she became very seasick and it was difficult for her to keep up with Pat. (Courtesy of Lillian Ciuccio.)

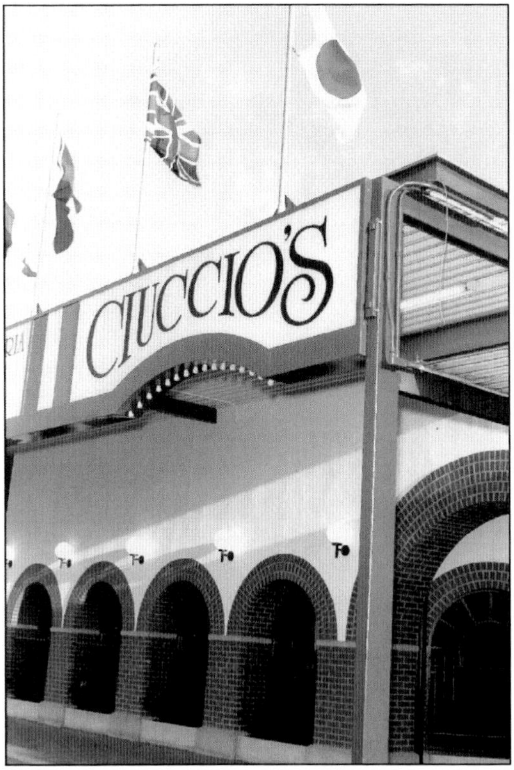

CIUCCIO'S RESTAURANT. Pat Ciuccio opened Ciuccio's Restaurant and a delicatessen next door to it in Hyde Park Plaza in 1980 and sold it in 1985. In 1949, Ciuccio owned and operated a restaurant located in "the bottoms." He served all his patrons from the warehouse district and commission houses from 2:00 a.m. to 2:00 p.m. His wife, Lillian, always worked at their businesses. Today she helps her son James Vito Ciuccio and Richard Ferguson operate Giminetti Baking Company on Gilbert Avenue. (Courtesy of Lillian Ciuccio.)

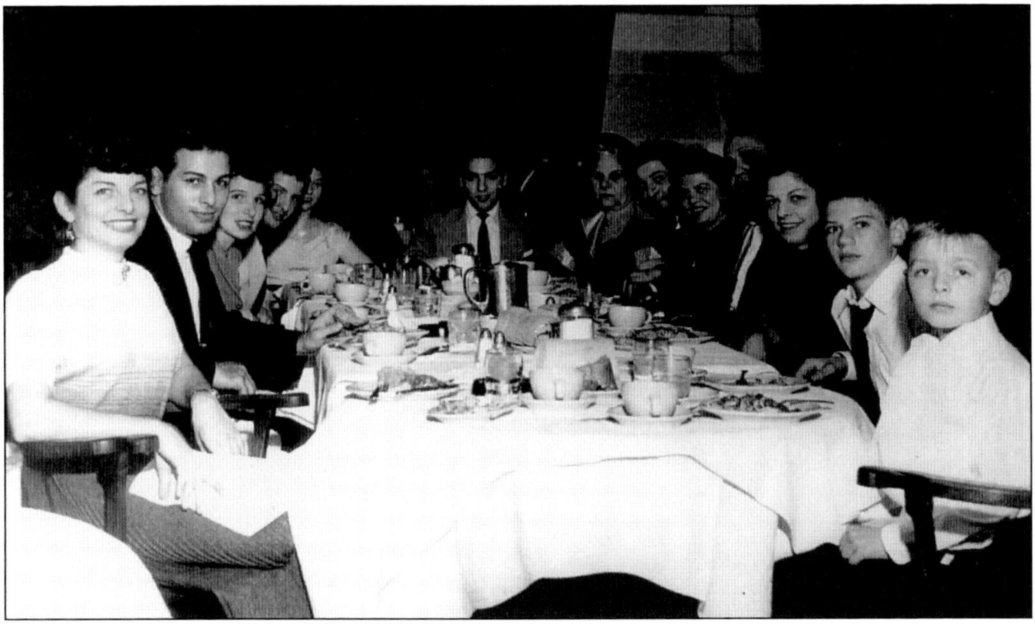

BUCALO FAMILY, 1952. Dining at Caproni's restaurant, the Bucalo family enjoys the celebration of a cousin's wedding. The Bucalo family members are, from left to right, Carol, Frank, Joyce, Sam, Angela Bucalo Glaser, unidentified, Rosalie (mother), Ross (cousin), Frances Bucalo Futrell, Frank Chessario, Rose Bucalo Chessario, and grandchildren Jerry Futrell and Charles Peters. (Courtesy of Sam Bucalo.)

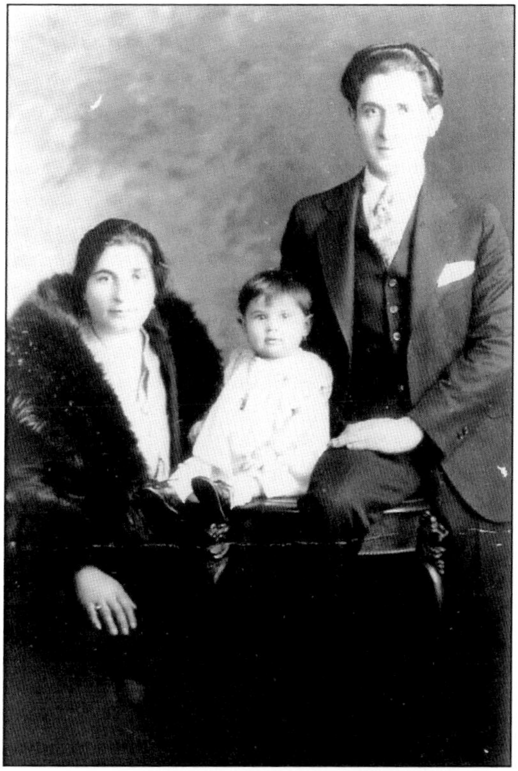

ADELINA, MARY, AND CARMINE NESI FAMILY. Carmine Nesi first arrived in America aboard the *Duca D'Austa* on September 4, 1920, at the age of 20. He was a shoemaker by trade and was coming to visit his cousin Francesco Mazzei at 1332 Main Street. After returning to Italy to marry his wife, Adelina, he returned on September 28, 1928, and stayed with his brother Giovanni. Adelina soon arrived and they began their family; Mary was born in 1929, Frank in 1931, and Mike in 1933. (Courtesy of Marlene Nesi.)

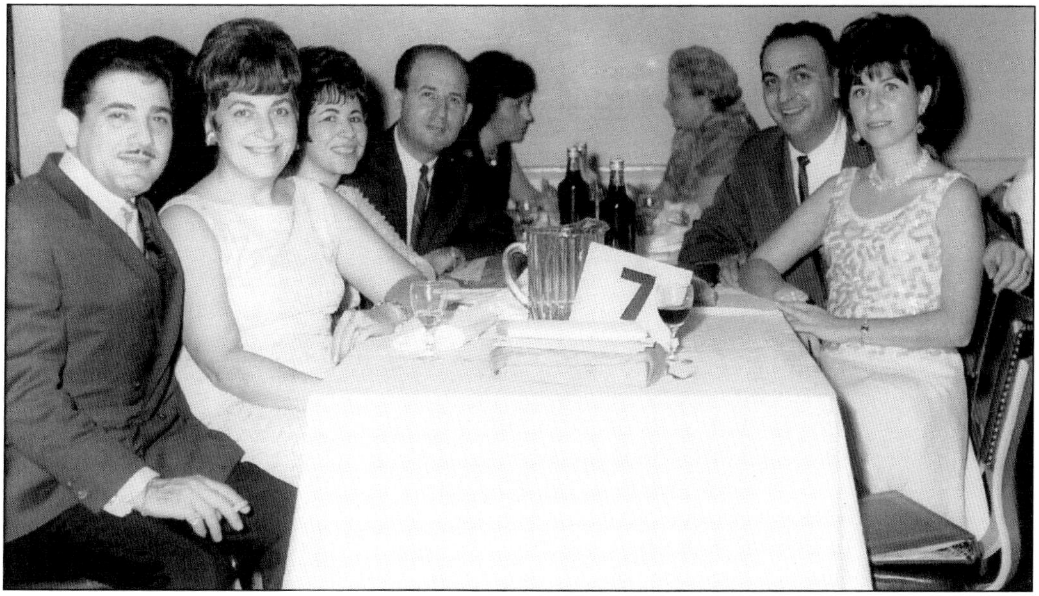

LA SOCIETA DI FUSCALDESE FEMMINILE DINNER DANCE. Female descendants from Fuscaldo formed their society, La Societa Di Fuscaldese, in December 1959 and will celebrate their 50th anniversary in December 2009. The society enjoys sharing its heritage and awards an annual scholarship to a high school or college student. Seated at the Ramundo table are, from left to right, Peppe Ramundo, Yvonne Ramundo, Barbara Ramundo, Mike Ramundo, Lena Vilardo, Mena Santoro, Frank Nesi, and Marlene Nesi. (Courtesy of Marlene Nesi.)

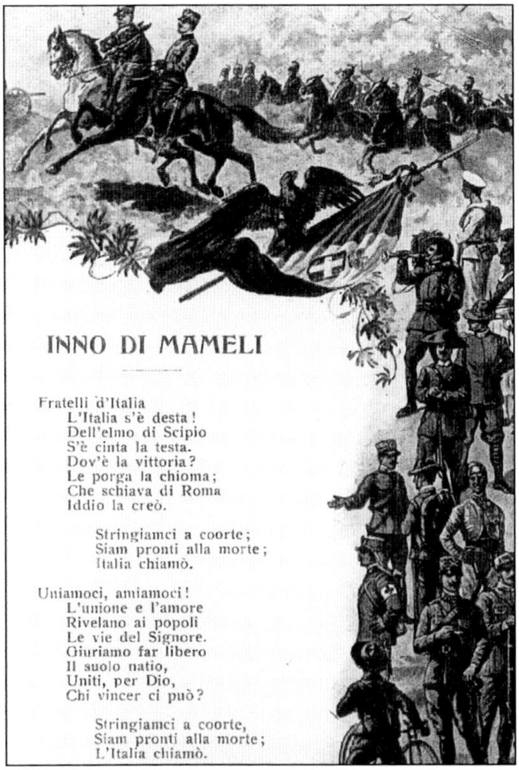

"L'INNO DI MAMELI." This Italian poem was written by Goffredo Mameli and relates the Italian struggle for unification and independence. It was put to music composed by Michele Naovaro in 1847 to become the national anthem of the Republic of Italy. The anthem, "L'Inno Di Mameli," is the first stanza of the poem, sung twice, and then the chorus. It has been the official anthem of Italy since 1948. (Courtesy of Nic Castrucci.)

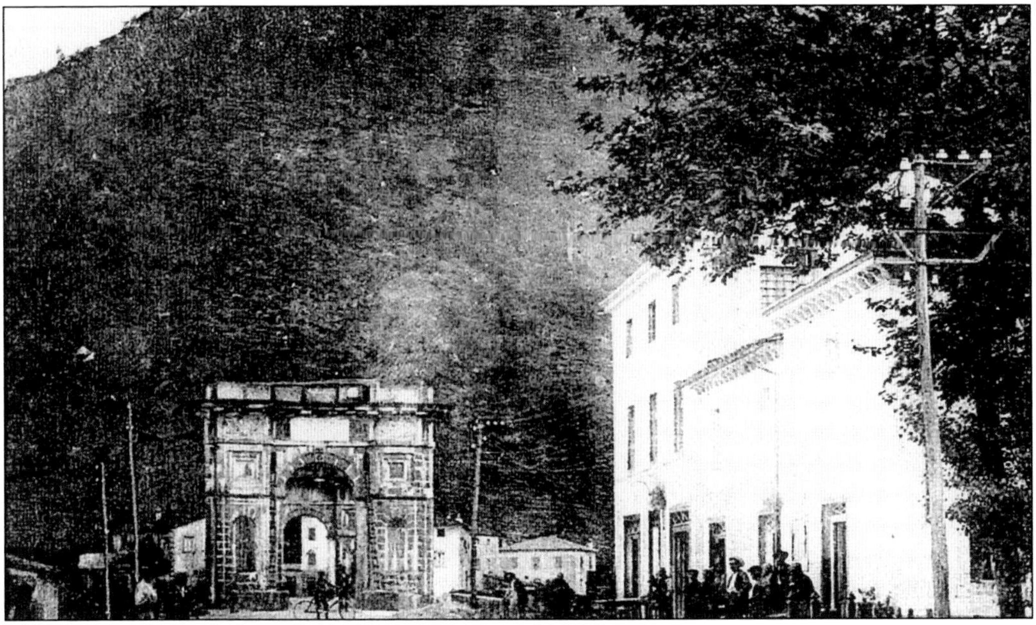

BAGNI DI LUCCA, ITALY. The charming town of Bagni di Lucca was well known for its thermal baths as early as the 11th century. In the early 19th century, Bagni di Lucca reached its peak as one of Europe's most fashionable spas, frequented by emperors, kings, and aristocrats, as well as the most famous artists. Visitors came not only for thermal cures but also for the casino (1837), one of Europe's first licensed gambling houses. (Courtesy of Nic Castrucci.)

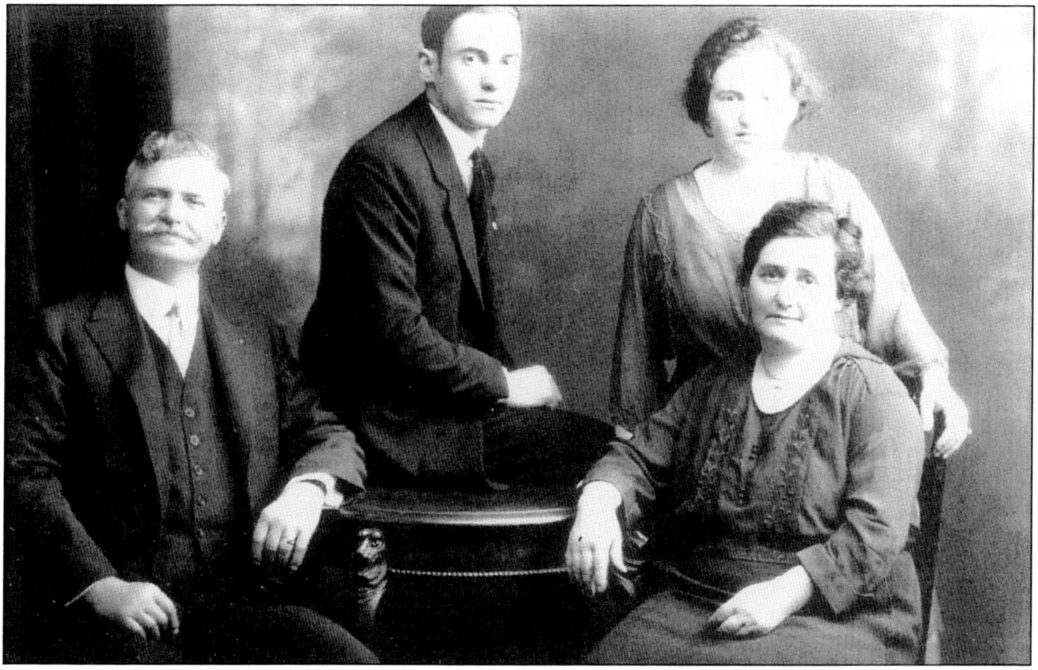

Guistino Castrucci Family. Guistino Castrucci (seated at the left) immigrated to America from the town of Bagni di Lucca, province of Lucca, region of Toscana (Tuscany), Italy, in 1900. His wife, Denisa (seated at the right), arrived on May 23, 1912, at the age of 38 aboard the ship *Moltke*. Also with her were their children Leda and Aldo. At the time of their arrival, Guistino resided at 707 Broadway Street and had his own statuary shop. (Courtesy of Nic Castrucci.)

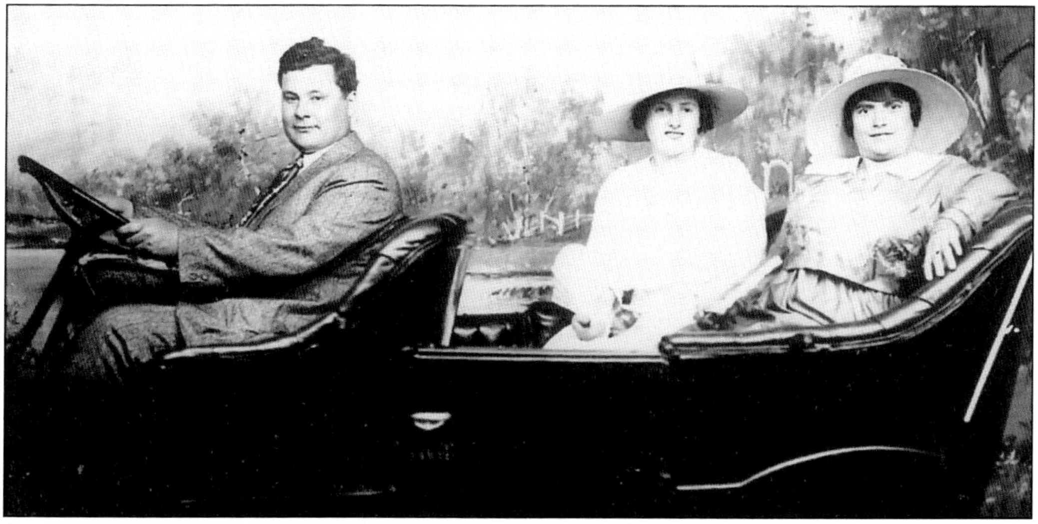

Car Ride, August 31, 1930. The Castruccis posed for this photograph at an amusement park in Cincinnati. Seated are Guistino, Denisa, and Leda. Today the Castrucci descendants operate car dealerships throughout the Greater Cincinnati and Northern Kentucky area. (Courtesy of Nic Castrucci.)

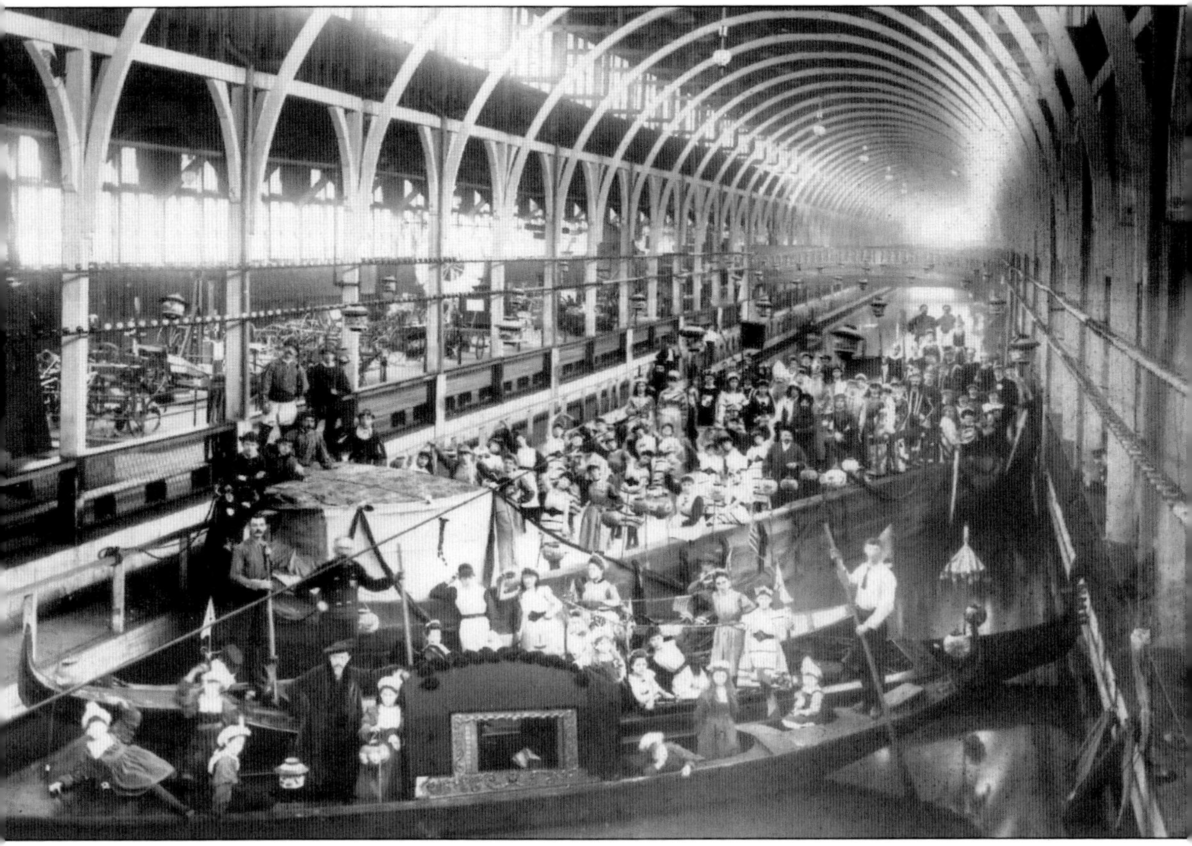

CENTENNIAL EXPOSITION. The 1888 Centennial Exposition of the Ohio Valley and Central States showcased the products of Cincinnati business owners as well as inventors, artists, and varied industries. Temporary structures were built in front of Music Hall, and another building was constructed from Twelfth Street to Fifteenth Street over the Miami and Erie Canal. A fleet of real Venetian gondolas carried dignitaries and partygoers to the exposition via the canal. When the exposition ended, the buildings were burned to the ground. Use of the canal diminished in 1906, and preparation began to build the Cincinnati subway. During the years 1920–1925, after spending a $6 million bond issue, it was filled in and paved over to form what today is Central Parkway. The city ran out of funds before the subway could be built. (Courtesy of the Cincinnati Museum Center, Cincinnati Historical Society Library.)

Four

Italian Heritage

The Italian population of Greater Cincinnati has never forgotten its heritage. From the early years of life in America, it found ways to stay in touch with family and friends in Italy. A close connection remained with the Italian government that was reinforced by the Italian consul in Cincinnati and through Sacred Heart Italian Church.

Today social clubs continue to be a part of the community just as they had been in the late 19th century. While dozens of social clubs existed then, they were usually tied to their place of origin in Italy or their employment. Today organizations such as the Order Sons of Italy in America, Cincinnatus Lodge No. 1191 (established in 1922) and the United Italian Society (founded in the late 1920s), two of the largest Cincinnati Italian societies, plan social events for their members. They continue to cook and serve spaghetti and ravioli dinners at the Italian Center in Camp Washington for the benefit of Sacred Heart Church. Smaller societies such as La Societa Di Fuscaldese Femminile, founded in December 1959 and comprised of female descendants of Fuscaldo, Italy, and the Societa Di Contadini Italiana, which began in 1907 and celebrated its 100th anniversary in 2007, continue to celebrate their heritage. New organizations, such as Mezzo-Mezzo Social Club, hold fund-raising events, which are open to the public, to support local charities. The Santa Maria Institute, which began with $5 in seed money, is now an organization with an operating budget of $2.3 million.

The first Italian magazine, *Veritas*, established in 1926 and later named the *Santa Maria* in 1930, provided information to the early Italian immigrants. The United Italian Society, its patrons, and its advertisers now support *La Voce Italiana* quarterly newsletter, an offspring of *La Voce Del Populo Italiano*, with all types of news about Italy, the United States, and the Greater Cincinnati and Northern Kentucky communities. They also sponsor the Italian programming that airs on WAIF 88.3 FM radio. Captured in this chapter are some of the events of the last 100-plus years.

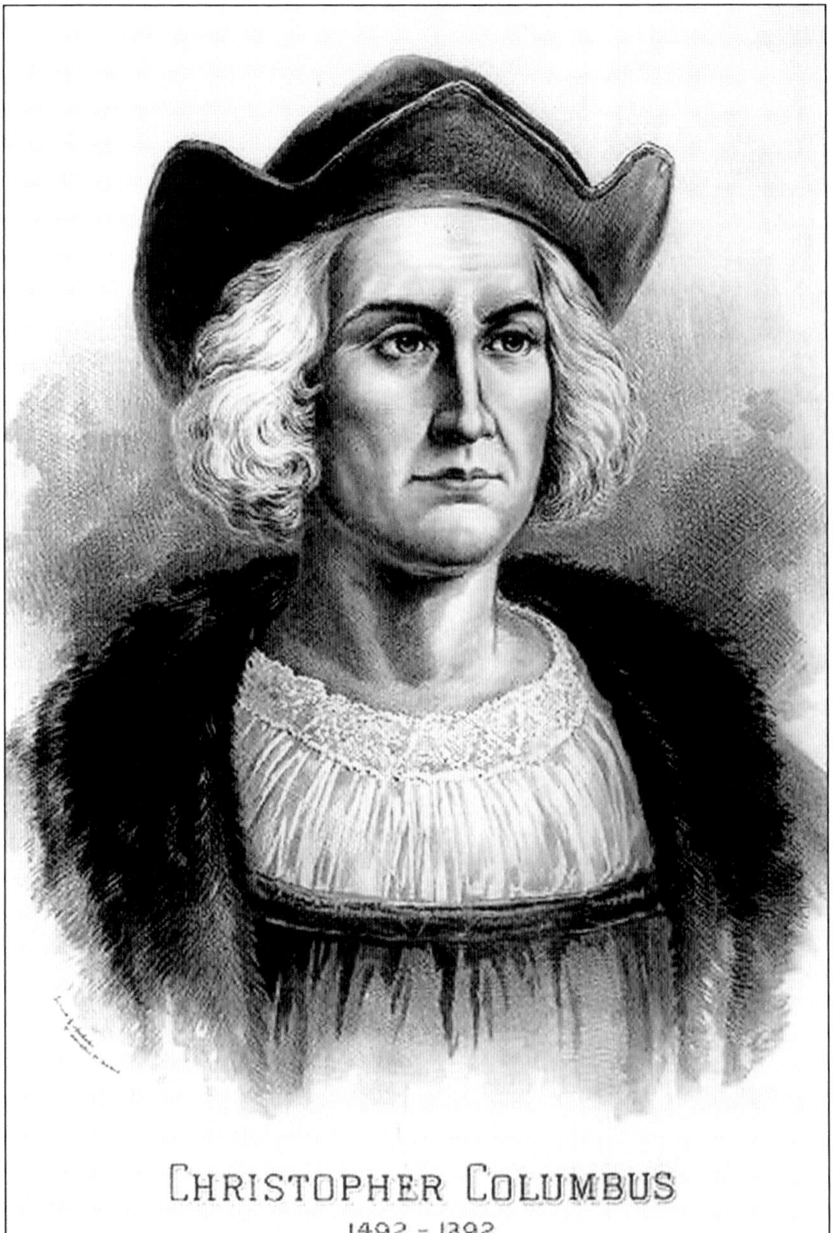

Christopher Columbus. Born Cristoforo Columbo, named after St. Christopher, the patron saint of travelers and bearer of Christ, in 1451 in Genoa, Italy, Christopher Columbus became the famous explorer who discovered America on October 12, 1492. His parents were Domenico Colombo, an Italian weaver, and Susanna Fontanarossa Columbo. Columbus was the eldest of five children. He first went to sea at the age of 14 and eventually settled in Portugal. There he married Felipa Perestrello Moriz, a woman of nobility, and they had a son, Diego, who was born in 1480. With the death of Felipa in 1485, Columbus and his son moved to Spain. It was there that he eventually convinced Catholic monarchs King Ferdinand and Queen Isabella to sponsor his journey in search of trade routes to the west. Columbus died on May 20, 1506. (Courtesy of the Library of Congress.)

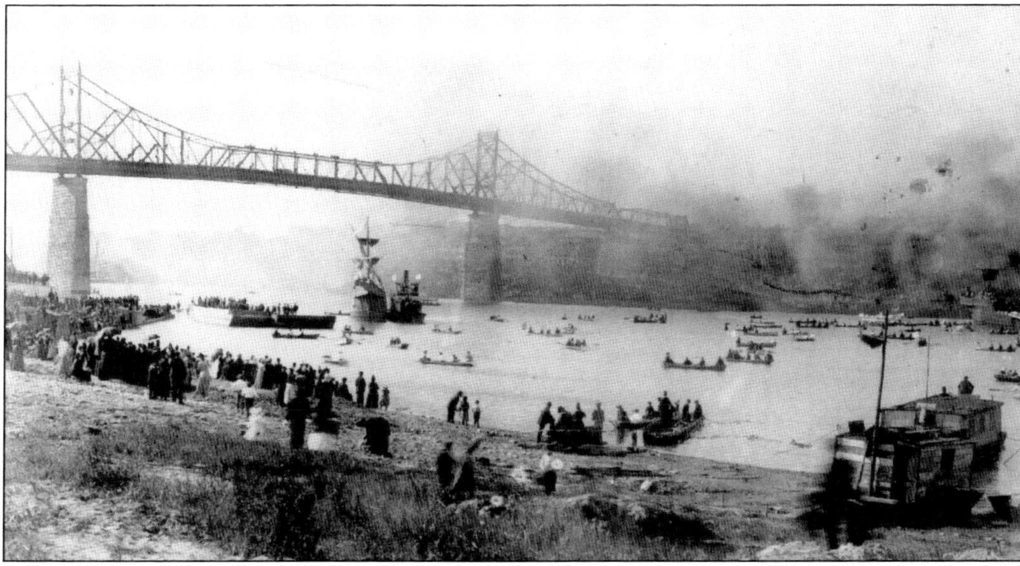

THE 400TH CELEBRATION OF COLUMBUS'S DISCOVERY, 1892. In recognition of the discovery of America on October 12, 1492, by Christopher Columbus, the entire local community on both sides of the Ohio River celebrated the 400th anniversary of Columbus's arrival in America. Full-scale replicas of the ships the *Niña*, the *Pinta*, and the *Santa Maria* sailed on the Ohio River. The festivities included elaborate parades with over 1,000 marching children, along with Catholic and civic societies and organizations, decorated floats and wagons, and music provided by area drum corps. Local militia and military troops from Fort Thomas, Kentucky, also participated in the festivities. Storefronts and buildings were decorated with American flags, as well as those of Spain, Italy, and France. Italians of Greater Cincinnati continue to celebrate this day with an annual banquet in recognition of their Italian heritage. (Courtesy of the Cincinnati Museum Center, Cincinnati Historical Society Library.)

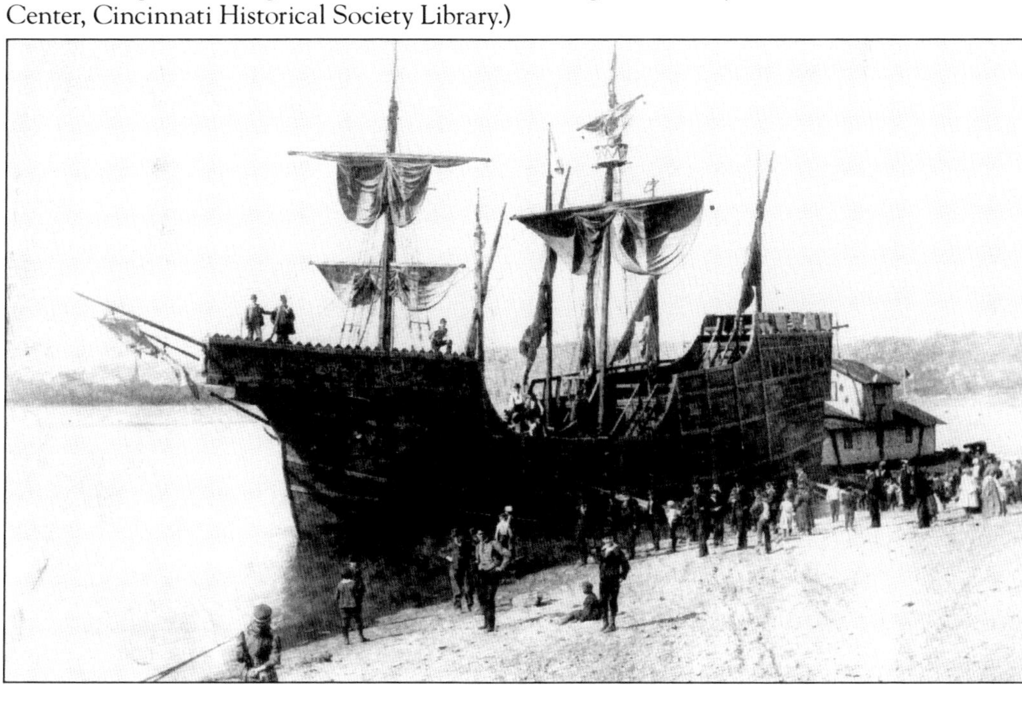

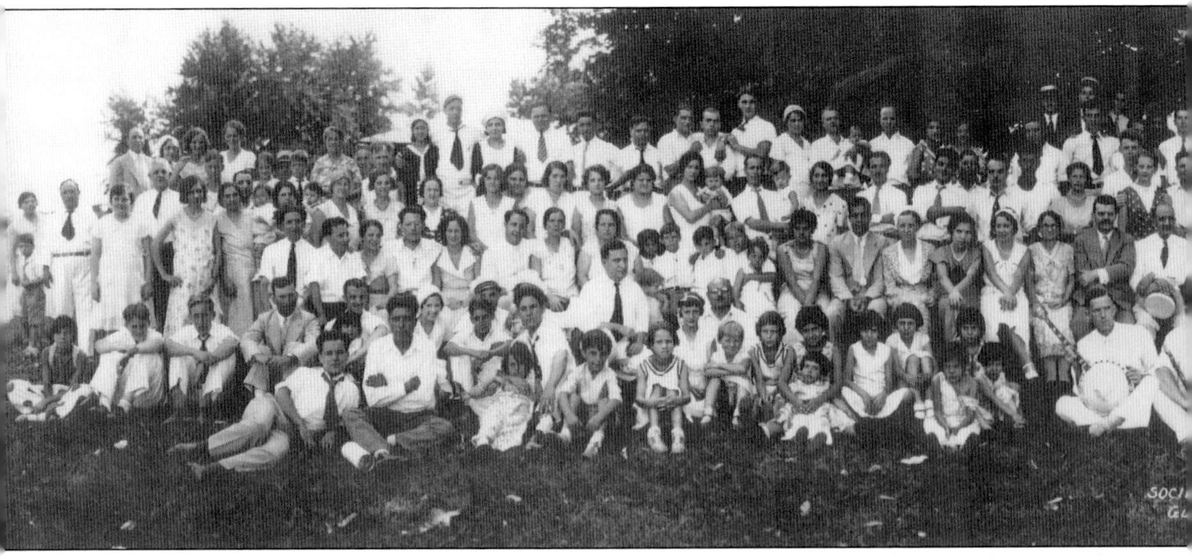

Societa' O.M.S. Fuscaldese Maschili, July 24, 1932. This photograph was taken at the second annual outing at Gutzwiller's Grove, a popular picnic location. La Societa Di Fuscaldese Maschili was comprised of men only who emigrated from Fuscaldo, Calabria, Italy,

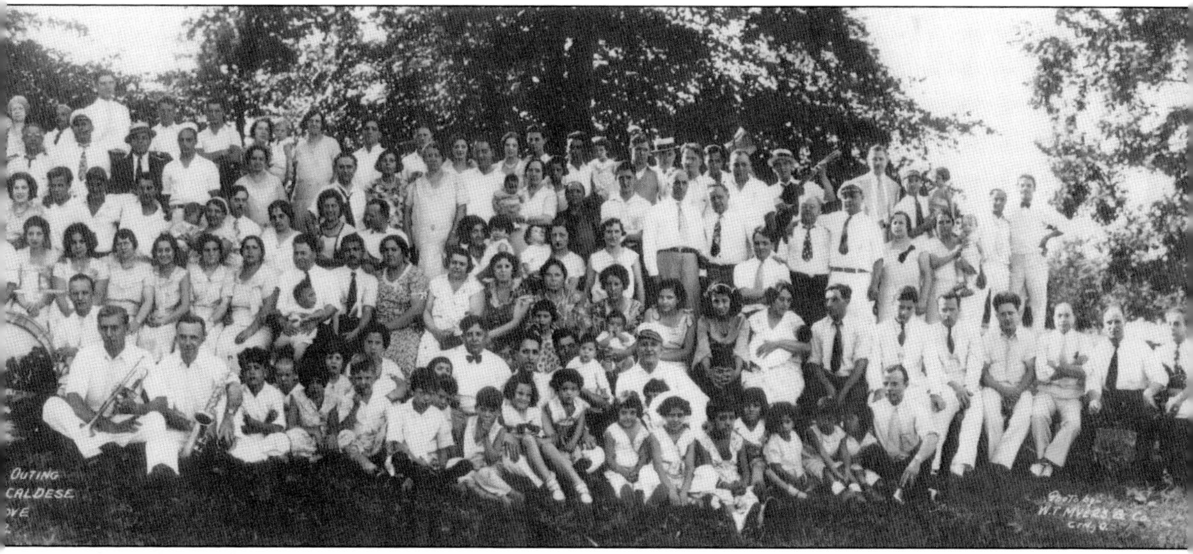

or their descendants. The organization was disbanded around 2002. (Courtesy of Joe and Rose Santoro.)

AN AMERICAN NEWSPAPER DEDICATED TO THE WELFARE OF THE AMERICAN ITALIANS
OFFICE: 4 WEST 7th STREET
MAin 6640

LA VOCE INDIPENDENTE

THE VOICE OF THE AMERICAN-ITALIAN PEOPLE OF CINCINNATI AND OHIO

April, 23, 1948

Reluctance to Cooperate Retards Italians Social and Political Progress in Cincinnati

CHIT CHATS

By Prof. Bravo

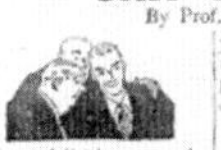

A specialist is a man who ncentrates more and ore on less and less.

Just had a glimpse at the ew Super-Ford that the nited Italian Societies are iving away, July 4th, at eir Italian Day picnic, to e held at Greenwood rove. IT'S A HONEY!

. . . Charley Arrighi is the ead man of the Parkview larkets in Cincinnati . . . oe Roberto, a nice young hap, is now connected with e Cincinnati Advertising ompany . . . Mike Giglio now the owner of a large uto cleaning company, cated at 243 Fodsick St. . . Lou Costello of movie ame is an Italian, and we ... agged his car while he was elivering goods in his own tore. 'Tis unfair, Nino, but ...

you open?" Deacon Jones roused a bit and sleepily replied, "Open? Why I just dealt!"

Sacred Heart Church Social

The annual Spring Social given by the Corona Club of the Sacred Heart Italian Church will be held, Sunday, April 25th, from 3 to 6 p. m. in the Church Parish Hall, 527 Broadway. Features on the program include games, valuable door prizes, refreshments and other unusual and interesting enterainment. The proceeds will be used toward necessary needs for the Altar. The chairman will be Mrs. Albert T. Venosa. Mr. Herman Carletti will be the co-chairman, assisted by Mrs. N. Baioni, Mrs. Pat Mancuso, Mrs. P. J. Palazzolo, and Mrs. Leo Pera. We urge our readers to attend this outstanding ... they will feel better after contributing to this commendable cause.

CIANCIOLA-ARMSTRONG WEDDING

—Courtesy of Pogue's Studio

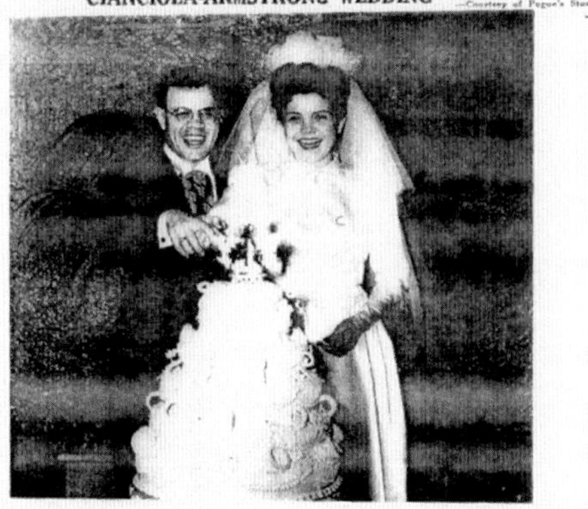

La Voce, without soft-peddling or mincing words, would like to know why several Italian fraternal societies, including many Italians not affiliated with any Italian organization, are forever recalcitrant when movements are set in motion to benefit the colony as a whole. Can it be the animosities and jealousies that go back a few generations; go back to the days when a handful of Italians (who had a handful of money) wanted to be known as "Padrone" of the Italian Colony. Let's not kid ourselves. This condition did exist, and we still have a handful of Italians who aspire to the title of "Padrone." Be that as it may, can it now be that as the years have sped by, and new blood has found its way to the surface, they are unwilling to fall all into step with progressive movements, and lag behind for no other reason than that of scoffing and criticising conscientious men and women who want to see American-Italians active in every sphere of American life. Much can be said, but it is best to leave some things unsaid for the reason that they have to be said to many people who are unreasonable.

More than a year ago the United Italian Societies of Greater Cincinnati, (with four dollars in its treasury) made a concerted drive for new members; members of progressive societies who were showing other societies the way to conduct charitable drives in order to aid the undernourished and destitute in Italy. Early in 1947, Anthony Cianciolo was asked to become president of the United Italian Societies. He accepted, and immediately started a series of benefit activities which netted approximately $7,000. Five-thousand dollars or more were quickly dispatched to Italy. Some through the Cincinnati Committee for Italy's Relief, and some ... Italian families, individuals, and institutions in Cincinnati. And today the United Italian Societies treasury has more than $2,000. This speaks well for the

LA VOCE, APRIL 23, 1948. The marriage of Patricia Armstrong to August (Gus) Cianciolo is an example of some of the local stories carried over the years in the *La Voce* newspaper. Shown below is the *La Voce Italiana*, "Italian voice," after a format change in March 2007. Its origin began when Columbo Melaragno brought *La Voce Del Populo Italiano* newspaper from Cleveland to the area in 1946. The quarterly newspaper continues to write bits and pieces of history along with activities and celebrations at home and in Italy. (Courtesy of Annie Cianciolo O'Donnell.)

La Voce Italiana

THE ITALIAN VOICE

Vol. VIII, Issue 1
March, 2007

Proudly Sponsored by
The United Italian Society

CINCINNATI, OHIO

A Rewarding Experience to Remember

Welcome to the first issue of 2007! I'm sure you are all just as excited to read it as I am, and I'd like to begin by congratulating Editors-in-Chief Linda Gromen and Rose Santoro, Managing Editor Alan Biondi, as well as the entire *La Voce Italiana* staff for successfully taking over this operation. It can be a daunting job that requires a lot of time, effort, and many different skills, but being the Editor-in-Chief over the last four years has been one of the most rewarding experiences I personally have ever had.

As many of you know, when *La Voce*'s torch was passed to me from Nick Stevens in 2003, I had some pretty large shoes to fill. It took me many issues to get into the swing of things! It wasn't until after I recruited Joe (my then fiancé, now husband), that we eventually made a newspaper making us, as well as our contributors, proud. It has been a pleasure to work with Ameri-

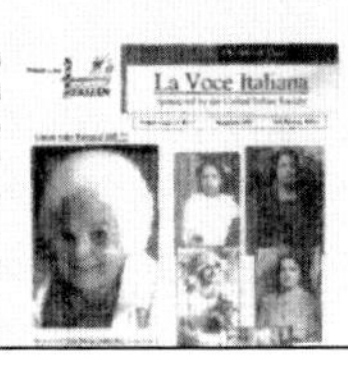

Gromen (UIS Vice President) wrote one brilliant literary review after another. Rose Santoro and Alan Biondi (UIS Trustees), Shirley Stevens (UIS Fundraising Chair), and Phil Sabatelli (current UIS President) all

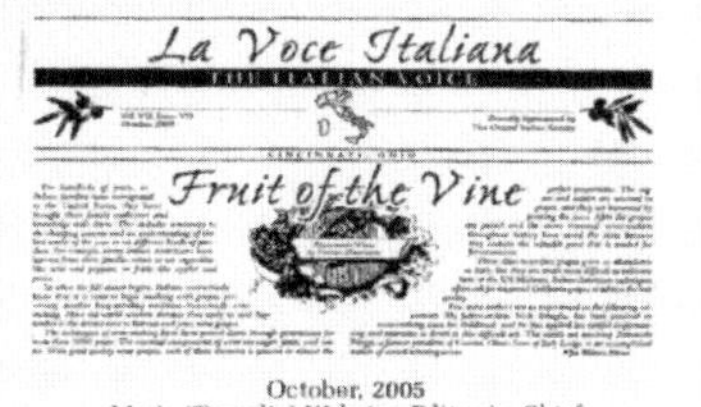

October, 2005
Maria (Tunaglia) Webster, Editor-in-Chief

contributed countless articles covering Italian culture and traditions. Our faithful news correspondent (and Sons of Italy member) from my hometown Canton, Ohio, Armando Pileggi shared numerous articles with us on Italian history and music. Cindy Meale (UIS Trustee and

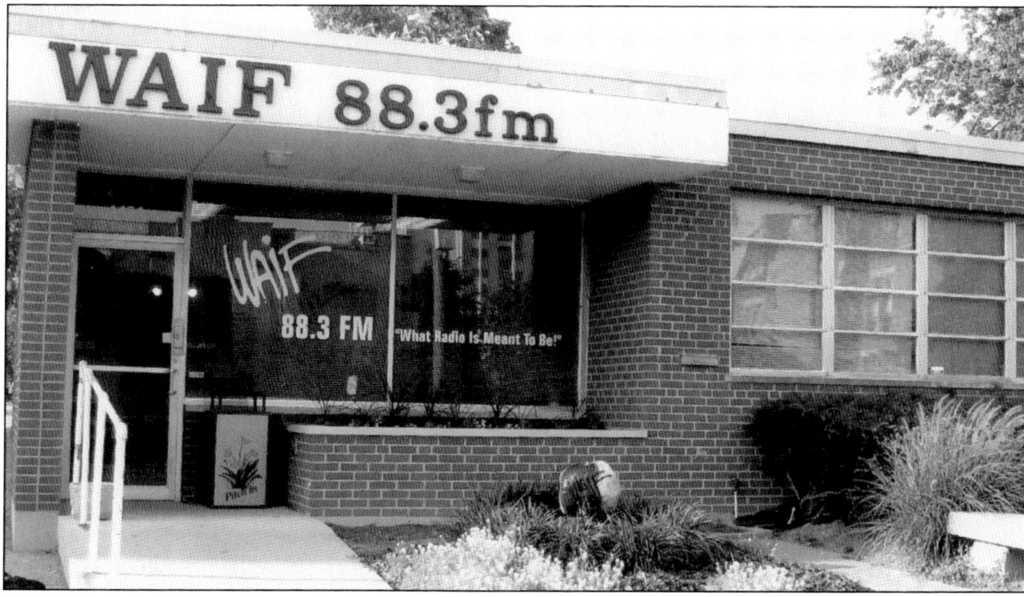

WAIF 88.3 FM. The radio station WAIF 88.3 FM is located at 1434 East McMillan Street in Cincinnati and is the home for ethnic heritage programs featuring talk radio, music, and current events taking place within the community. Its programmers all work on a volunteer basis. The station's broadcasts can be heard within the Interstate 275 area in southwestern Ohio, Northern Kentucky, and southeastern Indiana, as well as over the Internet. (Courtesy of Mario and Gina Onorini.)

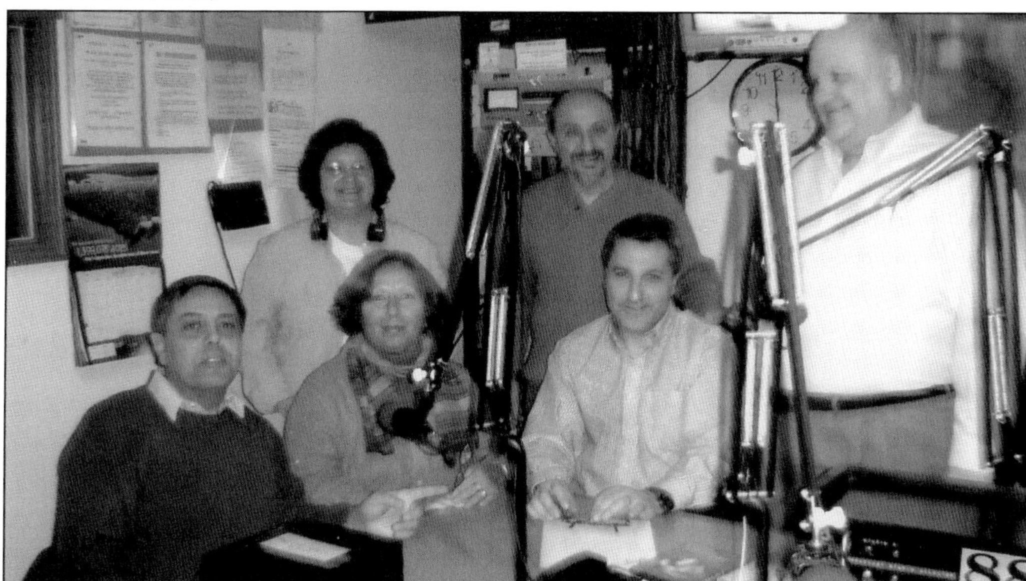

WAIF 88.3 FM PROGRAMMERS. Shown in this photograph are, from left to right, the original programmers for WAIF's Italian heritage program, Gerardo Perrotta, Paola Girelli Harding, Michele Alonzo, and Pietro Cassinadri. Standing in the back row are the current programmers, Gina and Mario Onorini. WAIF went on the air in 1975, and the Italian program *Italia Ieri e Oggi* ("Italy, yesterday and today") continues every Tuesday from 6:00 p.m. to 7:00 p.m. (Courtesy of Mario and Gina Onorini.)

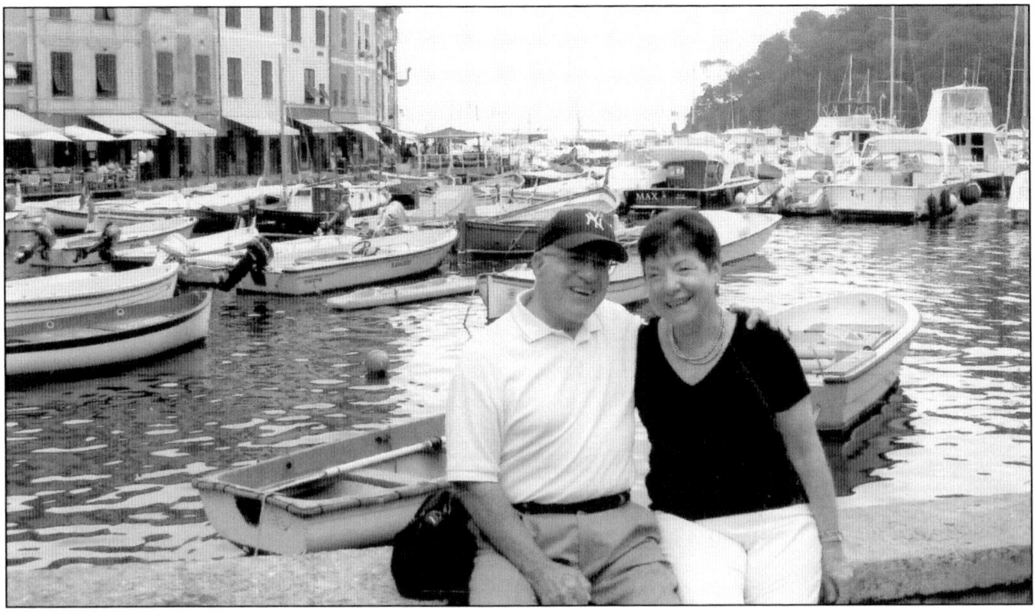

PHIL AND JUDY SABATELLI, PORTOFINA, ITALY. Phil Sabatelli is the son of Italian immigrants Phillip Antonio Sabatelli and Mary Salerno Sabatelli. He lived right next door to San Antonio Church in South Fairmount from 1943 through 1950. He fondly remembers the procession with the Madonna di Constantinopoli statue through the streets of South Fairmount, complete with the church festivals, pizza, and fireworks. Sabatelli is the current president of the United Italian Society in Cincinnati. (Courtesy of Phil Sabatelli.)

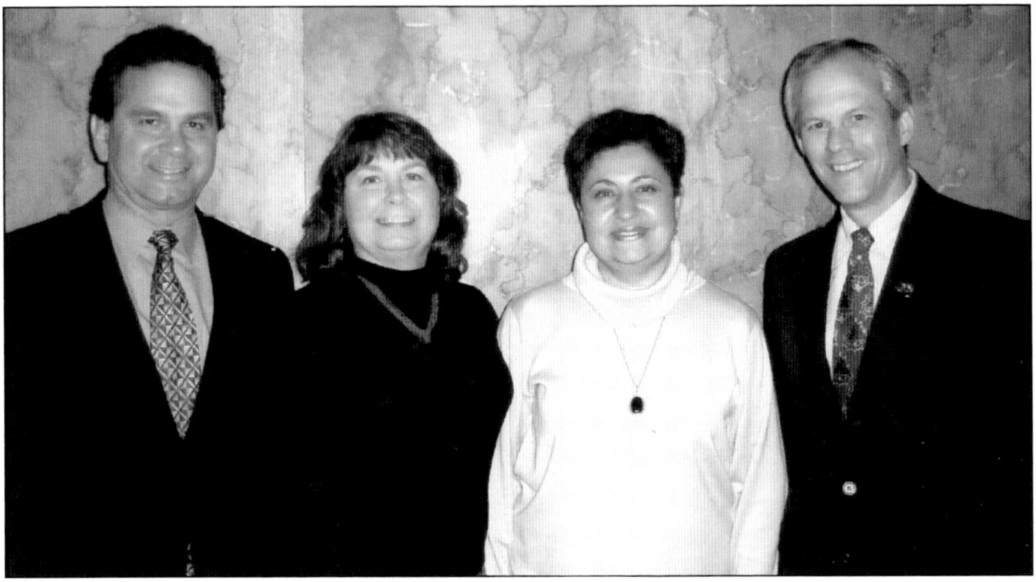

THE 110TH ANNIVERSARY OF SANTA MARIA. The legacy of the Sisters of Charity of Cincinnati, which began in 1897, continues today through SMCS, as the agency continues to "help families help themselves." Shown here at the 110th anniversary brunch are, from left to right, authors Philip G. Ciafardini and Pamela Ciafardini Casebolt, Nune Krayterman, development director of SMCS, and H. A. Musser Jr., president and chief executive officer of SMCS. (Authors' collection.)

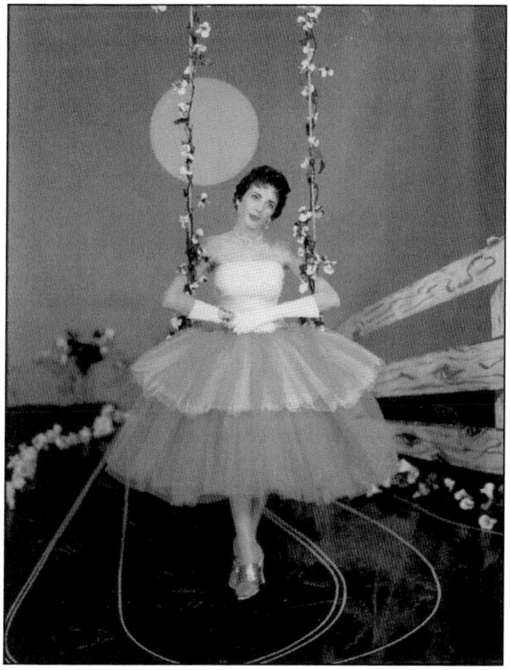

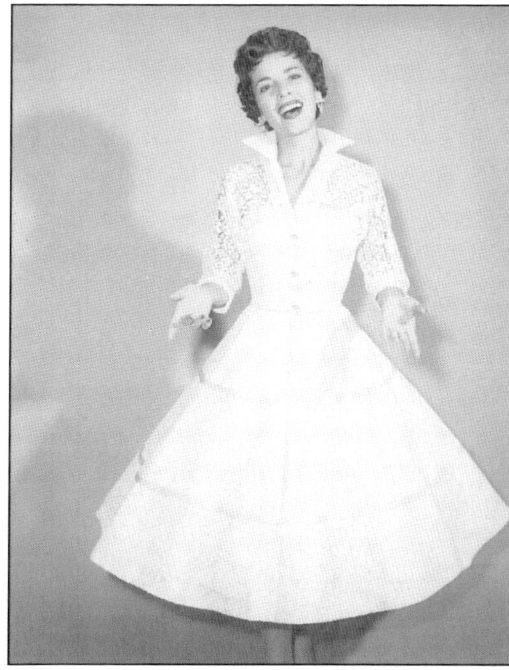

DOTTY MACK. Dotty Macaluso, stage name Dotty Mack, was born in Cincinnati and grew up to perform in early television on *Girl Alone*, *The Dotty Mack Show* (1953–1956 on ABC), and *The Paul Dixon Show*. Her specialty was to lip-synch current hit records. Mack is shown here wearing two of the many beautiful dresses she wore on the shows. (Courtesy of JoAnn Macaluso Beckman.)

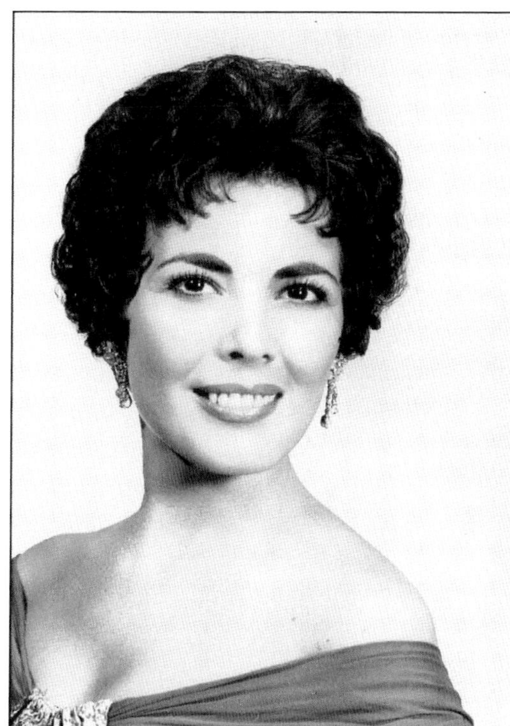

ITALIAN DAY QUEEN, CONEY ISLAND. The first Italian Day was celebrated in the summer of 1952 and was organized by the Italian societies. The glamorous Dotty Mack reigned as the Italian Day queen in 1954 and performed with her WCPO-TV performers Colin Male and Bob Braun on August 5, 1956, at Moonlight Gardens. Mack's Italian heritage was always important to her, and she enjoyed celebrating it with family and friends. (Courtesy of JoAnn Macaluso Beckman.)

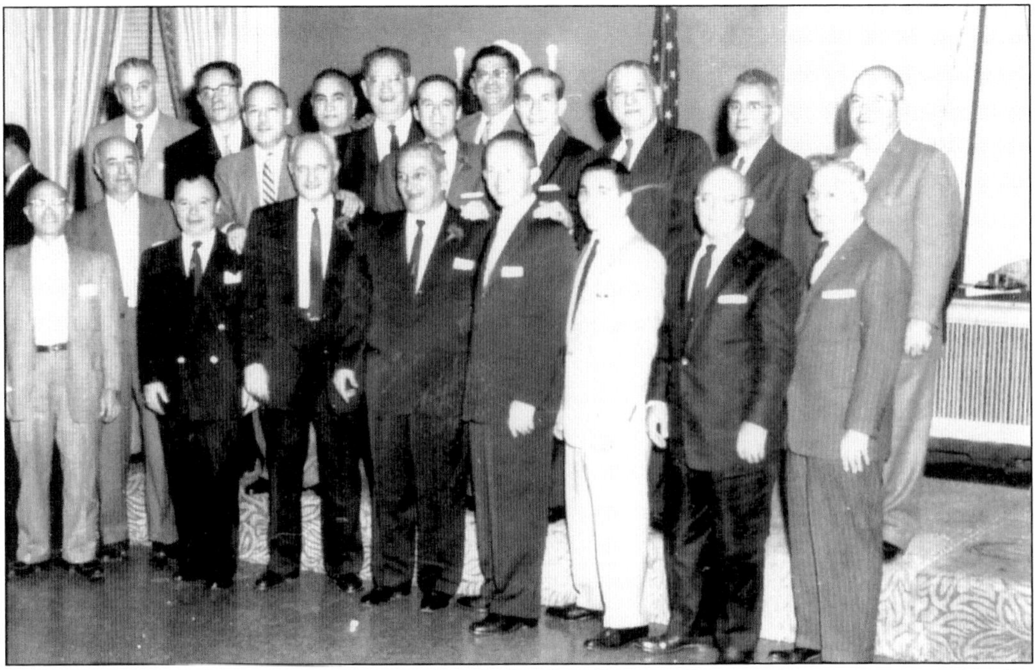

COLUMBUS DAY CELEBRATION, C. 1954. Columbus Day is always a joyous occasion for the Italian community in Cincinnati. Religious events, parades, and banquets are ways in which the community celebrates the day. The first Columbus Day banquet took place in 1923 and has remained an annual event through the Order Sons of Italy in America. A young Ronald A. Panioto is standing in the first row, third from the right. (Courtesy of Marlene Nesi.)

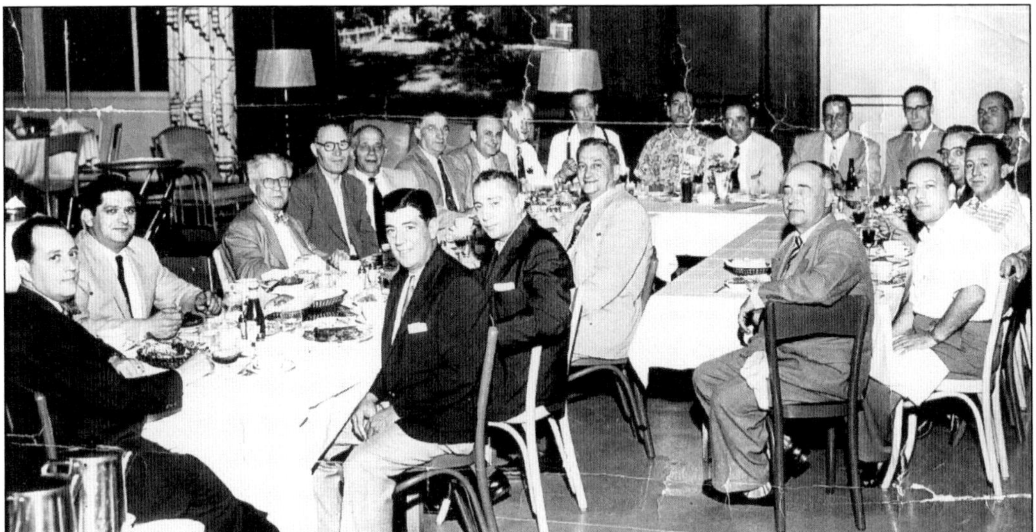

ORDER SONS OF ITALY IN AMERICA, CINCINNATUS LODGE NO. 1191, 1955. Order Sons of Italy in America was established at the national level by Dr. Vincenzo Sellaro on June 22, 1905, with the structure of national, state, and local lodges. Its founding principles were liberty (freedom of assembly, speech, and opportunity, economic freedom, and freedom of thought, conscience, and religion), equality (all men are created equal), and fraternity (help the community and continue with the ancestral traditions.) (Courtesy of Pat Iacobucci.)

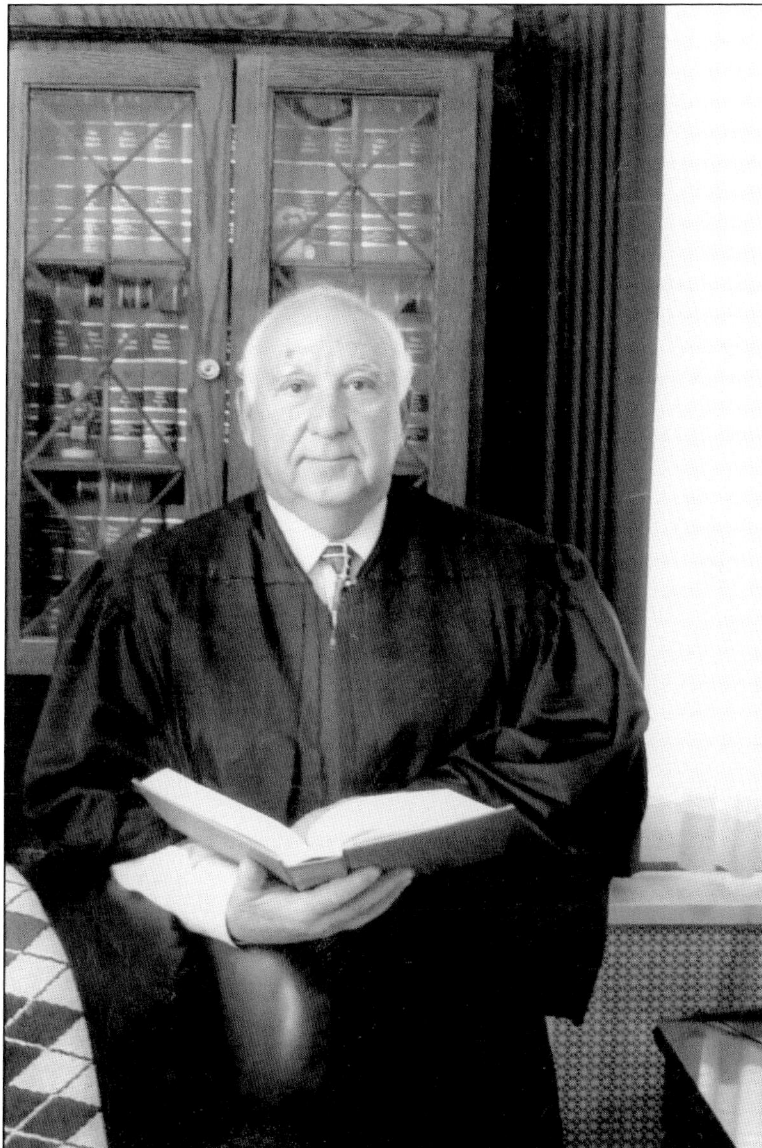

The Honorable Ronald A. Panioto. Judge Ronald A. Panioto, the son of Salvatore and Josephine Panioto, was educated at Hughes High School, the University of Cincinnati with a bachelor of science in commerce, and the Salmon P. Chase Law School with a Juris Doctor degree. After receiving his admittance to the Ohio bar, he became a prosecuting attorney. In 1977, he was elected the first judge of Italian descent in all of southern Ohio as judge to the Hamilton County Municipal Court, and in 1981, he became the presiding judge of Hamilton County Common Pleas Court, Domestic Relations Division. In 1990, the Italian government awarded the highest civilian honor, the *cavaliere dell ordine al merito della Repubblica Italiana*, to Judge Panioto for his outstanding contributions to the community. Judge Panioto continues to celebrate his Italian heritage by cochairing fund-raising activities such as Sacred Heart Church's spaghetti and ravioli dinner, as president of the Order Sons of Italy in America, Cincinnatus Lodge No. 1191. He was also the president of the United Italian Society from 1971 to 1993. (Courtesy of Marlene Nesi.)

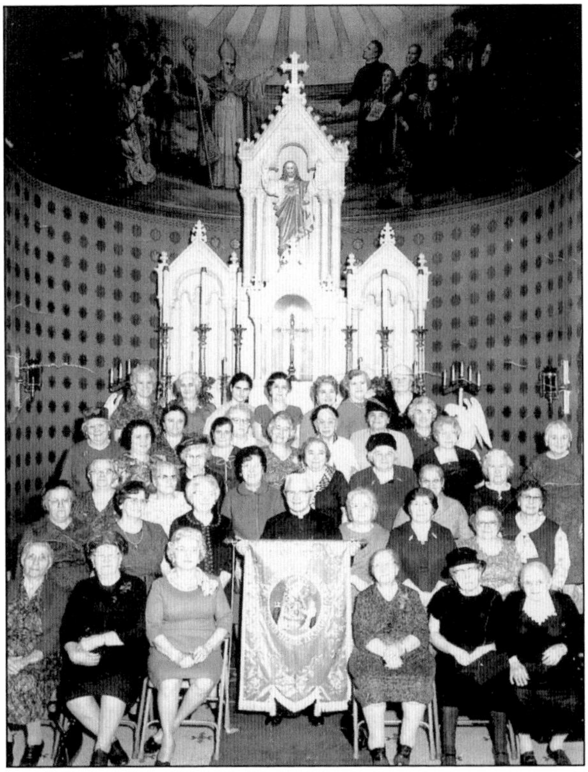

MADONNA DI POMPEI SOCIETY, CHRISTMAS 1967. Shown with the Madonna Di Pompei Society is Fr. Louis Bolzan, C.S., author of *Memories of an Italian Parish*. The tradition of preparing spaghetti and ravioli dinners for the benefit of the church began in August 1911 on the property of S. Brichetto in south Norwood. In 1928, the Madonna di Pompei Society prepared the meals, and the event was held in basement of Sacred Heart Italian Church. (Courtesy of Tony Pierani.)

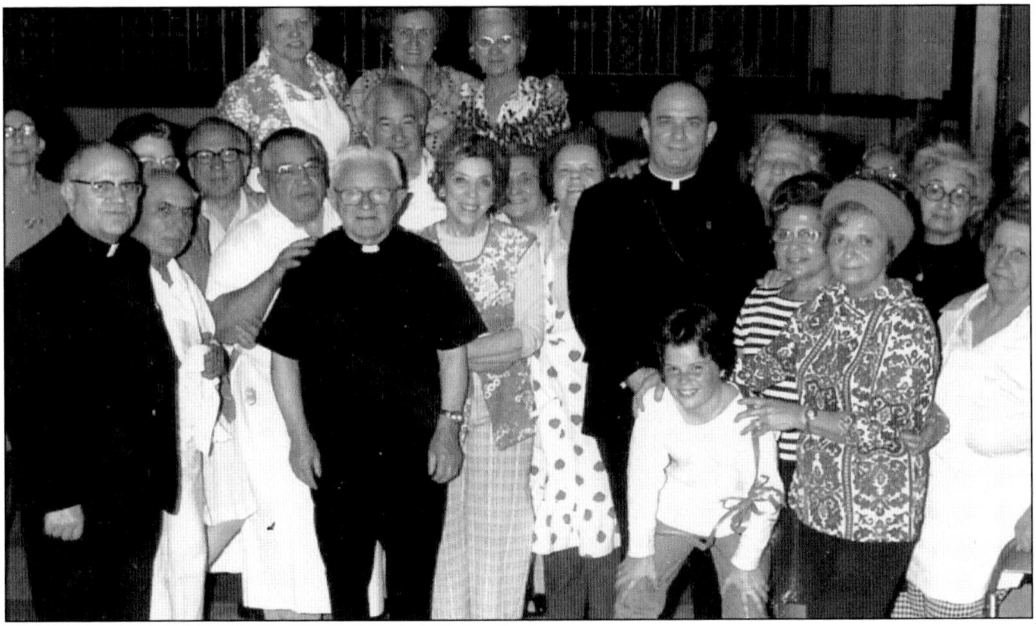

RAVIOLI AND SPAGHETTI DINNERS. The tradition continued with the move of the parishioners to Sacred Heart Church in Camp Washington. It was first celebrated there on Palm Sunday, March 19, 1970, and continues twice a year, on Palm Sunday and in October. Shown with some of the ladies of Sacred Heart Church are, from left to right, Fr. Mario Rauzi, Fr. Louis Bolzan, and Archbishop Joseph Bernardin (originally Bernardini). (Courtesy of Fr. Mario Rauzi, C.S.)

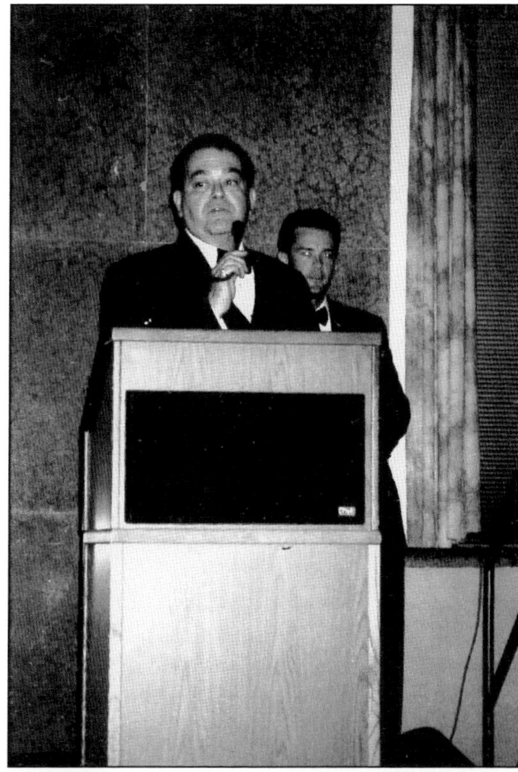

SPRING SCHOLARSHIP DANCE, 2007. Scholarship presenters Joe Pitocco, at the microphone, and Pete Scalia present a $5,000 college scholarship, which was decided by a four-person committee, to Lisa DiStasi at the Cincinnati Museum Center. The Mezzo-Mezzo Social Club was formed in the fall of 2003 and participates in area fund-raising events and arranges social events for its members and the general public. (Courtesy of the Mezzo- Mezzo Social Club.)

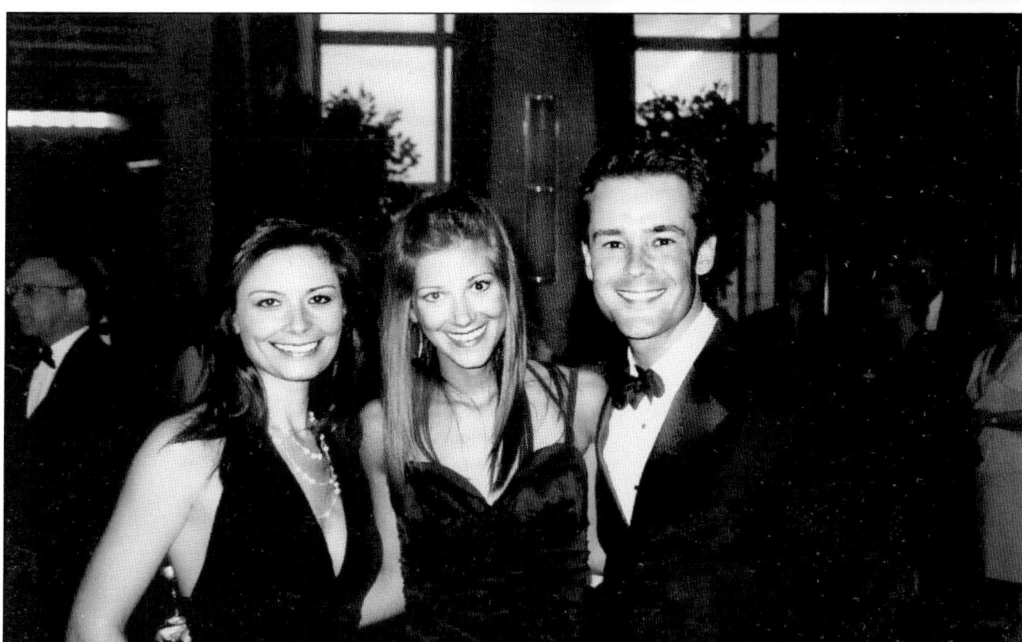

LISA DISTASI, 2007 SCHOLARSHIP WINNER. Pictured from left to right are Missy Scalia, Lisa DiStasi, and Pete Scalia. DiStasi is the daughter of Mary Ann and Dino DiStasi and at the time was attending her third year at the Ohio State University. (Courtesy of the Mezzo-Mezzo Social Club.)

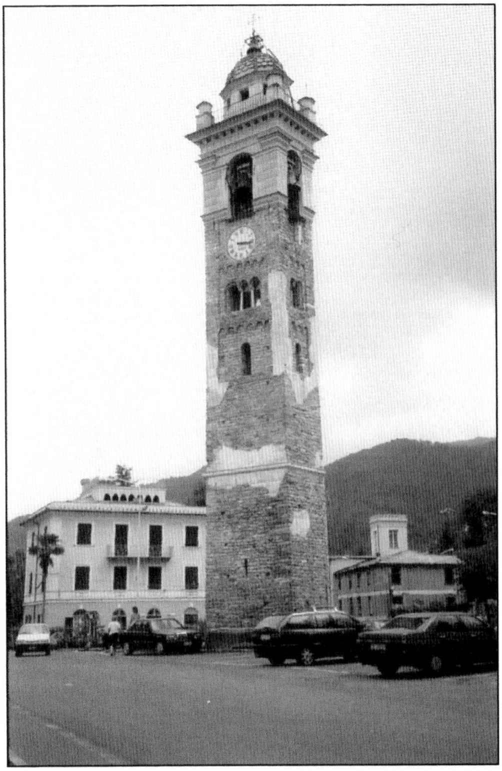

SAN GIOVANNI BATTISTE CHURCH TOWER. Overlooking the town square in Cicagna, Italy, is the original tower of the church where Sr. Blandina Segale and her siblings were baptized in the mid-1800s. The tower is over 1,000 years old. San Giovanni Battiste (St. John the Baptist) is the patron saint of Cicagna. (Courtesy of Roland and Nancy Becker.)

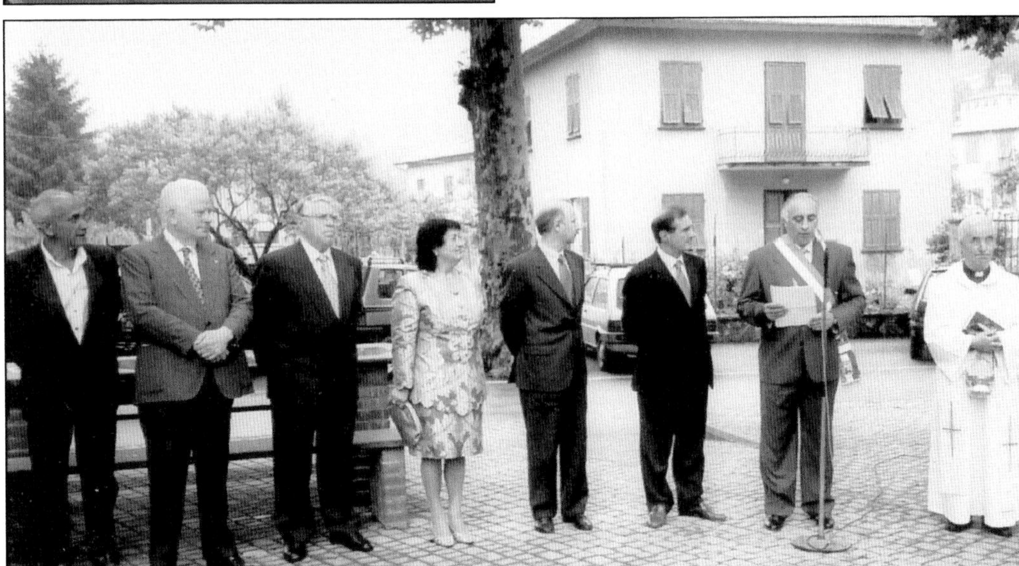

DEDICATION, JULY 11, 1998. On this eventful day, Mayor Claudio Crovo of Cicagna (second from the right) was joined by mayors from other towns located in the Fontanabuono Valley for the dedication of the square in honor of Sr. Blandina Segale. Also participating is the parish priest of Cicagna (far right). Joining the Segale family of Italy were over 38 relatives of the Becker and Stagge families who traveled from America for the dedication. (Courtesy of Roland and Nancy Becker.)

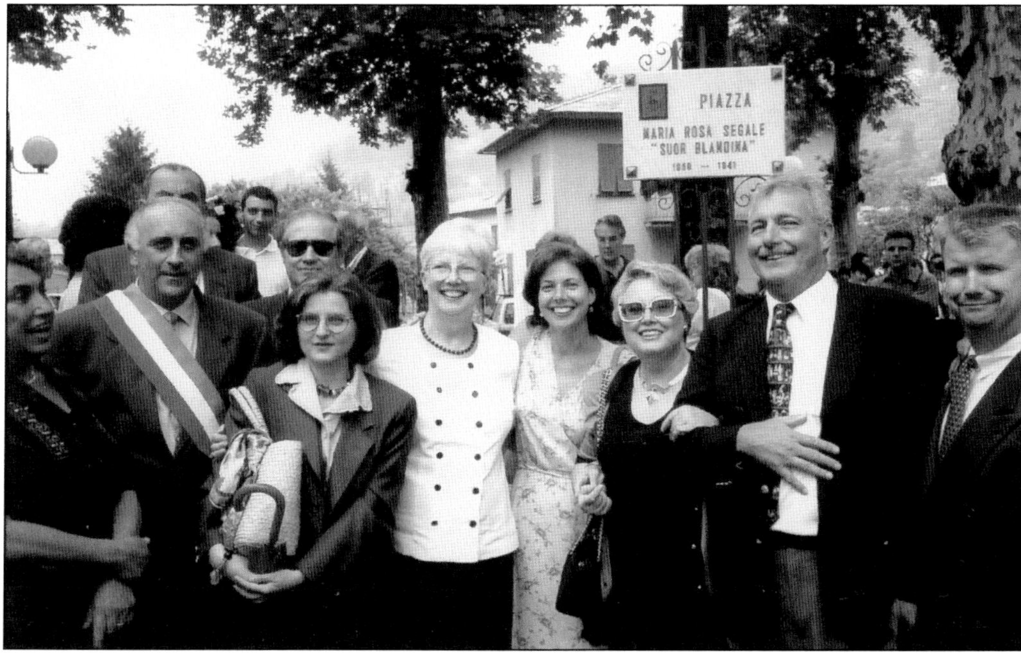

SR. BLANDINA SEGALE, 1850–1941. Standing beneath the plaque are, from left to right, Olga Rosa Segale, Mayor Claudio Crovo, Maria Elisabetta Ruggiero, Nancy Becker, Amy Becker, Donatella Aurili Ruggiero, and Roland Becker and his son Dan Becker. Standing behind Maria is her husband Vincenzo Ruggiero. Donatella, a teacher from Genoa, Italy, spent over 20 years researching the life of Sr. Blandina Segale. She and Carla Casagrande Maschio of the Civic Library in Cicagna were instrumental in having the square dedicated in Sister Blandina's honor. Members of the Segale, Becker, and Stagge families are shown below. (Courtesy of Roland and Nancy Becker.)

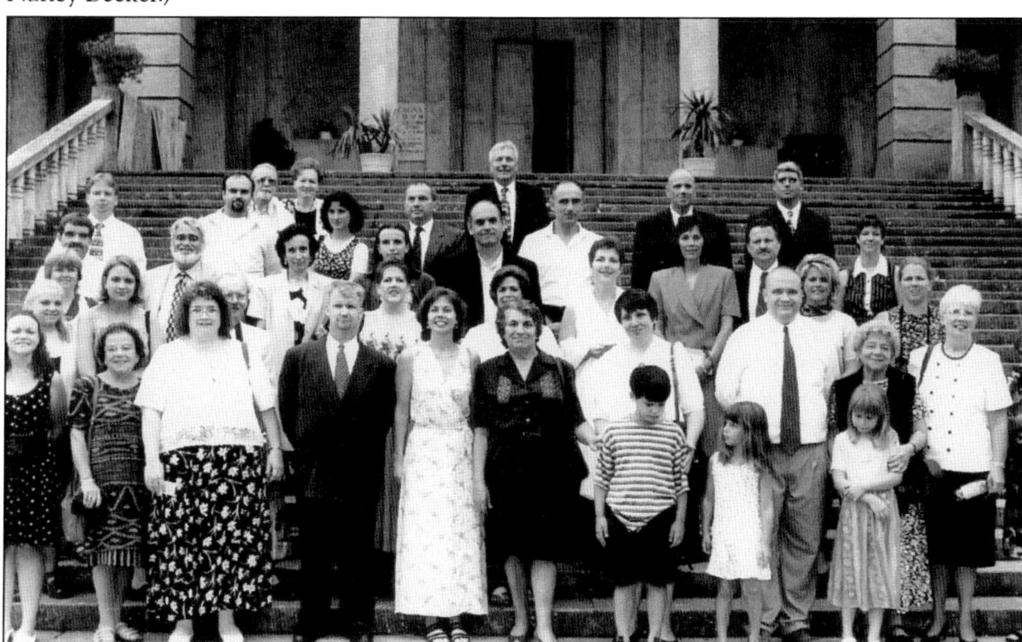

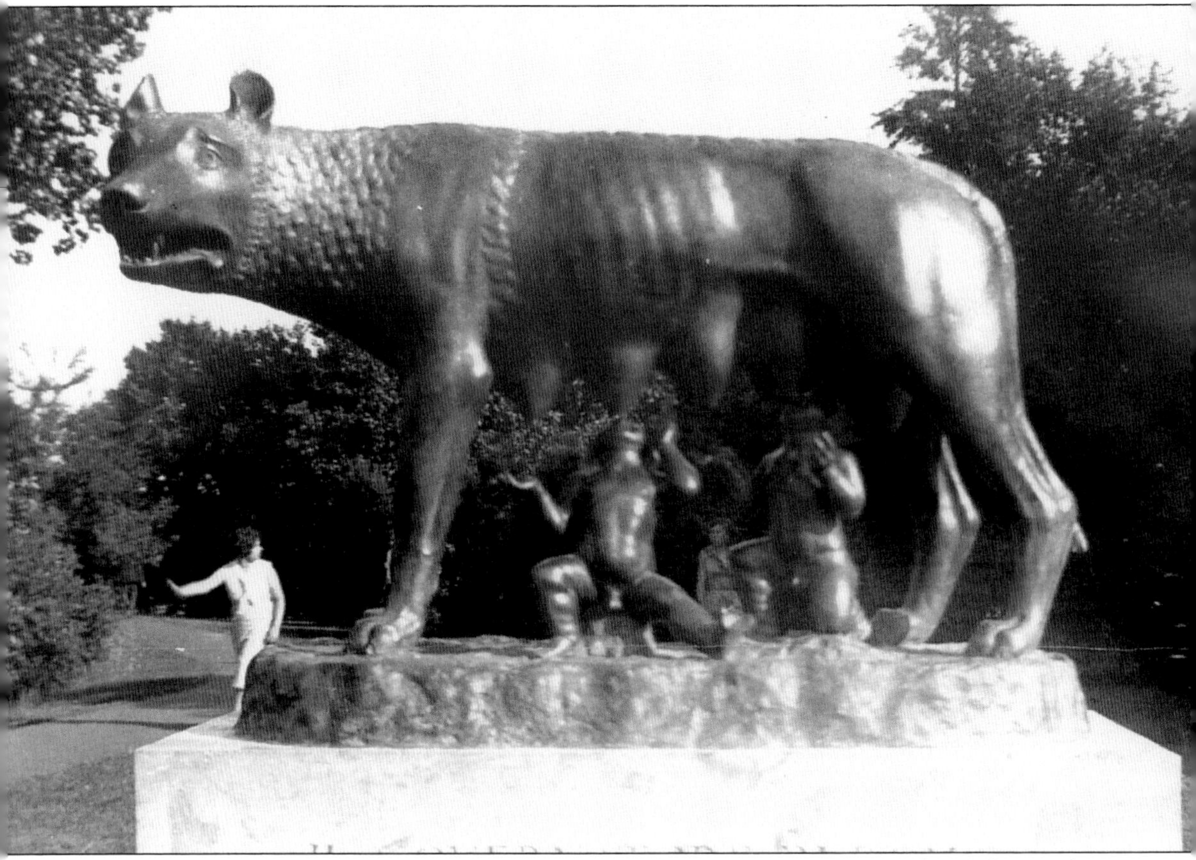

Roman *Lupa* with Romulus and Remus, Eden Park, 1931. Located in Eden Park near the Twin Lakes area is the bronze replica of the *Capitoline Wolf.* The legend says that Romulus and Remus were nursed by a she-wolf. Romulus became the first king and founder of Rome. The statue was a gift from the Italian government to the City of Cincinnati and presented through the Order Sons of Italy in America, Cincinnatius Lodge No. 1191, in 1931. The statue serves as a reminder of the bonds of friendship and spiritual ties between the City of Rome and the City of Cincinnati, both cities of the legendary "seven hills." (Courtesy of Gerardo "Curly" DiTullio.)

BIBLIOGRAPHY

Bolzan, Fr. Louis, C.S. *Memories of an Italian Parish: A History of the Sacred Heart Italian Church of Cincinnati, Ohio.* Cincinnati: Heskamp, 1974.

Connolly, Mary Beth Fraser. "'Devoted to the Interest of the Italians': The Sisters of Charity and the Santa Maria Institute in Cincinnati, Ohio, 1890–1930." PhD diss., 2005.

Dyson, John. *Columbus for Gold, God and Glory.* New York: Simon and Schuster/Madison Press Book, 1991.

Martinelli, Joe. *Little Italy, May, Burbank and Boone Remembrances.* New York: Rockhouse Press, 2003.

Minogue, Anna C. *The Santa Maria Institute.* New York: America Press, 1922.

Morison, Samuel Eliot. *Christopher Columbus, Mariner.* Boston: Little, Brown and Company, 1955.

Ruggiero, D. Aurili, N. Becker, C. Casagrande Maschio, A. M. Converso Mallucci, and M. E. Ruggiero. *Sister Blandina Segale: History of a Departure and a Return.* Translated by Fiona Bowler Ambrosino, 1998, *Edizioni Tizullio Bacherontius.*

San Antonio Church. A golden jubilee (1922–1972) directory.

Sacred Heart Church, Camp Washington, Cincinnati. A centennial jubilee (1889–1989) souvenir.

Sacred Heart, Cincinnati, Ohio, History 1893–1943. Printed Parish History Collection, Box 86. University of Notre Dame Archives.

Sacred Heart Italian Church, Cincinnati. A diamond jubilee (1893–1968) booklet.

Santa Maria Journals of Sister Justina Segale, S. C. J-1 through J-5, period of August 1897 through May 22, 1918. Archives of the Sisters of Charity of Cincinnati, Mount St. Joseph, Ohio.

Segale, Sister Blandina, S. C. *At the End of the Santa Fe Trail.* Milwaukee: Bruce Publishing, 1948. First published 1932 by the Sisters of Charity of Cincinnati from original serial form in *Santa Maria,* 1926–1931.

www.firstworldwar.com

www.santamaria-cincy-org/history.htm